Individual Morality

'Morality' is concerned with the questions 'What do we mean by "right"?' and 'What is the point of doing right?' *Individual Morality* is a study of the moral sense as an aspect of human natural history – of its origin and purpose in individuals and society.

Man is inescapably the custodian of evolving life on this planet. Moral values are thus those values which should allow him to operate creatively. The individual is naturally designed to enter adult life equipped with a responsive moral outlook, as distinct from a sense of guilt drummed in by an education based on rules and the fear of breaking them. The development of this capacity is the means towards a full maturing of responsibility.

Few will fail to find Dr Hemming's book both stimulating and profoundly encouraging. It is particularly to the point at a time when people throughout the world are beginning to react consciously against bureaucratic controls and the *status quo*, when the young are openly challenging older generations to justify claims to authority and wisdom.

THE NATURAL HISTORY OF SOCIETY
EDITOR: ALEX COMFORT

BY THE SAME AUTHOR

TEACH THEM TO LIVE

MANKIND AGAINST THE KILLERS

PROBLEMS OF ADOLESCENT GIRLS

JAMES HEMMING

Individual Morality

NELSON

THOMAS NELSON AND SONS LTD
36 Park Street London W1
P.O. Box 2187 Accra
P.O. Box 336 Apapa Lagos
P.O. Box 25012 Nairobi
P.O. Box 21149 Dar es Salaam
77 Coffee Street San Fernando Trinidad

THOMAS NELSON (AUSTRALIA) LTD
597 Little Collins Street Melbourne 3000

THOMAS NELSON AND SONS (SOUTH AFRICA) (PROPRIETARY) LTD
51 Commissioner Street Johannesburg

THOMAS NELSON AND SONS (CANADA) LTD
81 Curlew Drive Don Mills Ontario

THOMAS NELSON AND SONS
Copewood and Davis Streets Camden New Jersey 08103

First published 1969
Copyright © 1969 by James Hemming

17 138023 1

Printed in Great Britain by Western Printing Services Ltd Bristol

DEDICATION

To *Homo sapiens*
with affection and respect

No one can live his personal life without principles. Society would be a nightmare if it did not maintain values upon which people can rely. Mix these two facts with the current speed of change. Add the rigidity of traditional moral thought. Then you reach the quandary of the individual in the modern world, seeking the moral sense of his personal life. This book is an attempt to explore some of the aspects of this search.

JAMES HEMMING

CONTENTS

THANKS AND ACKNOWLEDGEMENTS

To write a book that is at all discursive places one under a grateful obligation to so many people – the other books, the conversations, the comments, the criticisms – that it is quite impossible to make proper acknowledgements. I would, however, like to add to my general thanks, especial appreciation to Mr C. G. Lister and the Rev. Chad Varah for critical comments on Chapters Eleven and Twelve, to Professor Philip Mayer for permission to refer to his work on the Red Xhosa (shortly to be published), to Mr W. T. Miller for the gift of a photograph from his private collection, to Mr Patrick Nuttall for assistance with certain palaeontological references, and, very especially, to Mrs Joanna Miller for her patient, unremitting help with typing, corrections, and proof-reading.

I would also like to express my particular thanks to Mr J. B. Priestley and William Heinemann for permission to reproduce a rather long extract, to Faber & Faber for permission to include two extracts from poems by the late Dag Hammarskjöld, and to Sir Julian Huxley, Professor John MacMurray, Professor Robert Redfield, and Dr Anthony Storr, from whose work I have quoted in several places.

NOTE ON REFERENCES

In order to avoid a proliferation of footnotes in the present book, the main references have been grouped together at the end of the text.

ILLUSTRATIONS

(Between pages 166 and 167)

1 Animal 'altruism'
a Courage (*photo by W. T. Miller*)
b Friendship (*Frank W. Lane*)
c Tolerance (*Frank W. Lane*)

2 Children are naturally indomitable
a (*Radio Times Hulton Picture Library*)
b (*Syndication International*)
c (*Rex Features*)

3 Sacred symbol: tjuringa stone (*Australian News and Information Bureau*)

4 Signpost in the wrong direction: IXth Article of Religion (*Lambeth Palace Library*)

5 The defeat of prudery
a Ann Packer (*United Press International*)
b Lady athlete of 1908 (*Radio Times Hulton Picture Library*)

6 The drive to be
a Channel swimmer (*Syndication International*)
b Learner climbers (*Syndication International*)
c Frank Tyson (*Syndication International*)

7 Creative self-expression
a Joseph Herman (*Radio Times Hulton Picture Library*)
b Sculptor modelling (*Fox Photos*)

Part One

THE BACKGROUND

1

WHAT MORAL CRISIS?

WE are living in the time of a world-wide exploration of values. The old absolutes, whether religious or ideological, have lost their edge. Up and down the world, and from all kinds of backgrounds, people are arguing as never before about the principles on which to run their lives. What values? What purposes? What behaviour? Where does the authority lie? The young, particularly, are restless. From Sydney to Moscow, from Beirut to Boston, from Delhi to Brazil, those in authority are being challenged to justify themselves.

There is also evidence of an increase in individual desocialization, alienation, and stress: the delinquency figures, the drift to drugs, apathy, character disorders, feelings of purposelessness and lost significance, wanton destructiveness, despair, suicide. It is not only that all these exist in society – they will in any circumstances – but that they are insidiously increasing. It is as if more and more people were passing a vote of non-confidence in life as it is. Civilization appears to be getting over-strained.

The temptation at such a time is to seek a solution in some supposedly better state of society that existed before the uncertainty set in. 'Back to the old gods' has usually been the slogan when societies have faced critical times in the past. But the old gods have never provided the answer. The way out of a crisis is to look forwards and try to identify ideas and values to deal effectively with the new conditions that have themselves precipitated the doubt and malaise. Today this task faces the world. Here we shall mainly be considering the individual quandary as it exists in Britain in particular and in western civilization as a whole.

For a start, we have to dispose of a myth – that modern man is in a condition of moral decline. This gloomy assessment implies that people are today less truthful, less honest, less faithful, less compassionate, less well behaved than they were at some time in the past. It does not diminish the reality of the moral crisis facing us to say that there is no evidence to support the view that society has declined morally. Imperfect we are – inevitably; foolish we are – often; rank bad – frequently. But worse we are not. There never was a moral golden age. The pessimists who denigrate the present should read more history.

Let us take a glance backwards into the past, by way of illustration. In the second half of the eighteenth century Smollett comments on the times:

'Commerce and manufacture flourished to such a degree of increase as had never been known in this island; but this advantage was attended with an irresistible tide of luxury and excess which flowed through all degrees of the people, breaking down all the bounds of civil policy, and opening a way for licentiousness and immorality. The highways were infested with rapine and assassination; the cities teemed with the brutal votaries of lewdness, intemperance, and profligacy.'

These were the times when publicans hung up signs 'inviting people to be drunk for the small expense of *one penny*, assuring them they might be dead drunk for *tuppence* and have straw for nothing'. Not much evidence there of notable rectitude. Life two hundred years ago was, for most people, crude and cruel and squalid to an extent we should find intolerable today. Slavery was legal *in England* until 1772.

Shall we, perhaps, find a moral golden age a little later in our history, in the expansive days of the nineteenth century when Britain trebled in population and the Bible and Union Jack went together round the world? Here is Wordsworth's comment at the start of the century:

> The wealthiest man among us is the best:
> No grandeur now in nature or in book
> Delights us. Rapine, avarice, expense,
> This is idolatry; and these we adore:

He goes on, assuming as moralists for ever do, that virtue was the habit of the past:

> Plain living and high thinking are no more:
> The homely beauty of the good old cause
> Is gone; our peace, our fearful innocence,
> And pure religion breathing household laws.

Shades of Smollett! He had died only thirty years before.

Take what yardstick you like to measure the moral condition of society during the nineteenth century, at any point you like, and you will nowhere find a situation that, by comparison, makes modern society look decadent. The reverse is true: by comparison with the present, the past appears insensitive, inhumane, crude, and depraved.

Suppose we consider concern for others as a measure of social virtue. Never has so much care been provided for those in need as today. We have to set against modern welfare and justice how things were a century and more ago: child chimney-sweeps, the hanging of children, the harsh treatment of criminals, public executions, schools where flogging was a constant occurrence, the subjugation of women, brutality to the mentally ill, and much else besides.

Honesty? Consulting the crime records – or Dickens – suggests no Victorian era of virtue. Sexual propriety? A hundred years ago young girls could be sold into prostitution to fill the brothels and houses of ill-fame that were scattered plentifully around big cities. In 1839 it was estimated that there were in London 933 brothels and 844 houses of ill-fame to serve a population of two million. Brothels, in the nineteenth century, were big business, and laws to forbid living on the immoral earnings of women, after several rebuffs in Parliament, did not reach the statute book until 1885.

Illegitimacy? In the middle of the last century the illegitimacy rate for Cumberland was 108 per 1,000 live births; Norfolk, 105; Hereford, 100. The rate for Middlesex was only 40 per 1,000, but the low figure may be accounted for by the fact that abortion and infanticide were common in the big cities. In London *alone*, between 1855 and 1860, an average of 226 children under two were murdered annually – those were the ones on whom inquests *were* held. In 1967, the total of all murders in England and Wales, including cases of manslaughter, was 219.

Hooliganism? Nineteenth-century London was frequently shaken by the destructive antics of informally organized hooligan gangs of young aristocrats. These young roughs, having idled away their days, spent their nights beating people up, smashing coffee stalls, alarming women, and such like – the Bucks, the Corinthians, and all their imitators and hangers-on. Such bands were following, somewhat less cruelly, in the tradition of the nefarious Mohocks who terrorized eighteenth-century London:

'Nobody who was alone was safe from their cowardly assaults. They attacked at random any unarmed person who was out after dark. They assaulted unprotected women; they drove their swords through the sides of sedan chairs; they pulled men from coaches and slit their noses with razors, stabbed them with penknives, ripped the coaches to pieces and, in some cases, killed.'

It is a curious fact that from the eighteenth to the twentieth century hooliganism itself has become more civilized. As compared with the hooligans of present-day Britain, their earlier counterparts seem very much more heartless. Mid-twentieth-century hooliganism is ugly evidence of frustration among some of our young males; it is not evidence of a contemporary moral decline.

Love of violence? Today all violence is immediately blown up larger than life by the mass media and eagerly absorbed. Is this thirst for violence itself evidence of decline? Evidence of something missing in the satisfaction of living maybe, but not evidence of decline. Violence has always been a best-seller. In the middle of the nineteenth century, an ill-printed, poorly written ballad on the theme of some particularly gory murder could, according to Thomas Burke, 'reach the quarter-million', and that at a time when a considerable proportion of the population was illiterate: in 1838–9, 33 per cent of men and 49 per cent of women were unable to write their names on their marriage certificates.

Some people point accusingly at the gas chambers of the last war as irrefutable evidence of man's moral degeneracy. But is it? The significant point about the war against Fascism is that mankind *was* revolted by what was happening in Germany and elsewhere. The civilized world rose against the loathsome social disease and smashed in five years the New Order planned to last a thousand. At earlier times in history, political acts of hate as murderously destructive in intent were tolerated, even applauded, in the conduct of religious rivalries or war. At the Massacre of St Bartholomew, 1572, tens of thousands of Huguenots were slaughtered. In celebration, Pope Gregory XIII 'commanded bonfires to be lighted and a medal to be struck'.

Such horrors of the past were not all that anomalous in view of the fact that there is firm Old Testament justification for acts of total destruction to eliminate ideological opponents. Saul was commanded: 'Now go and smite Amalek, and utterly destroy all that they have, and spare them not; but slay both man and woman, infant and suckling, ox and sheep, camel and ass.' Elijah, on Mount Carmel, ordered the massacre of 450 of the prophets of Baal. The Victorians and Edwardians appear to have regarded such bloodbaths as a fully justified way of annihilating the enemies of the Lord. These accounts were read in churches for the edification of young and old. The awful thing that the Nazis did was to take this hatred and insensitivity towards a rival ideology – the abominated out-group – to its terrible, logical conclusion. Heinous indeed, but not without precedent. The subsequent revulsion felt around the world was a measure not only of horror but also of man's advance in humanity and tolerance.

This is not meant to be a sneer at our ancestors – they were what they were, and what we are: mixtures of kindness and cruelty, sensitivity and blind indifference, virtue and vice. But they were not, by any comparison, our moral superiors. On the contrary, allowing for ups and downs and setbacks, the kindliness and sensitivity of human societies have slowly been becoming more and more in evidence as the centuries have passed. Progress in humanity is undeniable.

What, then, is all the fuss about? It arises from several sources. Established authority is now widely challenged; this makes people nervous. Secondly, people are apprehensive because, in some fields of life, person-to-person integrity has diminished, and commercial expediency has taken its place. You buy something in good faith; it falls apart, and nobody seems to care. A pipe bursts; the plumber promises to come for certain, but never turns up. A heavy bill for car repairs arrives; you pay it and then discover that the work has not been properly done. There is a feeling that you cannot rely on people as you used to be able to. That is the practical everyday aspect of our moral quandary. Another aspect is the crisis of outlook and attitude, arising from the transformed situation of modern man. Hundreds of years of 'normal' development have been telescoped into the last fifty. Astride the present, with one foot still in the past and the other reluctantly moving towards the future, man feels uncertain and lost. The old bogies that dogged his life and kept him busy for centuries – disease, cold, hunger, darkness – are, over wide areas of the earth, in retreat. Man has only to find out how to co-operate honestly and effectively and the quality of the human lot throughout the world can be lifted to heights unimaginable a century ago. Yet, instead of excitement and satisfaction, man feels anxiety and frustration, and guilt. He is losing heart because it all seems too much for him. He is somehow failing to connect with the possibilities.

This faltering in commitment and vision is evidence not of moral decline but of failure to develop the level of moral maturity that man's new powers and responsibilities make necessary. To be as good as ever in the past, however good that may have been, is not good enough. We shall have to learn to be morally more mature than ever before. The human species, now very largely in control of this planet, is out of the nursery, with its set rules and taboos. The days of certainty have gone. We are facing an unpredictable future. As we move into it, we have to find, test, and learn to share principles that will enable us to enter into our inheritance as responsible wardens of our own lives, of society, and of the world on which we live.

The core of the problem is that the rapid process of change to which men are struggling to adapt themselves has knocked away the very props with which people, throughout history, have been supported morally. It is not through idealizing the past and heaping blame on present failures that we can tackle the moral crisis of our age, but by understanding the nature of our condition and the strains it is imposing on individual life and the social framework.

One dramatic change with profound moral implications is the change from small communities to mass conurbations as the characteristic habitat of man. In 1850, in Western Europe, three quarters of the population were engaged in growing food. A hundred years later the position has become reversed. In Britain today 80 per cent live in towns. A stable, intimate community is known to be a dependable moral support. It creates a milieu of values, relationships, mutual obligations, and example which is a dependable source of moral strength. Earlier England was well aware of the potential delinquency of the individual left without community controls. The very word 'vagabond' means 'wanderer', the man apart from his community, the masterless man, and therefore the potential rascal. The social prophylaxis used against such people in the first Elizabethan age was to whip them out of town.

Today the close-knit community has largely gone; we are all vagabonds, more or less, therefore lacking that 'moral backbone on the outside' which an intimate and enduring community life provides. Furthermore, a mass society is an impersonal society, a society of specialist functions, strangers in brief contact, high mobility. Mass society also produces pace and stress which can themselves be demoralizing. Too much to do in too much of a rush means that something has to go, or be dealt with slapdash. Each defeat leads to lowered aspiration, hence to frustration and finally, perhaps, to a habit of defensive indifference.

The alternative to moral behaviour sustained by community relationships is for the individuals comprising any community to attain sufficient moral autonomy to stand on their own feet. Such people are also the *source* of community in the modern world because they are equipped to create community everywhere they go. Contemporary man has to strive to be morally autonomous, capable of *creating* community, and concerned for others all at the same time – a being of heightened moral capability.

This is a much harder task than conformity, but in our restless, mobile, technological world, nothing less will do. For one thing, individual moral immaturity and advanced technology do not go together. A single individual running amok can do immense damage. Isolated, egocentric, socially immature personalities with chips on their shoulders have always been a part of the human scene. Shakespeare's Edmund, in *King Lear*, was just such a one. But if a personality of this kind is provided, as a gift from modern technology, with a high-speed rifle, supplemented by the refinement of telescopic sights, he can kill the President of the United States. The rakes of earlier times in their horse-drawn carriages slew a chicken or two and knocked somebody down occasionally; their equivalents today in ton-up sports cars can destroy whole families by a moment of rash ostentation. The egocentric power seeker, whether on the side of management or workers, in Parliament or out, can strike at the country's heart. Today, in fact, social irresponsibility is not only a regrettable personal insufficiency. It can, in a hundred ways, be intolerably dangerous. Yet the very nature of modern society encourages the growth of social irresponsibility; it is a catch-as-catch-can affair, ultra-competitive, ultra-atomized, needing to be offset by a *deeper* moral insight than was ever needed in the past.

The extension of democracy itself has weakened another source of moral support for the individual. The coherence of communities depends in part on ideas held in common. In the past this coherence was built on ideas generated by tradition and sustained by those in authority. This kind of rigidity still obtains in authoritarian régimes. Where freedom of thought is tolerated, all ideas are open to question. Over time, this leads to the fragmentation of many established ideas. The result is an open society, highly stimulating to some, but disturbingly confusing to others. The competition for the minds of men that goes on in such a society can easily reduce those less able to tolerate uncertainty either to seek the security of unquestioning acceptance of one or other of the conflicting ideologies, or to slip into a condition of ideological apathy: 'Nobody knows, therefore I needn't care.' Each produces its own frustrations. Those defended within a rigid ideology are constantly bombarded by the facts that are inconsistent with the ideology; those sunk in apathy cannot quieten entirely the nagging inner yearning to find meaning and coherence in life. We are today urgently in need of a common ground of awareness and understanding which can give some kind of unity and direction to our open society without destroying the rich – and valuable – variety it engenders.

People are also likely to feel, directly or indirectly, the shock of losing their special place in the universe. Men draw strength and significance from feeling central and important. Until very recently man was able to regard himself as unique. But, in the last quarter of a century – all *very* recent – he has been shifted from his reassuring centralness in the scheme of things. Go back a decade or two, and the astronomers were themselves defending the position that life on earth was a once-for-all special event. Few would do so today. There are about thirty times as many stars in 'our' galaxy as there are people living on the earth. There are 100,000 million observable galaxies, and nobody knows how many more beyond the range of observation. If planets capable of supporting our kind of intelligent life are associated with only one star in a million – and they are likely to be more frequent – that still adds up to millions of millions in the observable universe alone. Should we be foolish enough to scorch life off the surface of our little earth by an ultimate exasperation at our own inability to resolve our differences constructively, this will, it seems likely, be less of a loss to life in the universe than the death of a single individual diminishes life on this planet.

People react differently to this new perspective. Some feel a disturbing loss of prestige; some feel a terrifying loneliness; some have a well-nothing-really-matters-then-does-it? reaction; some are excited at sharing in so vast a scatter of life. What no informed person can do any longer is bask in the warmth of feeling he is a special creation. He is a part of nature. That must suffice. The fictions of grandeur are no longer tenable; we have to found our sense of dignity and value on something sounder than an illusion of absolute centralness. This, too, is part of the quandary of modern man.

In addition, we have lost our models. A moral prop for man down the ages has been the assurance that, however feeble one might be oneself, there were the unblemished great ones to admire and emulate. Depth psychology and modern communications have successfully squashed that. Men – all men – are shown to be patchy and incomplete. Resentment at losing the immaculate models of valour and rectitude has led to a reactive wallowing in human imperfection, and we get the unhelpful image of the anti-hero – as one-sided a picture as was the hero formerly.

Notice, too, the setback that man has suffered as a consequence of losing the purpose supplied by traditional Christian belief. When belief held firm, an ultimate purpose for everyone's life was given in the certain assurance of an after-life. But now, for many, that certainty has weakened, or gone. When that happens, personal life and all the future has to offer may for some seem pointless. Is not the search for something in psychedelic happenings a desperate attempt to whip significance out of life in spite of a terrifying apprehension that it may be leading nowhere, may add up to nothing?

At the same time as man is reeling under the consequences of change and challenge – consuming mountains of aspirins, tranquillizers, and sleeping-pills every year while doing so – achievement follows achievement with great rapidity so that something that would have kept eighteenth-century man talking for months may rate only a single headline. But here, too, moral questions stare us in the face. What are we to do with it all? Does it matter what we do? The old rule-books do not offer us any satisfactory answers. There aren't any absolute guides any more. The signposts are down on the road to the future. We have to think problem after problem through *de novo*.

Yet another moral problem of our times is the startling extension of personal decision in the life of individuals. The expansion of opportunity, the emancipation of women, and the increase in average spending power have together enormously extended the range of our self-determination. Before the First World War, the majority of lives were narrowly confined by circumstances; today most people are free, or at least much freer, to make the major decisions governing their lives. What shall I do for a living? Where shall I live? How shall I spend my money? Whom shall I marry? (Mobility has made this choice much wider.) How many children shall we have? What, overall, shall I *do* with my life? Such self-determination demands constant decisions, and decisions can only be made, unless frivolously, on the basis of values and purposes. What, in such an open-ended situation, shall the values and purposes be? Every modern man who has reached an adult level of self-consciousness finds himself forced to work at that conundrum: each man individually but also all of us together. Personally, socially, nationally, and internationally man has to decide what values matter and why they matter. He has to identify the principles for a shared positive morality through which to live fully in the ever-changing present, and to shape the future as it grows.

The impact of all this change and uncertainty especially affects the young. Adolescents and young adults pick up the climate of their times. If they are surrounded by confusion, they will be under greater risk of becoming confused themselves and the struggle to emerge as integrated personalities will be that much harder. Young people have never had it so good materially as today, and never had it so difficult psychologically. Moreover, they are bigger, stronger, fitter, and are maturing earlier, than ever before. This means they have far more energy to dispose of. In the 1930s, 10 per cent of children in industrial areas bore the mark of rickets on their bodies; iron deficiency was found in over 50 per cent of cases among eleven- to fifteen-year-old children examined at the Peckham Health Centre. Today such gross malnutrition is very rare indeed. Conformity is much more likely among sick and undernourished young people than among those full of health and vitamins.

Health and confusion combine in the young as uncertainty and stress. These will mount unless a convincing framework and a satisfying purpose for their lives give the young an adequate outlet for energy and aspiration. At present, evidence of mounting stress is plainly observable. During the 1967 conference of the National Association of Mental Health, 'Young Minds at Risk', Dr P. R. Boyd pointed out:

'If we examine the trend over the last nine years for juvenile crime we find an alarming picture in the age group 14–20. In 1956 the number of males per 100,000 found guilty of indictable offences was 1,400, a figure that had remained stable for the previous nine years. However from 1956 there has been a steady and sharp rise to a figure in 1965 of over 2,800; in other words, the figure has actually doubled itself in the last nine years. The trend is almost certainly persisting, and it is greater than in any other age-group.'

During the same period the rise in other stress symptoms among this age-group – maladjustment, neurosis, suicidal tendencies, and drug-dependence – has also been marked. Between 1965 and 1966 registered drug addicts among young people increased from 145 to 329. These young people, whatever their symptom of stress, are victims of a society that has not worked hard enough at the task of reorienting itself to the dramatically new situation in which *Homo sapiens* of the twentieth century finds himself.

This is the kind of moral crisis we are in today. New problems are facing us; old props have gone. We cannot go on for long fumbling and stumbling, living from hand to mouth. We should rather, learning from the past and looking to the future, work out at least a rough route-map that gives a pattern and purpose to personal and social life and restores to man the dignity and significance he is at the point of losing. Man is worried about himself. We have to try to clear his brow a little. This book is a review – an outline sketch – of some of the areas in which the thinking has to be done and the new orientation searched for.

2

CHANGING FOUNDATIONS

It is time to look at what is meant by moral values and on what their validation rests. Morality is often linked in people's minds with lists of rules – the Thou-shalts and Thou-shalt-nots which it is 'good' to obey and 'bad' to ignore. But moral codes are fairly recent arrivals on the scene, originating only a few thousand years ago. Moral behaviour – moral values in action – goes back into a much deeper antiquity.

We have to start with the social life of animals. If creatures are to live together, whether birds, beasts, insects, or fish, they can succeed in their communal life only by virtue of behaviour that allows necessary co-operation to take place. At the very minimum, there has to be the degree of co-operation that permits mating to occur and the next generation to be reared. To achieve this, as the ethologists have shown, the two sexes, particularly among birds, often develop elaborate rituals through which individual antagonisms are stilled and a bond of mutual trust established.

Even at this rudimentary level we find the need for one in-dividual to set the advantage of another before its own, and for the group as a whole to make sacrifices to defend the species from threat or destruction. A mallard drake, usually a greedy creature, will, during a certain period of the nesting season, stand aside while his mate eats. A mother will risk death to save her young ones. Birds will sometimes mob a cat. A male chimpanzee, by nature cautious, will seize a club and rush at a stuffed leopard that has been placed menacingly near. In all such cases, however experienced inwardly, if at all, we see the rudiments of the moral situation: the immediate advantage of the individual in conflict with the needs of others – self-sacrifice in action.

The obligation upon man consciously to control his motives and energies, so that the needs of individuals within society and the needs of society itself can be secured, and sustained in balance, goes back at least to the emergence of *Homo sapiens* from the earlier hominoids that preceded him. By studying the behaviour and ideas of primitive societies still in existence – the Australian aborigines or the Indians of the Amazon forest, for example – and by supplementing this information with that provided by archaeology, we can ascertain that men and moral order are inseparable. Moral values were not, as it were, injected from on high into unregenerate man at a certain point in history; they have always been present, though usually taken for granted rather than argued about. Professor Robert Redfield writes in *The Primitive World*: 'Even the little glimpses of religion and sense of obligation to do right which are accorded the archaeologist show us that twenty-five thousand years ago the order of society was moral order.'

Along with moral order to secure social coherence have gone systems to assure its continuity. Early human society achieved this mainly in two ways: by a compact social structure and by supernatural sanctions. Society itself was a closely knit community in which moral values were held in place and constantly confirmed by custom, tradition, ritual, and ceremony. There was a right and wrong way of doing everything: planting crops, grinding corn, making bargains, finding a wife, conducting war. The difference between right and wrong, even in most practical affairs, was not seen as a technical difference between an efficient and an inefficient method, but an ethical difference between a proper and improper way of doing things. Crops that failed were usually held to fail not because of bad land, bad seed, or careless husbandry, but through some ritualistic error in the tilling and planting, or through the machinations of evil magic. So with all human action of any consequence.

This technical-ethical unity of social organization is found in the most primitive of societies that still exist for us to study. Writing of the Australian aborigines, Professor O' Reilly Pidding-ton states: 'The close inter-relationship of myth, ritual, procreative beliefs, local organization and economic life is one of the most marked features of aboriginal life. The horde territory, its increase centres, and its natural food resources, so vital to the life of the aborigines, thus acquire a social and spiritual as well as a utili-tarian significance.'

Pre-literate societies had three ways of transferring information from one generation to another: by word of mouth, by art, and by ritualization. Ritualization in everyday affairs assured that some skill discovered in the past would not be lost. In course of time, the ritual took precedence over the skill which might be-come ossified because of this. One of the tjuringa stones of the aborigines symbolizes the care of yelka nuts and is the personal property of the family of which a member, in the long, long ago, discovered a quicker way of cleaning the nuts. This tjuringa is a sacred object which relates the present to the past and commemo-rates an important tribal discovery. The 'new' method of cleaning nuts is still in use among aborigines today. The dual effect of ritual – it preserves and it ossifies – is an important factor in the evolution of human thought and human society.

The moral compactness of primitive society at a higher level of social development is brought out in Professor Malinowski's study of the fishing communities of the Trobriand Archipelago:

'Within each canoe there is one man who is its rightful owner, while the rest act as crew. All these men, who as a rule belong to the same sub-clan, are bound to each other and to their fellow villagers by mutual obligations; when the whole community go out fishing, the owner cannot refuse his canoe. He must go out himself or let someone else do it instead. The crew are equally under an obligation to him; each man must fill his place and stand by his task. Each man also receives his fair share in the distribution of the catch as an equivalent of his service. Thus the ownership and use of the canoe consist of a series of definite obligations and duties uniting a group of people into a working team.'

Again, when Professor Malinowski is describing the co-operation between two village communities:

'The inland village supplies the fishermen with vegetables; the coastal community repays with fish. This arrangement is primarily an economic one. It has also a ceremonial aspect, for the exchange has to be done according to an elaborate ritual. But there is also the legal side, a system of mutual obligations which forces the fisherman to repay whenever he has received a gift from his inland partner, and vice versa. Neither partner can refuse, neither may stint in his return gift, neither should delay.'

The other virtually universal method of underpinning the moral order was to found its rules, rituals, and relationships in some kind of supernatural order with its divinities, its characteristic world view, its explanation of ultimate origins, and its representatives on earth. Supernatural systems to be found within the human race and throughout history vary in quality, humanity, and sophistication, but everywhere play a similar role in human affairs. The gods of such moral orders are essentially guardians of the 'right' ways of doing things – demanding, punitive, appeasable, potentially helpful. Originally this guardianship extended into every area of human activity. In Leviticus, for example, principles of nutrition and hygiene are stated as divine laws. The habit of mixing moral and hygienic values is still with us today.

Moral values, then, are simply those values which, over the course of time, come to be regarded as essential to the good conduct of personal and social life. Traditionally they have been based on some concept of divine or quasi-divine revelation which, once for all, laid down regulations governing human affairs. Hence, they have been regarded as not only right in themselves but also as expressing the divine will for men.

So long as the sacred order, the perspective that went with it, and the values linked to it, remained unquestioned, people cherished these values because of their presumed special origin: the ancestors, the gods, the prophets, God. In addition, the values were honoured because they served to unify a people, differentiating 'us' from 'them', imparting a sense of superiority over against others. The influence on people of these values was not only to encourage obedience and generate guilt (when disobeyed), but also to provide a foundation for a sense of identity and self-respect. To do the divine will was to become at one with the divine purpose and to gain self-value and serenity.

To understand the moral situation today, we have to realize that the compact, self-perpetuating moral order is now a thing of the past. We are in a changing world and need a more flexible, more personal, and therefore more responsible moral order to go with it. Absolute authority has gone. In place of a single system of beliefs we have the open society. The authority operating in the modern world is, apart from the authority of the law, the authority of knowledge, relationships, situations, purposes. This is a pattern of authority calling for constant thought, constant judgement, constant sensitivity, constant humanity, constant responsibility – and a sense of direction. Western civilization is struggling to establish itself in the new framework. The nature of the task can best be seen by going back a century and comparing the past with the present.

A hundred years or so ago, John Smith, ordinary citizen, was, especially if he lived in the country, firmly held in his place in life by his employer, his landlord, his squire, his parson, his family, his community, and God over all. Wives were subject to their husbands. Apprentices were subject to their masters. Employees were subject to their employers. People were expected to be honest, truthful, reliable, *and obedient*. The child mumbling his catechism promised: 'To submit myself to all my governors, teachers, spiritual pastors and masters. To order myself lowly and reverently to all my betters. To hurt nobody by word nor deed.

To be true and just in all my dealing.' Conformity, or at least the appearance of conformity, was the lynchpin of moral order. It was a hierarchically ordered world, set in an easily comprehensible universe.

In such a framework, it might be hard to make a good living, but the conduct of personal life was comparatively easy. The range of choices for the ordinary citizen was narrow; most decisions were imposed by circumstances. The rule-books, as interpreted by pastors and masters, were to hand in case of doubt. All you had to do was to submit to authority and live out your days 'in that state of life unto which it shall please God to call me'.

This tidy, but restricted, system was built on an equally tidy set of beliefs. Man had been created perfect, some 6,000 years earlier, but had wantonly chosen to disobey God. This sin had brought into the world evil and suffering, which went on spreading from generation to generation so that every child was to be regarded as 'born in sin'. In due course God had taken pity on his corrupt Creation and had sent his son to save the world, by his teaching, by his example, and by his death: 'a full, perfect and sufficient sacrifice, oblation and satisfaction, for the sins of the whole world'. Thereafter man had only to believe in Jesus and the Christian faith, and to strive to follow its teachings, and he would inherit an eternal life which would more than make up for whatever had happened to him in this one.

This whole system had, in terms of human psychological needs, much to commend it. Although it condemned man as corrupt, it also gave him significance in the universe; every person saw himself as the child of a God who *cared*. It defined the limits of behaviour in an easily understood way, with its sets of rules, reinterpreted, at need, by those in authority. It maintained a status hierarchy in which every man 'knew his place'. It presented an explanation for the entire cosmology which even the least intelligent was able to grasp. It provided a ready means of assuaging guilt even if it contributed towards generating it. To the man who failed in his purpose here, it offered the recompense of a life hereafter. There was cruelty in it sometimes, but comfort in it always, and to those who accepted it actively rather than passively there was inspiration and challenge. Of the various alternatives available to man to see him through the childhood of the race, it was probably the best. But it was not true, or only true in an allegorical sense. It was certainly not true in the way that John Smith believed it a hundred years ago, or in the way Billy Graham, the fundamentalists, and near-fundamentalists believe it today.

The collapse of Christian dogma under the impact of modern knowledge and critical analysis paved the way simultaneously for the coming of the open society and for our contemporary moral crisis. Not since the Roman gods lost their grip on the credulity of the Roman intellectuals has so startling a transformation overtaken the ideology of a civilization. For the Romans, Christianity was ready to hand to replace the old beliefs. But, when Christian dogma in its turn failed to carry its old conviction, what was to serve as a foundation for moral values?

It so happens that at the very time John Smith was going about his business in the latter half of the nineteenth century a new enlightenment about the human condition, with profound moral implications, was bursting upon the minds of men through the work of Wallace, Darwin, T. H. Huxley, and others – the concept of evolution, first seen as mainly biological but gradually becoming expanded and refined until it embraced all aspects of life. This evolutionary picture presented man with a quite different image of himself, a dramatically different time-scale to go with it, and, increasingly, as the years passed, a cosmology that swallowed John Smith's homely concept in a magnificent, vast immensity.

This influx of new insight turned John Smith's ideology inside out. Man was not a fallen angel, but a rising animal, incomplete not through the machinations of his own evil will but because he is an imperfect, emerging, evolving creature by virtue of the creative process which produced him. This, once the fact of evolution had been established, became the only reasonable way to regard man, whether or not you believed a Supreme Being rather than some other dynamic lay behind the existence of the creative process itself.

The evolutionary perspective also revealed that, as a species, man is not to be regarded as a long-established failure but as a promising beginner. Man is around half a million years old – very young by the biological time-scale. The giant lizards had a run as the dominant species on earth for some hundred million years. By comparison man is hardly off the nursery floor, in spite of his accelerating development.

The burden of initiating evil was also lifted from humanity. Evil, it now was plain, had not been brought into the world by the sin of man but appeared to be an unavoidable by-product of the creative process itself. This was a staggering topsy-turvy thought for the pastors and masters of John Smith. They had grown used to regarding the Creator as above failure or compromise, impeccable, all-loving, and almighty. But here, in the record of the rocks, in the evidence of creatures still living, was testimony that there had been false starts and dead ends in evolution, that 'all things' were by no means 'bright and beautiful'. The plague bacillus, virulent bacteria, butcher birds, gaboon vipers, and the liver fluke were as much created things as butterflies and spring flowers. God did not necessarily have to be dismissed from human conjecture; but he certainly had to be redefined. An all-loving *and* almighty God 'out there' no longer squared with the evidence. Swinburne, anticipating some theologians of our day, wrote:

> This thing is God:
> To be man with thy might,
> To grow straight in the strength of thy spirit,
> and live out thy life as the light.

And what of the 'soul' of man – the striving, searching essence of personality and all the higher qualities that go with it? The soul was thought to have been exclusive to the human race. This idea, too, has had to be dropped as the years have passed. Judging only in terms of man and the higher animals that today share the world with him, we find in these primates the rudiments of the subjective awareness so marked in man. Yet between the higher apes and man is a wider gap than between man and the recently discovered man-apes or ape-men whose bones and arte-facts indicate they had more highly developed brains than those of the apes. We know nothing of the thoughts and feelings of these long-extinct creatures. We have reason to assume, however, that their subjective awareness lay somewhere between that of the higher apes and our own experience. It seems likely that, in due course, other 'missing links' will be discovered. Thus, we can no longer regard the soul as bursting into full bloom within the psyche of man, but as emerging gradually in the process of evolution.

The new enlightenment, along with the other advances in scientific understanding of the past two centuries, while undermining the absolutist foundation for moral values, has offered new foundations in their place – roots for human values in the creative process itself, and in the nature and needs of man. To the first of these sources we will now turn.

Looking back down the 2,000 million years or so during which the story of life has been unfolding on earth, we can observe certain continuities of trend as creatures have evolved into more and more complex – or 'higher' – forms. We are, of course, biased observers. What operates to prepare for, or promote, human advance we regard as 'good'; what is inimical to it we consider 'bad'. But our viewpoint is not merely subjective. We are a part of life and biased in its favour, but it seems valid none the less – if any judgement is ever to be regarded as valid – to accept the direction of evolution as indicating an upward trend: that a worm is a more significant entity than a single living cell, that a horse is a more significant creature than a worm, and that man is a more significant creature than a horse, if only because each is more conscious than the other.

If this evolutionary direction is accepted as 'good', then certain elements of it can be identified as especially pertinent. These warrant our attention. We represent self-conscious life at a stage when it can turn back and examine the processes that have produced it. These processes can be taken as indicators of likely future trends in development.

One of these abiding trends has already been mentioned: the gradual extension of the range of consciousness. As Teilhard de Chardin has pointed out, to go backward in time down the life-scale is to observe a progressive diminution of consciousness until it ceases to be detectable. Reversing the perspective, we can watch awareness of the environment expanding from a bare response to the immediate environment – sense without sight or smell or hearing – up through the development of the special senses until, in the primates and, later, man, we find a complex balance of the senses and an overtopping consciousness to interpret their messages; and functions of mind extending beyond consciousness as such into imagination, judgement, and creative thinking. Finally, man adds the product of his inventive creativity to his senses, extending their range, through microscope, telescope, and other devices, to the almost infinitely small and the almost infinitely distant, and bringing the whole surface of the globe within range of his eyes and ears.

The principle we can abstract from this is that consciousness is 'a good thing'. As Samuel Johnson put it, 'it is better to know than not to know'. There are, of course, exceptions. Ignorance is sometimes bliss. But as a principle the more conscious we are of our environment the better. The converse of this is that withholding from people information that is relevant to their lives is wrong. Supplying them with misinformation is also wrong. If we apply that to the education of children, the management of industry, the operations of government, the biasing of news, and the protestations of unscrupulous advertisers, we can at once see how relevant this particular principle is to our times. To withhold relevant information intentionally is, to the mind, the equivalent of deliberately starving the body. The future will no doubt regard it as equally criminal.

But the extension of consciousness has not only been a matter of knowing but also of feeling. Higher organisms are more sensitive than lower organisms. Higher animals offer plenty of indication that they can feel put out, care for one another, pine if separated, play and dream, gain or lose self-esteem, feel guilty. To develop the range of feeling in ourselves and encourage its development in others would seem, therefore, good by the evolutionary criterion, and the reverse, bad. Fear of feeling is a self-diminishing, often a neurotic, tendency.

Yet another indicator that we can trace up through evolution is the greater individuation of members of a species. Individuality is analogous to consciousness: it becomes less and less marked as we press back in the life-scale. Reversing the perspective, two beetles of the same species are different, but not much. Mice or sparrows may show considerable individuality of character and temperament. Monkeys and apes, as recent observers have discovered, show marked differences of personality. In man, individuality is more definite still. A high level of individuality and a more complex capacity for life are thus found together. Individual variation, we might say, is pro higher-order life and standardization is anti higher-order life. The standardized creatures survive by filling a niche, but at the price of being limited and set.

The degree of individuality we have attained in our open society is one of its main features and one of its main problems. In earlier societies the range of individual behaviour was much narrower because standardization of behaviour by social expectation was much more powerful; new ways of doing anything were regarded with suspicion, if not condemned as impious. The open societies, such as we have today, value change and encourage variation. This gives all sections of society – not just the privileged – a chance to explore their individuality.

If we accept the evolutionary trend of greater individuation as a good thing, a number of supplementary principles accrue. Individuals have a responsibility to themselves to develop their individual uniqueness. We should seek to help others in their struggle to become themselves. We should never try to standardize human beings by aiming to force them into a preconceived mould; should welcome variety in one another, personally and socially. We should be tolerant of nonconformity. As Sir Julian Huxley has often stressed, exclusiveness is biological death; interaction with difference is one of the great sources of life. Hidden within individuals are untold latent potentialities. These emerge under the challenge of the environment, material or social. Human beings, since they are social animals, need the security of warm interpersonal and group relationships; they also need the stimulus of interaction in order to grow. These are laws of life and should be venerated as such.

Let us notice how these developmental principles deriving from evolution accord with our intuitive evaluation of good and bad societies. We feel democracy is the right system for society, even if it sometimes seems muddled and slow in its methods. We are apprehensive of dictatorships, even when they are wise and benevolent. In fact, autocracies fall down on every principle stated above. In order to exist as themselves they must limit individuality, distort information, curtail the consciousness of ordinary people, blunt sensitivity, maintain hierarchical exclusiveness. Dictatorships sometimes have the short-term advantage of producing a temporary efficiency in the attainment of limited aims, but they have soon to start moving towards democracy again or they destroy themselves by becoming set, and quenching the creativity within their people. A corollary to this is that, if any nation developed a fully participant democracy, interacting vigorously with other nations, instead of the nationalistically oriented democratic-autocratic compromises we have so far achieved, it would release such a wealth of creative human energy that its capacity for self-transformation would amaze the world.

Evolution and the new cosmology viewed together present man with an even more profound responsibility than self and social development. Highly developed life in the universe is a rare and precious thing, even though probably far more widely spread than was once supposed. It certainly remains true that in the whole vast array of stars and galaxies, spreading for millions of light years in any direction that we care to direct our visual telescopes and our 'big dishes', we can discover nothing more significant than human personality. We represent – along with what other intelligent beings exist in the universe – the supreme achievement of life. And now our own history calls on us to accept that fact fully. Earlier man could rampage with the utmost destructiveness and barely scratch the surface of the globe, locally and temporarily. Today we have in our hands the power and the knowledge to destroy the substance, and if not the substance the quality, of life as we know it.

What the future will be like for our children and grandchildren and for other men far ahead of us in the mists of the future depends on how we use our present knowledge and power. To refuse to accept that responsibility is to be less than men. Already, magnificent creatures like the whale are threatened with extinction. Forests fall that our newspapers may be unnecessarily fat. Population spreads like a plague, stamping the earth bare and producing appalling overcrowding that blunts the power to live. Every day decisions are being made that will shape the future. To a degree we are all responsible for those decisions. Every day we make choices; every day we act. And how we choose and how we act affects others. The contemporary foundation for moral values is the acceptance of our responsibility for ourselves, for one another, and for the future.

This is a new moral situation for man. Social duty in the animal kingdom is instinctive. In simple societies it is largely intuitive – knit closely into a way of life and passed on from generation to generation almost unaltered. As A. L. Kroeber states in *Anthropology*: 'their sense of right and wrong springs from the unconscious roots of social feeling, and is therefore unreasoned, compulsive and strong'. In this kind of society, part of moral obligation is seen as to retain the social order intact and the ideas that go with it. Today our moral responsibility is quite different. It is to steer change and development aright and to identify and sustain the principles of personal, social, and global life that permit us to do so. In a changing society the moral aim is not to conform but to transform. Certainty has gone and we have to depend on ourselves. As Harold Blackham says in *Religion in a Modern Society*, our modern open society 'is a permanent incompleteness, leaving open the interpretation of the world and the choice of values, and therefore reminding everyone that this is a personal responsibility'. Which brings us to the question whether humanity has got what it takes to measure up to this immense responsibility.

In *Towards a Psychology of Being*, Professor A. H. Maslow writes: 'When the philosophy of man (his nature, his goals, his potentialities, his fulfilment) changes, then everything changes, not only the philosophy of politics, of economics, of ethics and values, of interpersonal relations and of history itself, but also the philosophy of education, the theory of how to help men become what they can and deeply need to become.'

That about sums it up. It sounds like a big task of readjustment. It *is* a big task, one that in this book we can only touch on here and there, searching for the moral reorientation that will put us in the way of tackling the job. *But can* Homo sapiens *do it?* The time has come to take a closer look at man himself. Has he the will, the imagination, the vision to move on into the future?

3

THE MEASURE OF MAN

WE have now to examine whether man can create a moral order commensurate with his new powers and responsibilities or whether he has overrun his moral resources. Is he on the threshold of a new freedom or is he about to forge new fetters to contain and limit the fruits of his exuberant inventiveness? Is he flexing his muscles for a great leap forward or is he at the end of his tether? It depends on his actual potentialities. What is the nature of man as a person? We cannot get anywhere much until we have made up our minds about that. The world is our sample and all history and prehistory our data. That, however, is too broad a front to work on here. In this chapter we shall limit the perspective to considering man's idea of man as it has developed in western civilization.

Definitions of man have been the sport of writers since the beginning of our civilization. In any substantial dictionary of quotations you will find, under 'Man' and 'Men', not to mention 'Woman' and 'Women', a dizzy assortment of viewpoints. Some are reverential, some are sneers, some are jokes. 'Man is a two-legged animal without feathers,' is one of Plato's comments;

Shakespeare's Falstaff refers to him as 'a forked radish'. Cervantes gives us: 'Every one is as God made him, and oftentimes a great deal worse.' But honour is paid, among the puzzlement: 'What a piece of work is man! how noble in reason! how infinite in faculty!' – thus speaks Hamlet. 'Great things are done,' says Blake, 'when men and mountains meet.' Tennyson intones: 'For man is man, and master of his fate.' Pope's 'Essay on Man' runs to over 1,300 lines in an attempt to square the account, but, having encouraged us with the assurance that 'The proper study of Mankind is Man', he still teeters in uncertainty in his assessment:

> Chaos of Thought and Passion, all confused;
> Still by himself abused, or disabused;
> Created half to rise, and half to fall;
> Great lord of all things, yet a prey to all;
> Sole judge of Truth, in endless Error hurled:
> The glory, jest and riddle of the world.

The debate continues – inevitably: man is a mixture.

It is a regrettable fact, however, that, whereas the philosophers, poets, dramatists, essayists, and novelists have swept over the whole range of human possibilities, other influential voices have consistently belittled man, being obsessed with his potential weakness, and almost oblivious to his equally obvious strength. This is damaging because the value an individual places on himself affects his behaviour. To be at his best, a person needs 'a positive self-concept'. We also know that human beings react with extraordinary sensitivity to the expectations of others. Experiments have shown that children reflect their teacher's anticipations about them to a remarkable degree. If a teacher believes a group of ordinary children is especially bright, he will convey his conviction to the children so that they tend to do especially well. Industrial managements, it has been clear for a long time, get the sort of behaviour in their labour force that their approach and assumptions generate. One kind of management will engender co-operation, interest in work, and reliability, while another management, with similar industrial objectives and a similar labour force, provokes antagonism, indifference, and irresponsibility. A man's behaviour at any time is not only the outcome of his potentialities and previous experience but also of the expectations he has about himself in the immediate situation, and the expectations that others have about him.

It is, therefore, closely pertinent to our assessment of the moral capacity of contemporary men and women that, throughout history, man has had his self-respect hobbled by a consistently bad image of himself promulgated by authoritative ideas operating in the society around him. This cannot but have the effect of obscuring his vision about his full capabilities, and lowering his sense of value and, therefore, of responsibility. An individual is unlikely to behave responsibly in a situation where he feels he has no value as a person. A low level of self-esteem need not be too destructive in a static, autocratic society which is stratified in terms of implied worth, but it becomes a major source of moral weakness in a changing open society, where every individual stands or falls by his own autonomous development. Which is the reason why the rejected, and self-rejecting, are today such a problem to themselves and to society.

Psychologically, the whole matter of the acquisition or loss of a sense of personal worth is subtle and complex. Babies and small children, being small and weak, yet subject to inner passions and outer criticism, readily acquire a crippling sense of inadequacy and inferiority. If loved, reassured, and encouraged, they can transcend this check on self-esteem and find positive ways of compensating for it and gaining confidence. A society should be concerned to help them do so. But some societies, including our own, aggravate and reinforce initial self-doubt by surrounding parents and children with depressing ideas about the corruption of human nature. It is important to understand this climate of despondency in which our society has been sunk. So long as it remains, it will obstruct the moral and creative potentiality of western man. To give ourselves a chance we have to understand and rectify the historical and contemporary distortions of the human self-image.

The idea of man as an evil creation was in evidence much earlier than Christianity, but the Church Fathers built this misrepresentation into social thinking in a particularly discouraging form following a crisis in the early Church in which a British theologian, Pelagius, and Augustine, later St Augustine, were the principal protagonists. We have been bearing the brunt of this error ever since.

The substance of this fifth-century dispute was that Pelagius believed man had within him the power to transform himself, whereas Augustine clung to the conviction that man is corrupt by nature: 'guilty in the sight of God and deserving of damnation, unless by baptism he enters into the redemption secured by Christ's Passion, and that secondly his will is enslaved to evil desires (concupiscence) until it is liberated by God's grace'. The dispute raged for seven years. Finally, in a council at Carthage in A.D. 418, attended by over 200 bishops, Augustine won, eighteen bishops resigned, and what was fundamentally nothing more than a committee decision became the established doctrine of the Church.

This doctrine – that man is devoid of virtue from within himself until rescued from his unregenerate condition by divine grace – persisted century after century, reinforced Sunday after Sunday throughout Christendom, unrelieved by any more hopeful note. A thousand years later we find this pessimism about man being reaffirmed in the Articles of Religion promulgated in 1562. Article IX states: 'Original Sin . . . is the fault and corruption of the nature of every man, that naturally is ingendered of the offspring of *Adam*; whereby man is very far gone from original righteousness, and is of his own nature inclined to evil. . . .' By this time, too, the idea had become deeply ingrained that man's vigorous physical desires were, of themselves, evil. Article IX concludes: 'Concupiscence and lust hath of itself the nature of sin.'

Since the sixteenth century, this jaundiced view of man has been constantly reaffirmed by the substance of sermons, the Litany, and many prayers – the sources from which, until very recently, most of the people of our culture acquired their evaluation of themselves. Says the Church of England Litany, in frequent use until well after the First World War: 'Remember not, Lord, our

offences, nor the offences of our forefathers; neither take thou
vengeance of our sins: spare us, good Lord, spare thy people,
whom thou hast redeemed with thy most precious blood, and
be not angry with us for ever.' The General Confession, still
used regularly in churches, carries on the same negative tradition
about man: 'We have left undone those things which we ought to
have done; And we have done those things which we ought not
to have done; And there is *no* health in us.' (My italics.)

As Pelagius himself pointed out, the doctrine of inherited
corruption is itself morally corrupting. So, too, is the doctrine
that physical desires are, in themselves, sinful. Although only a
few people nowadays consciously hold these beliefs, their long
inculcation must still be having a widespread influence in society.
The persisting ideas that sex is 'dirty' and that the uninhibited
enjoyment of life is somehow wicked may well have their origin
here; and it seems likely that much irresponsible behaviour arises
as the aftermath of the view that man is no good of himself.

With the extension of the scientific exploration of nature and
of man, one might have supposed that man would quickly
have escaped from the taint of self-rejection. We now realize
that man's 'shadow-side' is an aspect of his potentially creative
dynamic. As there is imperfection in evolution itself, it is not
surprising that there is in man both incompleteness and a capacity
for bad behaviour. Man is, among other things, a system of
energy, and we must expect this energy to be misdirected sometimes. The real problem is how to actualize our powers creatively,
not that we have within us potentially dangerous and destructive
energy. But this liberating reorientation of thought has not
yet become a part of social consciousness.

Indeed, the negative evaluation of man has re-emerged in a
secular form as the model which presents modern man as a
savage overlaid with a thin veneer of civilization, as though man
were pretending to be humane whereas he is really a monster.
This concept of man is a mass of inaccuracies. The idea of the
'savage' is itself a projection of human fears of the unknown.
Primitive societies show a range of behaviour between one and
the other as varied as the range between nations in 'developed'

areas of the world. Some are gentle; some are warlike; some are tensed and ambitious; some are relaxed and easy-going. It all depends on the sort of terrain the people live in, the societies they have built up, and the kind of interaction they have with their neighbours. The brute savage that people have at the back of their minds when they talk of civilization being 'only skin deep' is as much an image of fantasy as was Rousseau's 'noble savage'. It is a projection of their own fears about the uncivilized residues within themselves. Look where we like around the human race, we see people living together in various ways, but almost always co-operatively within their groups and always with a sensible, if imperfect, framework of internal social order. Bertrand Florney writes in *Jivaro*, his study of a primitive head-hunting tribe in the upper Amazon: 'But one thing is certain: the Jivaros are not savages. There are no such things as savages.' Professor Redfield speaks of 'the traditional moral solidarity to be found in any isolated folk society'.

In a way, of course, we *are* potential cave men – but there is nothing alarming or disparaging in this condition. Man stopped evolving biologically when he was still at a primitive stage socially. Says Sir Julian Huxley: 'Man's inherited mental powers cannot have changed appreciably since the Aurignacian cave-dwellers' – which is around 25,000 years ago. What, mainly, has been happening since is the cumulative advance of society which offers each generation of children a modified environment and, therefore, an opportunity to bring to fruition potentialities that would have found no stimulus to full development in more primitive times. There is not much point in being a Beethoven if the only musical instrument available is a nose flute; or in having the potentialities to become a 'born pilot' before the days of aeroplanes.

To this extent the society makes the man, or, rather, a man is the outcome of the interaction between his potentialities and the environment, plus a rather subtle element which we can call integration, or focus, the quality of achieving harmony and concentration of powers within the personality itself.

It follows that, if a modern child at birth were transferred to the conditions of Stone Age cave-dwellers, he would grow up like one: a member of his Stone Age society, *not* a brute. It is equally true that, if a Stone Age cave-dweller could have been transferred at birth to a contemporary civilization, he would have grown up into a modern adult. The reality is the potentiality of a child to take on a myriad different forms according to the environment in which his growth takes place. This does not mean that there is not in every person a uniqueness craving fulfilment. There is, and this is one of the vital elements in the whole conundrum of personal emergence. As a society is, so will the uniqueness shape itself, personal yet socially modified, through the dynamic interaction of individual and environment.

Another reinforcement of the idea of man's supposedly sordid nature – a savage under the skin – has come from the wide acceptance of the outlook of classical Freudianism. Freud attacked with great insight and courage the sexual obscurantism of his time, opened up to view the dynamic range of the human psyche, and established important mechanisms that underlie human interaction, but he himself projected on to man a deep pessimism about human nature which tinged his overall view of the human condition.

Freud's perception of man had all the brilliance and all the narrowness of genius. The time has come frankly to admit the incompleteness of his perception. Freudian man is presented as primarily driven to seek gratification, particularly sexual gratification. This is a half-truth. Of course man does seek gratification, and why not? Life is to be enjoyed, not denied. Sex *is* obviously a dominant human impulse. But man is also striving for self-fulfilment, which embraces the satisfaction of his biological appetites but goes beyond them. Man is a creative, goal-seeking creature by nature, eager to explore and control his environment; he is inventive, inquiring, hungry for significance and status, yearning for self-realization.

The Freudian system explains man's creative propensities as nothing but substitutes for the blocked gratification of sexuality. It denies creativeness a place in the human psyche in its own right. It denies spontaneity. This interpretation of human behaviour does not stand up. The Neolithic Polynesians who discovered New Zealand were driven by something other, one may suppose, than ungratified sexual need when they covered 1,500 miles of the Pacific in open canoes with their upper planks tied on, so that the travellers had to bale constantly to keep afloat. A man concentrating on an idea, or a symphony, or an invention does not really behave as though he were acting to alleviate the inhibition of his primary impulses. Freud writes: 'Much of our most highly valued cultural heritage has been acquired at the cost of sexuality and by the restriction of sexual motive forces.' Then how does it come about that some of the greatest creative periods of human history – Ancient Greece, Renaissance Italy – were particularly free from sexual prudery and inhibition in those social groups in which the creative energy was manifest? The well-to-do citizen of ancient Athens, for example, had readily available, if he wanted them, a wife, mistresses, concubines, and boy friends.

The partial perception of Freudian theory is nowhere more clearly displayed than in its approach to child behaviour. It correctly observes the infant's fascinated interest in his bodily sensations and functions and in his genitalia; it fails to take sufficient regard of the indomitable courage with which a young child tackles the task of standing and walking, and the insatiable curiosity he turns loose on the world around him. It correctly observes the child's aggressivity, tantrums, and anger, but almost overlooks the resolute will with which the child proclaims his personal identity to those near him. As Anthony Storr writes in *Sexual Deviation*: 'It can be assumed that, from the very beginning of life, there is present a drive towards self-realization, towards finding one's own identity as a person, and that this is a motive force as powerful as sex itself.' Adler and Jung both recognized this drive; Freud neglected it. And here Freud was wrong.

Freud himself came to see the insufficiencies of gratification theory, and proposed an alternative scheme: the theory of life and death instincts (Eros and Thanatos). This, in turn, is inadequate to explain man. The Eros–Thanatos theory interprets human activity as a combination of two instincts: the positive, life-affirming drive to create, and the negative, destructive impulse towards death. Freud explained the death instinct by supposing that all instinctive life is under the impulse to regress to an earlier state – hence what is living yearns to return to an inanimate condition. This leaves Eros – the life instinct – totally without explanation. Freud admitted this frankly, and so revealed that he was loth to accept the simple truth – that man is driven, by his nature, to be creative; that the constructive in man is a more powerful force than the destructive. If this were not so, we should not be here.

But even more damage has been done to the image of man by the Freudian gloom than to rob him of the self-respect arising from his positive creative potentialities. The concept of the death instinct led on to the idea that man, of his nature, generates destructive impulses that constantly seek an outlet. No one would deny that envy, hatred, malice, and all uncharitableness bob up readily enough from the human psyche. Man is capable of destructive aggressiveness, cruelty, and viciousness, but the explanation of their origin is not to be found in a rooted instinct that *has* to seek an outlet. The truth is that man has a self to be established and energy to be disposed of. Aggressiveness mounts if he feels himself to be frustrated, challenged, threatened, trapped, or uncertain about his status. Aggression is a *necessary* biological reaction to assist the individual in overcoming obstacles as they arise. There is plenty of aggression and destructiveness around because much of life, right from very early childhood, is threatening and frustrating so that there is in society at any time abundant free aggression ready to be displaced on to any convenient object, person, or group – a thwarting row, or loss of face, at breakfast makes us more likely to kick the garage door. But it is not true that, wherever there is a human being, destructiveness is willy-nilly mounting inside him and needing an object to release itself upon.

A relaxed, amiable school or factory or family is as it is, not because people there are repressing their aggression but because life is reasonably fulfilling and, in consequence, not much aggression is being provoked. Recent work on primates in their natural habitats, as compared with those living under the frustrations of captivity, endorses the view that aggressiveness is not a necessity of behaviour; it is something held in reserve for special situations. Freud, although he believed it possible to 'sublimate' sex into something else, seems to have felt that destructiveness had to be directly expressed: 'The holding-back of aggressiveness is in general unhealthy and leads to illness.' Once again, this is a half-truth. It is unhealthy to refuse to accept our aggressive reactions. They need airing. They need an outlet. But to have reached a stage when it becomes frequently necessary to let fly without restraint is not a mark of mental health. By and large, the overtly aggressive people and societies *are* the disturbed ones. Nazi Germany was not mentally healthy. Tyrants, like Nero or Shaka, are liable to go mad. Behind destructiveness is a thwarting of personal growth, and it is this we should pay attention to rather than riding away from the real problem on a new mythology of human savagery. Violence is a constant potential in human nature and will be dealt with in greater detail in a later chapter. Here we can just state that man is not doomed to live with a destiny of unbridled aggressivity. The primates, including man, when given reasonable conditions of life in free association with others, are not particularly aggressive creatures, and what aggression they show is limited to the context of maintaining the dominance hierarchy – behaviour which, in itself, helps to preserve their society. Whereas Freud's gloomy view of man may well be attractive to those who seek a mirror for their own pessimism, knowledge acquired since Freud's death refutes much of his despondency. The neo-Freudians have themselves mitigated the pessimism, but its influence lives on.

Yet another attack on man's integrity has come from those who have written in such a way as to undermine man's confidence in his own reason. Man, the argument goes, uses his reason as a cover for his real motives. By rationalizing his behaviour, he both flatters himself and aims to deceive his neighbours. Rationalization *is* a human stratagem and it was right to point it out. The damage is done when, at the next step, the suggestion is made that human reason is *nothing but* a device for rationalizing selfish and irrational behaviour. The falsity of this belief is easily exposed. For one thing, if man had not a genuine respect for reason there would be no temptation to rationalize; for another, if the opponents of reason are right, then their elaborate statements are, by definition, mere rationalizations of their own unadmitted impulses and we can discard them as superficial. Furthermore, the towering achievements of the human intellect make nonsense of the anti-intellectuals who live by the results of human reason while they sneer at its honesty as a human function. Once again we find ourselves faced by an *incomplete* perception which is taken beyond its brief and ends up by belittling man.

The siren voices of consumer commercialism have added their quota to other dominant ideological influences in denigrating man. Many politicians have fallen into line and are taking it for granted that all that really matters in life is purchasable and that we shall inevitably all be happy if we will only put our backs into doubling the standard of living in twenty-five years.

The widely sold image of man as 'economic man' reduces his stature by presenting him as primarily omnivorous for commodities and by presenting the measure of fulfilment as how many of them he can acquire. A not inconsiderable number of people get the message and behave not only as if it were true but also as if it were the whole truth – and then wonder why the flavour has gone out of life. 'I'm all right, Jack' is, often enough, a self-justification voiced against a niggling doubt. Marx, incidentally, did not define man as 'economic'. He described economic man as arising from the thwarting of man's true nature.

Of course money is good. Prosperity is good. Having things to buy is good. Social justice is good. Social services are good. But these things are the means to life, not its ends. The voice of commercialism is deluding because it states as loudly and often as it can that possessions are ends in themselves. This despite evidence to the contrary. Money talks, but *sometimes* the satisfaction of working at a particular job, or with particular people, talks louder. People value not only money, but also warmth and trust and respect in their relationships, and a sense of making a valuable contribution by what they do. So we find a steady, if small, stream of people leaving lucrative posts where they have established themselves successfully to become teachers, or to work in the social services, taking time out for retraining *en route*. In large numbers, students are turning to studies that lead on to social service. These are not saints or deviants; they are ordinary people who want their lives to add up to something in their own judgement of what life is about. Their behaviour is symptomatic of the sense of something missing in life which is today widespread in society; a sense of frustration in people about the use to which their lives are being put. These people, and others, are in revolt against the frustrating implications of man viewed as 'consumer'.

The daily press and other mass media add their quota to reinforce modern pessimism. A research worker from outer space, making off with a supply of popular newspapers as his data, could readily establish that earthmen were a quarrelsome, murderous, lecherous bunch of thieves and rascals with a tiny minority of decent people struggling to get a hearing, and all living in the midst of constant horrifying disaster. The steady flow of news about human failure and misfortune has a double impact. It obscures the part that love, self-sacrifice, and creative effort and achievement play in the day-to-day life of mankind, and it blunts sensitivity by forcing people to build a protective resistance against the ceaseless catalogue of human suffering. The world is now one world and has a world-wide information service. It is good that people should know what is going on. But a better balance between the positive and negative would assist modern man to be more objective about himself.

It has been necessary to deal at some length with the distorted image of man, developed out of traditional Christianity, classical Freudianism, anti-intellectualism, commercialism, and the mass media because they have done much, in combination, to produce the prevailing climate of near-despair about the nature of man manifest in society at present, the whole way from nihilist writing, drama, and films to remarks on the top of a bus. What is the alternative picture?

For a start, man, we now know, is *by nature* social, capable of love and co-operation, able to sacrifice his personal advantage, at times, for the common good. Were this not so, the human species would never have reached the stage of civilization at all. Selfishness is an ever-present aspect of human behaviour, but the world can go on only because co-operation and concern for others are always, together, a greater force in society than selfishness. We notice and condemn selfishness just because it shows up against a background of dependable mutual consideration. The really selfish driver on the road sticks out. If everyone were to behave as he does, motor transport would be impossible.

Man is not only a social being, he is also a person facing the daunting task of actualizing his uniqueness in a world in part alien because it has not been planned to fit his individuality. He has to make the grade out there, with others, in society. This takes courage. He did not select his inheritance, and he did not choose his society; his task is to make something of himself in the situation in which he finds himself: to survive, to grow, to emerge.

The life of modern man is largely in his own hands, directed by his own choices and decisions. We will not here pursue the dialogue about free-will, as to whether choice itself is not determined by circumstances on the one hand and unconscious impulses on the other. Making decisions is hard work and *feels* valid. At the very least, individual consciousness is at the centre of all the influences bearing upon it and makes the act of choice between the alternatives, however distorted this choice may be by irrational impulses and however limited by situational necessity.

Man is goal-directed. Every man, except when in a condition of depression and defeat, looks ahead with plans for the future. Young people long to become their best selves. They dream of success and strive for it unless they have become too deeply discouraged about their own powers. Even the apathetic and cynical young people are – in their fantasies – significant.

Man, in a condition of mental health, is bent on the constant extension of his powers. Even in play he never lets up, but constantly faces himself with new challenges, for the fun of over-coming them and extending his range of control. Skill is greatly admired in every society. Man strives naturally because he is the end-product of a striving evolution. Cooped up in sameness, he gets bored. What's over the hill? What's across the ocean? What's at the bottom of the sea? What's out there in space? Even the ordinary unspectacular people are enjoying a sense of continuing achievement in their own quiet way: 'Next year I'll try sowing the runner beans a bit earlier.' 'Don't you think it would look better in here if we had the table the other way round?'

Man is a warm, loving, affection-seeking creature. He needs association with others as well as the opportunity to be alone. Also, life in the bustling, competitive modern world brings set-backs, hurt, discouragement. People seek opportunities to rest, relax, lick their wounds, rebuild their hopes, be consoled. So human nature needs not only challenge and independence, but also comfort, compassion, warmth, and love. Personality discovers itself in community and sustains itself through love, which is itself another kind of discovery.

People value warmth and love more than they are commonly ready to admit. Groups of general foremen in the building industry were asked, under conditions of anonymity, which two of five choices they would wish to retain, supposing they had to lose three. The choices were:

(a) One third of your income.
(b) A house of your own.
(c) Someone to love.
(d) Someone to love you.
(e) Your left hand.

Different groups, each comprising fifteen to twenty men, an-swered the question while attending a residential course which took place from time to time over a period of several years. Results were remarkably consistent. In all cases but three, the total of group choices (two per man) placed either (c) or (d), and often both, at the top. In the three exceptional cases, (e) came first.

The cumulative scores were: 1st (c) (478); 2nd (d) (466); 3rd (e) (266); 4th (b) (159); 5th (a) (100). An interesting reflection on a society which is supposed to be materialistic and hard-faced.

What of sex? The role of sex in human development is considered separately later on. Suffice it to say here that we can no longer regard sex as merely a gratification – a dainty tit-bit of experience that is naughty but nice. Sex is a component of personality that, given a chance to grow, itself heightens sensitivity and responsibility. It illuminates and strengthens the inner world of being. To quote Professor G. M. Carstairs, Professor of Psychological Medicine at Edinburgh University: 'A rewarding experience of sex gives more abundant life. To be without it limits your capacity as a human being.' Man is driven askew not by his robust sexual impulse but by the frustration arising from compelled abstinence or *from his own misunderstanding of the nature of the sex relationship*. People can be driven to despair by too much sexual experience as easily as by too little. What people are seeking for, however blindly, is sexual fulfilment, which is morally formative because it deepens human feeling and the capacity for human relationships.

There are a few points still to add. Man yearns for acceptance, recognition, prestige, status. This confirms his value to himself and sustains him for further striving. Although the fact is frequently overlooked, status is a dominant factor in society as it is throughout the animal kingdom. The converse of man's love of recognition is his deep uncertainty about his own worth.

Man struggles to make sense of his environment and of his experience. Every man believes something. Every person runs his life to some principles. The questions are: What beliefs? What principles? Even the unprincipled sail away on the belief that 'It's all a fiddle, anyway'; and nihilists are dedicated to their nihilism.

The total demands of human striving are not easy. Under stress comes the temptation to run away from reality into fantasy; to give up challenge in favour of dreams. What so often can swing the balance is confidence or lack of it. Man starts out in the world small and weak, and never quite gets over this experience of initial personal inadequacy. Hence, he is hypersensitive to set-backs, hates criticism, is fearful and anxious, and the more so the less the capital of confidence from past achievement he carries into new situations.

The whole dynamic of human confidence is one of the keys to human behaviour. It can be watched in action in any close-matched contest, such as a game of tennis. One player gets on top, then a couple of errors by himself, or a lucky shot by his opponent, alters the balance of confidence. Now the opponent becomes more accurate and the other's touch goes; so, to and fro, the whole functional competence of each player in turn rising or falling with each gain or loss in confidence. Life is like a very complicated game of tennis with all our confidence temperatures making zigzags on the chart. We all need as much confidence as we can get. It is the vitamin of effectiveness.

As has already been noted, positive attitudes and relationships have their negative counterparts. Thwarted people get vicious. Rejected people become anti-social. Take away a man's self-respect and he will hate you. Undermine a child's confidence and you are likely to reap a whirlwind of deliquency. Life denied turns sour and gets ugly. Setbacks readily produce a sludge of self-pity. And all failure, meanness, hatred, and malice bring with them demoralizing guilt. These negative aspects of humanity are as real and ubiquitous as the positive aspects, but, in the past, they have been given too much attention at the expense of man's positive dynamic. Living is quite a tough assignment. Man needs all the encouragement he can get. Instead he has been overshadowed by ideas about himself that have constantly corroded his powers and potentialities. The time has come to question this negativism. It is from the realization of his positive qualities, not from wallowing in his failures and imperfections, that man acquires the moral fibre without which living slumps into futility.

Let us return to our questions. Is modern man capable of handling the new responsibilities being heaped upon him by his own discoveries? Is he morally mature enough for freedom? The answer would seem to be 'yes', on two conditions. He needs to have established in society a new and more encouraging picture of himself and his role – a more *accurate* picture – as the basis for the extension of confidence he requires to tackle effectively the complex present and the perplexing future. Given confidence and courage, man is potentially invincible. Secondly, as a self-dependent decision-maker, he needs sufficient clarity of principle and purpose to help him make good choices. Doing justice to man's image is the long-term job of the teachers, the writers, the dramatists – many of whom seem still to be stuck with the old concepts. We can take the clarification of principle and purpose a little farther in the next chapter. Where has twentieth-century man got to in the evolution of moral order in human society?

4

VALUES OF SELF AND SOCIETY

As we noted in Chapter Two, moral order, in nature and in history, manifests itself at different levels. Among animals, instinctive behaviour patterns demonstrate *in action* values we call moral, notably obligation, courage, unselfishness, self-sacrifice. In simple human societies – or, indeed, in any human society at a stable phase of its evolution – we find a self-perpetuating moral order which ties the community together in a network of relationships and obligations that are experienced with intuitive force as inviolate and unchanging. Writing of simple static societies, Professor Redfield states: 'Each precivilized society was held together by largely undeclared but continually realized ethical conceptions.' Individuals in such a society may deviate from the expected pattern of behaviour and know they are doing so, but nobody is in doubt about the rightness of the moral order itself, which is confirmed by a sacred authority of some kind.

Such a moral order is felt to be as much a part of the nature of things as sunshine and rain. No man in his senses questions it. Each child absorbs it. As the child grows, he takes on, one after another, the socially expected roles of his age-group together with the self-control they require; he identifies with his peers and his elders, striving to emulate and excel in the approved patterns of behaviour. Each stage of conformity takes him ahead of his previous role and prepares him for the more significant role which is to follow: initiation at puberty, or later, confirms his past advance and opens the way to new responsibilities and a new status. Whatever the age of a member of a primitive society, and whatever position he may attain within his community, all the forces of society – love and the withholding of love; praise and ridicule; reward and punishment; the sources of status; success in marriage and fellowship; the forms of ritual and ceremony – are concentrated upon the individual to ensure his conformity to traditional patterns of behaviour. Ultimately, if he attains the position of an elder, he identifies himself with the whole life of his community, past, present, and to come. The elders set the tone and climate for the next generation and the pattern is repeated with each generation in turn.

Not only do the living elders and chiefs represent on earth the personification of the social and moral order, but, after death, they become the venerated ancestors who have the responsibility of guarding and protecting the continuing life of their tribe. They are thought to react with anger to any breaches of custom, but also to intercede with the tribal divinities on behalf of the living. Thus there is a continuum of community-linked responsibility, starting from the time the child is first expected to undertake simple duties, extending from age-group to age-group, reaching fruition on earth in the tribal leaders, continuing after death in the ancestors, and leading on to the absolute authority of a supreme being or beings. Such is the pattern of the self-perpetuating moral order in its characteristic form. Its order is conformist, imposed, antipathetic to individual originality. It is the primitive stage of social order.

A more advanced static society – as, say, in medieval England – lives by the same kind of self-perpetuating moral order, although made more conscious of its own values through the ministrations of priests, its sacred books, and the institutionalization of religious beliefs. Even as recently as Victorian or Edwardian times, the moral order was very largely self-perpetuating in spite of the inroads of rationalism and industrialization.

A different system of moral order – or disorder – is found when a society and its ideas are in process of transition. This may arise when static societies expand or become more mobile so that they begin to interact with one another; or from conquest, which brings an invasion of ideas as well as of people; or from a natural catastrophe that alters the basis of life; or from the emergence of new knowledge, or patterns of life, that conflict with established order; or from the ideas of gifted individuals of a reflective turn of mind who see the insufficiencies in the established order and set out to renovate it; or from a combination of several influences acting together. Transition in the moral order is a time of pain and progress. It is experienced as the shaking of the foundations and produces widespread anxiety. Many people interpret the changes as degeneration and long for the old certainty and security. They are conscious only of the confusion arising from change and miss its creative aspects.

We are, at present, living through such a transition – with a difference. In the past, the uncertainties of transition – as in the Renaissance, for example, or in the years bridging paganism and Christianity – have, after a time, settled back into some new authoritarianism which has re-created a stable, self-perpetuating moral order, even if considerably more under challenge than that of a static pre-civilized community. Today no new *authoritarian* moral order is in sight except as some kind of neo-fascism which we seek to avoid. Constant change will be the natural condition of man's future, and, under this condition, a static moral order cannot serve. Instead we have to create, and learn to live with, a dynamic moral system which is firm enough to support personal and social life but is also resilient. We are not, to be precise, living *through* a period of transition; we are living *in* transition. This condition is reached when the extent of change between one generation and the next makes it necessary for each generation to rethink its moral position.

We should also notice another fundamental difference between a static moral order and a dynamic moral system. The morally static society is, by nature, highly sectarian because it is a network of rules and conventions defended against change, and therefore fiercely reactive to rival claims. The static society believes devoutly that it possesses the one and only pure moral order, created and watched over by its own superior divinity or divinities.

The break-up of static moral order by ever more rapid change makes belief in absolute divine sanctions, and claims to absolute rightness, equally obsolete. This does not necessarily drive out the concept of God, but it does turn the relationship between God and man into a private rather than a public relationship. The decline in absolutism and sectarianism within Christianity itself is clearly shown in two modern trends: the tendency to describe the individual's consciousness of God as a personal encounter, and the ecumenical movement, which can only exist, let alone prosper, if historic claims to absolute right are dropped by all participants. Dialogue is today extending farther still. Marxists and Roman Catholics are seeing value in exchanging their points of view. Within and outside religious institutions, static moral order is giving way to a dynamic moral system.

This does not mean, however, that we are in an era of a moral free-for-all. The alternative to absolutism is not a formless relativism. It is true that something thought right in one society may be regarded as wrong in another, but it is not true that no universal moral values can be found. Examples of relativism are common enough, especially in variations between approved and condemned social behaviour. A belch is regarded as vulgar in some parts of the world and as a well-mannered sign of appreciation in others. The Maoris used to put out their tongues as a mark of greeting. Some societies have approved the exposure in public of both the faces and breasts of women. Other societies have covered both. Yet others – such as our own – have accepted bare faces as normal but have regarded uncovering the breast as improper. In some societies premarital sexual relationships are frowned upon; in others the stigma is not on a young man and woman sleeping together before marriage but on their eating together before marriage. In some societies – including Ancient Greece – it was regarded as a social duty to leave weakly children out in the open

to die; in others such behaviour would have been fiercely condemned. Circumcision has been widely regarded as an important
religious ritual and obligation in many societies; others have
considered it an impious mutilation. In the ancient civilizations,
circumcision was practised among the Phoenicians, Egyptians,
and Hebrews, but not by the Persians, Babylonians, and Greeks.

The evidence of social and moral relativism should not dis-
tract us from the fact that other values are consistent throughout
the whole, or almost the whole, human race, and throughout
history also. These are the universal values of mankind; values
everywhere recognized, everywhere admired. Courage is one of
them, so is self-control, so is honesty between members of the
same community, so is the honouring of personal obligations and
group responsibilities, so is good workmanship, so is telling the
truth to kinsmen in important matters (trivial lying, which often
takes the form of boasting or protecting one's own self-esteem or
another's feelings, is usually tolerated), so, as a rule, is hospitality
to strangers and travellers. Generosity and kindness are widely
approved. And so forth. Professor Morris Ginsberg, speaking as a
sociologist, states, in *On the Diversity of Morals*: 'Amidst variations, moral codes everywhere exhibit striking similarities in
essentials.' Anthropologists seem to be in pretty general agreement
on this point. Professor Redfield quotes with approval Professor
Raymond Firth (*Elements of Social Organization*): 'As some factors
are discernible in the basic requirements of all societies, so
certain moral absolutes exist.' Another anthropologist, Professor
Clyde Kluckhohn, agrees in principle but prefers the term 'con-
ditional absolutes'. Human beings, living together, cannot avoid
arriving at certain values, limits and controls, and the universal
needs of human societies, and of individuals within the societies,
result in a degree of similarity in these values, limits, and controls,
however strange and exotic the accepted behaviour of particular
societies may be. For example, the existence, in a society, of
ritual murder, or cannibalism, or a policy of torturing captives,
does not mean that this society cannot at the same time exemplify
many of the general values of mankind; it always does.

Thus, moral order in human society, as we have known it

so far, may be regarded as a potential morality of mankind modified by local variations. Our task, today, is to sort out the wheat from the chaff and search for the moral principles through which we can sustain moral order in the midst of change. To succeed in this, we have to become conscious of the principles upon which a universal moral order depends. Let local variations be what they may, we need to know where we stand in relation to one another, as persons, as communities, and as nations. The days are over when we can have one moral order for 'our' people, and another for outsiders; when we can regard 'our' traditions and beliefs as absolutely right and the traditions and beliefs of others as, at best, inferior substitutes; when we can hope to run our lives, personally or socially, on vague intuitive ideas about right and wrong. We have to identify the principles for a dynamic moral system and bring them to consciousness, in order that they may inform our personal and social behaviour.

A contemporary moral system of this kind must, in the nature of things, be established on the common ground between us all, on universals we can all accept, on principles that can be discovered and confirmed in experience – demonstrably sound principles of personal and social life.

At first sight, it may seem to go against all that is right and proper to talk about moral order in such secular terms, but this, in fact, is no more than to accept the final stage of a long process of secularizing the supernatural which has been going on for generations. Originally, all behaviour, all knowledge, all relationships, all institutions, were rooted in concepts of the supernatural. Early farming was organized in terms of carrying out routines, often highly ritualized, which had been laid down by tradition, with divine sanctions as their guards. Building was similarly controlled by sanctified routines. Early medicine was concerned to manipulate supernatural forces, and illness itself was commonly thought to be evidence of divine wrath. Incipient astronomy regarded the movements of the planets as governed by spirits. So through all the range of human experience.

Gradually, in field after field, scientific principle has taken over from supernatural intervention. We have now reached the last regions of this transformation. For about a century we have been searching scientifically for the principles underlying the functioning of the human psyche itself – in psychology. And now, at last, we are challenged to discover and apply the principles of moral order. This is as much a job for man to do as growing food, building houses, curing disease, exploring the universe, or any other task of living that faces us.

We are not concerned here with differences in the explanation of how things come to be as they are between those with a specifically defined religious commitment and those with a humanist-agnostic outlook. To treat moral principles as open to human exploration does not specifically include or exclude the concept of God. The existence of God is no more and no less implied in the search for moral truth than in the search for scientific truth, truth in art, or any other kind of truth.

One reason why we are today in moral confusion is that we have been slow, in evaluating personal and social conduct, to move over from the supernatural to the natural. Where supernaturalism still rules in agriculture or medicine – to take just two examples – agriculture and medicine are in a state of confusion. This is the sort of inefficiency the Food and Agricultural Organization and the World Health Organization are constantly battling against in their efforts to raise the standards of life and health in under-developed societies. In our society we are submerged in a similar confusion in the moral field. We are still clinging to concepts of supernatural revelation and sanctions when we ought to be exploring the nature of moral reality.

The secular foundation for moral values is the actual situation of man in his relations with himself, with others, with life, and with the universe as we now apprehend it. The secular sanction is the need for man, individually, socially, and on a world scale, to continue to develop.

In every individual is a drive to self-fulfilment; in every modern society an urge to advance. Neither can be achieved unless we follow in our lives, and can depend on in one another, certain principles of being and relationship that are as pragmatic and inevitable as the laws of physics. These are the values of self and society. There are principles operating in this area of existence as there are in any other. If we understand them and live by them, we thrive; to neglect them too much is self-destructive and socially destructive. This is, in fact, what the great moral teachers have been saying all down the ages, but man has been so absorbed with ideas of divine revelation and personal guilt that the pragmatic wisdom of the messages has been largely missed. To have life and to have life more abundantly as human beings we have to live by the principles of human life. It is as simple – and as difficult – as that.

Before we can begin to frame a dynamic moral order out of pragmatic principles, we have to clear away a very ancient confusion – that the wishes of the self and the needs of society are inexorably in conflict. In a static society this is true because its distaste for originality and independence of thought sets it sharply against the creative potentialities of the individual. In a changing, emerging society, however, personal and social fulfilment are not, of necessity, mutually exclusive, but can be mutually supportive. Their unity is the condition for the release, and use, of the creative in man. As Toynbee puts it: 'A society is a system of relations between individuals. Human beings cannot be themselves without interacting with their fellows, and a society is a field of action common to a number of human beings. But the "source of action" is in the individuals. All growth originates with creative individuals or small minorities of individuals.' What we are searching for in modern society is a *modus vivendi* which permits this kind of creative interaction – persons, small groups, and the wider society fulfilling their potentialities in dynamic relationships.

How are we to identify the principles for such a moral order? We have to start with two fundamental choices: What kind of society do we want? What kind of life do we envisage for the individual? The two are interdependent.

Suppose, for example, we were to assume that an authoritarian society, because of its definite structure and the clear guide-lines it offers, is ideal for maximizing human happiness. We should then find ourselves saddled with such moral controls as absolute obedience to those in authority, unquestioning service to the state, an uncritical attitude to received information, and condemnation of nonconformity. Such controls are the logical and necessary principles of moral order in an authoritarian society. We have only to state them to see at once that they represent a social regression to the static society. The modern choice must be for a democratic society, since only such a society can harmonize individual fulfilment with social order.

What kind of democratic society? As we saw in Chapter Two, the right to vote does not of itself create a democracy. Neither does a two-party or multi-party system of government. The modern concept of a democracy is a society which draws people into continuous participation in their own affairs. Every kind of institution is affected: family, school, university, hospital, factory, what you will. Each is faced with a problem of managing its own developments and all in positions of management have a choice in the way the management is carried out. They can seek to impose decisions, or they can mobilize the personal participation of all who are involved as individuals and groups. Trist, Higgin, Murray, and Pollock have shown in their book *Organizational Choice* how, in the coal industry, organization in autonomous work-groups extends the responsibility, the creativeness, and the satisfaction of workers, as compared with more authoritarian systems. Moving into a quite different situation, we find the same principles demonstrated in a number of African primary schools that went over from the traditional sitting-in-rows classroom arrangement to small groups, into which a degree of self-management was built. Quality of work, vitality, interest, social responsibility and attendance were all reported to be greatly improved. Many other instances could be cited. The conditions for the growth and release of human potentiality include individual responsibility within purposeful group relationships: contribution combined with stimulation. A modern democracy is a social system organized in terms of this dynamic.

Once the decision is for modern democracy, a whole range of moral principles flows from that decision. To bring those principles into effect over against the antagonistic values that will also be present is the moral struggle of a democratic nation.

5

For the individual in the modern world we envisage the goal of personal fulfilment – self-realization. This, also, is a source of values. People, as we saw earlier, can only become themselves by interacting with others. A prime dynamic of individual fulfilment, therefore, is the quality of relationships attained with others. That simple truth brings a train of values in its wake: the principles governing creative human interaction.

To seek self-fulfilment is not an egocentric or an easy purpose; it is each person's most significant contribution to the creative process; it is the decision to strive, to suffer, to be, and to become. Self-fulfilment is a drive, in its way a duty, certainly not an indulgence; it is a much tougher option than conformity. Playing life safe in conformist submergence instead of coming out and being what we are is a betrayal of the life in us. This is the meaning of Jesus's parable of the talents. Milton also has something to say about this. Fervent puritan as he was, he had no use for respectable conformity: 'I cannot praise a fugitive and cloistered virtue, unexercised and unbreathed, that never sallies out and sees her adversary but slinks out of the race, where the immortal garland is to be run for, not without dust and heat.'

But self-fulfilment is not to be attained along the lines erroneously laid down by the *laissez-faire* economists, who believed that, if every individual sought his own advantage, then, by the combined efforts of each, all would attain a higher level of life. Such a philosophy misses the interrelatedness of things, the basic principle that nothing has any pure existence of itself but is what it is by virtue of its relationship with other things. Man is no exception; he is nothing in isolation. Each person is a potential, but what becomes of that potential depends on the patterns of relationship and interaction that are set up with the world outside the person, and which provide the opportunities for experience through which the individual becomes himself at the same time as he grows nearer to the outer world, understanding it more deeply, responding to it more sensitively. The road to personal fulfilment, therefore, is not via egocentricity but through the establishment of reciprocal, sensitive, creative relationships in friendship, love, work, play, appreciation.

This gives us an important lead in the identification of moral values from man's actual condition. They are the values which, in personal living, lead to fulfilment. Men are social beings and destroy themselves, in whole or in part, if they fail to become socialized. Men are creative beings who limit and thwart themselves to the extent that they fail to release their creative potentialities. Men need to contribute and to feel valued for their contributions. The principles governing the fulfilment of individuals as themselves, and in relation to one another, are supreme values in life, the guides controlling the continuing evolution of humanity within the creative process.

If we regard a society dynamically, in terms of evolutionary advance, then the principles by which a society organizes its affairs should correspond closely with the principles which maximize personal development. In other words, the social framework should extend and become stronger by the same processes of self-actualization through which its members thrive and grow as individuals. This is what democracy seeks to achieve and why it is superior, in evolutionary terms, to authoritarianism. Nevertheless, although it can in theory draw on more creative energy than any other society, democracy's task is not easy. It has to create a network of institutions, relationships, and purposes that will permit the drives and potentialities of its members to find the means to growth and expression in personal and collective life without disrupting the social framework. An open society makes possible all kinds of exciting opportunities for imaginative contribution and co-operation; it also makes possible an unlimited variety of conflicts. For this reason it needs a greater clarity in values and purposes than is necessary in any other form of society. Purposes and values are a unifying force and a democracy needs this ideological structure to give form to its high spontaneity.

Another natural source of moral values is the need for self-management. The dynamic of the psyche needs direction and control. Without focus it falls apart into a warring mass of conflicting impulses. Such a chaotic condition precludes self-fulfilment. One vital personal value is courage, not in the form of spectacular valour, but as the courage needed to face life as it comes. Without this, the personality gets cut off from that formative interaction with the environment through which growth occurs. Sufficient pertinacity is also necessary; to get anywhere in self-development an individual needs to keep going long enough to make a valid judgement about whether or not an activity should be pursued. A third vital principle of self-management is self-control. All human achievement – from playing a game to writing a symphony, from gardening to making love – comes from a balance between spontaneity and control. Too much control produces deadness and rigidity; too much spontaneity results in chaos.

Finally, we have to take account of the principles deriving from our responsibility for the future of the planet. Man finds himself to be a product of a creative process that, astoundingly and mysteriously, has produced both himself and the immense universe of which he is a part. He finds himself, after aeons of biological evolution, to be the highest manifestation of life on this planet, and the custodian of this planet.

He cannot absolve himself from this responsibility. It is there, now, and every significant decision that is made, or every failure to make a necessary decision, delineates the shape of the future – a future of millions of years, unless man wrecks the planet. However we look at man's role, it includes the obligation to work for the fuller release of the personal and social potentialities of man within a habitat that he should reverence, protect, and hand on, not only intact but enriched.

We see, then, that the principles of dynamic moral order fall into four groups: the principles of self-management, the principles of creative personal relationships, the principles of democratic organization, and the principles covering our responsibility for the future. If we start giving these principles names we find that many have long since been recognized. This we should expect, as man's moral wisdom has been gradually acquired and great moral leaders have arisen from time to time who have stressed the importance of certain abiding values. Other principles have emerged clearly only since the evolution of modern democratic systems.

Of course, dynamic moral principles are not like the absolute moral edicts of the past, and are to be regarded as subject to modification and expansion. But, in the light of our present knowledge, the following list of personal and social values would probably be acceptable to most people who are striving for self-discovery and self-fulfilment for themselves and others within the framework of democracy. Some are values as such; some are attitudes; some are qualities. All are attainments in terms of personal development, and rules of the road – ideals – for democratic life:

Love of life, and other people.
Self-respect.
Respect for others and for the dignity of the individual.
Honesty in dealings and relationships.
Consideration and concern for others.
Sensitivity about the feelings of others.
Insight into one's own feelings and behaviour.
Love of truth, and justice.
Unselfishness.
Tolerance.
Kindness.
Compassion.
Generosity.
Courage.
Pertinacity.
Self-control.
Responsibility for one's own actions.
Social responsibility.
Responsibility for keeping well informed.
Responsibility for the future of life on this planet.

Such values are not to be regarded as independent absolutes, but as component parts – the language – of a contemporary moral outlook. 'I must adopt some moral vocabulary if I am to have any social relationships,' writes Professor Alasdair MacIntyre in *A Short History of Ethics*. 'For without rules, without the cultivation of virtues, I cannot share ends with anyone else. I am doomed to social solipsism.'

The list could, of course, be altered. People might wish to include other values as essential to the creative fulfilment of personal and social life, or to exclude as redundant some of those named. But the list as it stands is well founded, not only in the moral wisdom of the past and present but also in the findings of developmental psychology and psychiatry. The values stated are as much principles of mental health as they are principles of moral virtue, which is what we should expect once moral values are identified as the laws of life, the principles governing how to live fruitfully.

The point of naming moral values is that now we have reached the stage requiring full moral consciousness – as distinct from the stages of instinctive moral action or intuitive moral acceptance – we need everyone to be aware what are the principles by which our society is striving to live, even though the antitheses of these values – greed, cheating, indifference, cruelty, irresponsibility, and the like – are also in evidence. This does not mean that the values should be imposed, but they should be known to be venerated, not as absolute rules but as accepted principles. Just as physical health in society is defended by general knowledge of the principles of nutrition, hygiene, and so forth, so are mental and moral health sustained by awareness of moral principles.

The recent emphasis on the power of unconscious components in human motivation has led people to forget the great influence of conscious ideas on the way people behave. If we believe a thicket is populated with vipers, we shall walk through it with care and apprehension whether or not our belief is true. In a country where all life is held to be sacred, animals are treated differently from one in which animals are thought to have been created as a lesser order to be used as man sees fit. Any individual is considerably controlled by the dominant ideas operating in his pattern of understanding, and any society by the ideas it is supposed to subserve. Thus, it is personally and socially important that creative ideas shall be alive in the minds of the community.

A part of the moral problem of the present is that some

erroneous ideas have become dominant while some valid ideas
have receded, or have not been grasped at all. Among the erroneous ideas about life widely current in our society are that you can
buy happiness; that you will get on fastest if you disregard other
people; that fulfilment as a woman depends on shape and appearance rather than personality; that success is a matter of luck, not
effort; and that everything is a fiddle. Such ideas are, in moral
terms, at the intellectual level of superstitions or old wives' tales.

But even if moral values are established as valid principles for
the good life, will people pay any attention if the values are not
backed by divine sanctions? It is curious to suppose that they will
not. Human beings search for knowledge and control relevant
to the fulfilment of their aspirations. This is true of knowledge
about life. Moral values have fallen into disfavour because people
have come to doubt their effectiveness and because the values have
been assessed not as important information about life but as
authoritarian dictates and prohibitions. Which, in fact, they
often are, until checked against the realities of existence and
accepted or rejected in terms of them.

Now that the heyday of absolutism is over, whatever struggles
of its shifting power may lie ahead, authority can no longer
spring from a single source; it must be sustained by generalized
influences. One is the enduring moral wisdom of the community.
People, because they *are* social beings, recognize dishonesty,
exploitation, unfairness, insensitivity, weakness, cruelty, etc., as
bad. A thief, swindled in a purchase, is as furious as the next
man. The law is another source, even though its authority can
rapidly become discredited if it lags too far behind developments. A new source of authority is modern knowledge – incomplete but helpful – about the nature of man. Most people want to
make something of their lives and to play their part for others,
and are prepared to put up with inconvenience, even suffering, in
the interests of doing so. But, in order to have the will for the
sacrifice, they must understand the dynamic principles involved.
A serious weakness in the moral situation of our times is the
appalling ignorance in society as a whole about the principles
lying behind life and growth. Once these have been properly

communicated, the authority of our human situation will become more effective.

People are just as likely, or unlikely, to pay regard to obviously well-founded moral principles as they are to any other established principles. A man who knows about cars usually maintains them at a good standard of mechanical efficiency. If heavy smokers were *convinced* they were heading for a premature death from lung cancer, most of those not actually suicidal would cut down. Now that the nutritional causes of corpulence are understood, most people take some account of the principles involved, and many apply them with heroic self-restraint. We have to organize and present the moral truth of experience with the same objectivity and frankness we have used in communicating other aspects of experience. John Wilson, in *Reason and Morals*, writes: 'We have not yet met a case where we have had proper experience and yet failed to agree. We can, therefore, only believe that proper experience will probably lead to unanimity in the acceptance of ultimate ethical criteria, just as it has led to unanimity in other cases.' What a modern society needs is to get the essential principles known, discussed, lived, and appreciated. This, today, is the only secure foundation for moral order.

The first part of this book has outlined the main styles of moral order that may be observed in nature and society, leading up to the modern style, which is that of a dynamic moral system based on generally accepted principles and individual moral insight. Man, we find, has now escaped from the rigid conformities of static society, and is beginning to shake off the limitations of sectarian thinking. As an individual he is free in a quite new way. But to describe his situation is only the beginning. Freedom creates its own problems of adjustment and readjustment. Situations happen and have to be dealt with. Personal potentialities are no longer confined within the straitjacket of an imposed order but become a personal responsibility. Perspective has to be re-examined. The natural history of man, the moral animal, is at a crucial stage. In the chapters ahead we shall explore some of his new problems and new possibilities.

Part Two

THE MORALITY OF FREEDOM

5

HOW FREE IS FREEDOM?

MAN is a freedom-loving creature, but it has taken him an unconscionable time to achieve the opportunity to be free. He has it now. What happens hereafter depends on his capacity to use his freedom in satisfying and creative ways. There is nothing any longer between mankind and a world of material plenty, ample opportunity, and freedom to live fully and abundantly – except man himself. This exciting possibility and responsibility creates a strange, heady milieu for man, a twentieth-century situation which it is hard for man to credit, let alone adjust to. It is all so new.

Back in those distant days when the human race was represented by rare bands of brothers roaming the wilds, seeking food, and hunting, man was free from many later oppressions but was at the mercy of ignorance, fear, disease, climatic changes, the failure of food supplies, and his own imagination. Later, when towns and institutions had developed, some crude threats to freedom were a little mitigated, but at the cost of domination by élites and conquerors. Up through the ages, as slaves, as serfs, as underdogs, the mass of the people have spent their lives under constraint, with only a select few enjoying anything like personal freedom. It could not be otherwise so long as wealth depended largely on the expenditure of human muscle and the total product was insufficient to provide abundance for any but a favoured minority. Under such conditions almost the whole lives of most people – the total of waking hours – were in pawn to those who had achieved power, or to the remorseless pressure of mere subsistence.

The modern machine age and know-how have changed all that. We still have the ups and the downs, the wealthy and the poor, but the contemporary economic system runs, not on a substratum of ignorant, impoverished, overburdened, under-nourished hirelings and dependants, but on an educated, well-fed proletariat with money to spend and free time to spend it in. This is the change that has produced the potentially vast extension of personal freedom in modern societies. It provides freedom of choice and freedom of action to supplement the other liberties – of thought, of speech, of association, of voting rights – that have been previously struggled for and, often, won. The expansion of freedom has inevitably coincided with the crumbling of the hold of absolute authority on human behaviour because, as we have seen, such authority makes sense only in a static or regressive society and does not fit a surgent changing one.

The popular name for the new social condition is the 'permissive society' – a society in which everybody has a wide range of personal choices; in which everybody has a reasonable chance of attaining to whatever he is capable of without artificial barriers being put in the way; in which the dictates of authority are critically assessed and, possibly, discarded; in which everything is explosively in a process of movement and change. It is true that, over wide areas of the world, the permissive society is still a long way off. But it is predictable, none the less; man has the means to make it everywhere possible within the lifetime of children now at school. Sooner or later, stumbling from one crisis to another, via untold error, waste, and regression, man will realize the possibility.

Moral order has to take new forms to accommodate this

dramatic change. Societies governed by tradition or élites operate through a morality of conformity. The new conditions require a quite different pattern: the morality of freedom. The two systems are framed differently and exist for different ends. The morality of conformity is rooted in unquestioning obedience to the rules of tradition and in a constant pressure to conform to the ideas and wishes of those set in authority; individual initiative is regarded with suspicion and constrained within narrow outlets; the goal of the system is the perpetuation of itself. The morality of freedom, in contrast, values and liberates initiative in thought, choice, and action, subject only to the limits that the liberty of others shall not be threatened by individual behaviour, nor the security of society itself. Its goal is the constant transformation of society into superior forms. The second kind of moral order is slowly emerging over against the first, which is, however, still very much with us. A modern democratic society carries within it, at the same time, authoritarian persons and institutions, liberated persons and institutions, and all varieties in between. It is in the process of transforming itself but the transformation has still a long way to go.

The sudden emergence of expanded personal freedom, and the lack of a coherent moral order to go with it, lead to a great deal of confusion. At the heart of the confusion is a misunderstanding about the nature of freedom. Some people think of the permissive society as though it were without any restraints, a society in which anything goes. But no society can exist without a moral order. Not even a small group of people – let alone a whole nation or a whole world – is able to get along together in amity and effectiveness without moral understanding existing between individuals, some values that all respect and can depend on in one another. Furthermore, far from personal responsibility being less in a permissive society, it is greater.

A major difference between an authoritarian society and a permissive one is that in the first people are closely subject to duress, whereas in the second we are largely under our own steam, responsible for ourselves and our own lives as never before, responsible for our thoughts, beliefs, actions, ideals, development.

Nobody, any longer, is going to do it all for us. We can, of course, nestle under somebody else's umbrella and conform without question, but that is to opt out of the permissive situation. What nobody can do with any hope of success is to equate responsibility with being under authoritarian restraint and assume that the modern alternative is irresponsible absolute freedom.

There can be no true personal freedom on those terms. To have more freedom is to accept more responsibility. This is self-obvious but hard to grasp for some who are new to freedom. The error is understandable. Only here a bit, there a bit, have the ordinary people won the right to self-determination from their rulers. Right up through the long struggle, freedom has seemed the quintessence of everything desirable. To those living under arbitrary authority, the condition of being free appears to be the ready key to a full and happy life. In the event, once freedom is attained, responsibility is found to emerge, writ large, as its natural partner. Emergent Africa's jubilant cry of 'Uhuru!' – 'Freedom!' – has already become the puzzled 'Freedom for whom?' 'Freedom for what?' But it is not only emergent Africa that is faced with this conundrum.

Free at last, or, at any rate, freer than ever before, how is modern man to use his freedom? To understand the nature of freedom is the first step. Freedom is compounded of man's capacity to sort out the possibilities for choice, and the opportunity to put his personal choices into effect. But self-determination is not possible without recognizing and accepting the limits on freedom. Freedom can become a reality of experience only if we understand and accept these limits.

Our social nature itself is one such limit. We cannot play ducks and drakes with the needs and feelings of others and ourselves remain psychologically free. Freedom, as Sartre has pointed out, is indivisible. To destroy the freedom of others is, ultimately, to destroy our own.

History offers us a small sample of people who have had both the power and the opportunity to live as they chose without regard to others. These were the tyrants. Far from these people ending up as free and fulfilled personalities, we may observe that precisely the opposite occurred. To claim absolute freedom as a right is to embark upon an insidious course of self-destruction. Indifference to the needs and feelings of others gradually produces psychological isolation, darkened by increasing guilt; then comes the dread that revenge or envy may at any moment lead to swift destruction; then mounting fear and suspicion, with an almost total curtailment of normal life and relationships, and finally a trapped and terrible paranoia. So a tyrant, with an empire or a nation to pluck clean, gets driven mad by the false goal of absolute freedom. At the end of his tether he is a terrifying automaton, scowling, isolated, hated, a lost soul for whom all flavour and significance have gone from life. Thus, Macbeth:

> Tomorrow, and tomorrow, and tomorrow,
> Creeps in this petty pace from day to day,
> To the last syllable of recorded time;
> And all our yesterdays have lighted fools
> The way to dusty death. Out, out, brief candle!
> Life's but a walking shadow, a poor player
> That struts and frets his hour upon the stage,
> And then is heard no more: it is a tale
> Told by an idiot, full of sound and fury,
> Signifying nothing.

The fact that a similar despair is echoed in much modern writing goes to show how easy it is to lament about the human lot instead of striving to improve it in terms of its inherent laws of life. One limit on freedom, then, is that those who wish to be free must take account of others. Freedom lies in reciprocity, not in isolation.

The actions of other people are another limit on every individual's personal freedom. We depend constantly on the reliable and responsible behaviour of others, and life would be nothing but a treacherous and frustrating confusion without it. Business executives, statesmen, and other leading people, speeding about their business around the airlines of the world, depend utterly upon the responsible behaviour of battalions of people. Behind every safe flight is the oil-refining industry, the engineering

industry, the skills of aeronautics and navigation, the integrity
of service mechanics, a complex network of administration, and
much else besides. At a less exalted level, the adolescent who
spends Saturday on a trip to see a friend depends constantly on
the responsible behaviour of others. He expects the pork pie he has
between trains to be wholesome, whereas, if someone somewhere
wasn't bothering, it might well give him food poisoning. He
expects the trains he uses to be on time, or thereabouts, and the
bus he catches from the station not to break down. In the simplest
affairs of life we are constantly anticipating responsibility in
others. Freedom apart from our own and others' responsibility is
unattainable, non-existent. Freedom is the opportunity to use
responsibility, not the opportunity to banish it.

Another limit on personal freedom is the need to accept and
respect principles of order that themselves increase freedom.
This is a difficult one for some people to stomach as they have met
order mostly in the form of arbitrarily imposed dictates. Hence,
they suspect all regulations. This is wholesome enough in its
way; it is a sound policy to probe the justification of any restriction, yet some restrictions are themselves a source of freedom.
For example, people are free to enjoy games *because* the games
are played to rules. Cricket would become nonsense if the
batsman was permitted to play with a bat of any width. Tennis
and football would lose their point if tennis courts and football
pitches had no restricting lines on and round them. The referee, or
the umpire, is a guardian of freedom because he is there to represent the agreed rules.

In many real-life situations, freedom and limits on freedom
are the warp and woof of liberty. Rules of the road are an obvious
example. Because we are all limited by the rules, we are all
freer to get more quickly and safely from one point to another.
If there were no rules of the road there would be no freedom on
the road; there would be only chaos. That freedom is related to
objectives to be attained is now beginning to be understood in
society. Thirty years ago the breathalyser tests would have been
howled down as a gross infringement of individual liberty.
Today they have been accepted as a necessary safeguard under

conditions of overcrowding on the roads. This does not indicate that people are becoming indifferent to their liberties, as some suggest, but that they are acquiring a more mature attitude to the nature of freedom. Once you raise the standard of living to a point when large numbers of people who were formerly unable to buy cars are now free to do so, you have to accept the consequences of the extension of that freedom in the limitation of another. A law is acceptable when it is seen to be the logical outcome of seeking to achieve approved objectives in a given situation. It is resented when it is felt to be a pointless imposition.

Every situation carries within it the principles of freedom characteristic of itself, and everyone has to accept these situational limits as a condition of effective self-determination. A man who becomes a doctor has chosen not only a career but also a life-situation that extends freedom in some directions and limits it in others. No one is so exalted that he can neglect the limits on his freedom. Princes, popes, prime ministers, managing directors, judges, and pop idols are free within limits, just as are those of lowlier status in the world. The limits vary for each person and for each situation, but they are always there and freedom in action and decision always require that they shall be respected. To be free, we have to know what roles we are filling and what situation we are in. Failing that, the forces we are not taking account of will become dominant and defeat us. As Spinoza said: 'Freedom is the understanding of necessity.' Echoing this in *Adventures of Ideas*, A. N. Whitehead spoke of 'the reconciliation of freedom with the compulsion of the truth'. We are a part of nature and we are free only in so far as we exercise our self-determination within the realities of human nature, of society, and of the environment that is the ground of our life.

Other limits on personal freedom arise not from the situation but from within ourselves. Ignorance and lack of skill are such limits. Whatever the activity, a level of appropriate skill is the foundation of freedom. The beginner in golf, for example, rigid in stance and tense in muscle, can only play *at* golf. Before he is free to play golf, he must have acquired a 'grooved swing' and be able to use a range of clubs with reasonable precision.

Until he has reached that stage, the constant intrusion of uncontrollable errors makes the outcome of every shot a matter of chance – obviously not a situation of freedom. A good skier seems free as a bird because a whole elaboration of built-in skills permits the free execution of any needed manoeuvre. He knows exactly what to do and when to do it.

Limits of ignorance and limits of skill are, of course, acting together in most situations. A man at sea in a sailing dinghy is in a condition of freedom so long as he knows how to handle his boat, knows its limits, can navigate well enough, and can judge the sea and wind aright. If these conditions are not fulfilled, he becomes nothing more than a floating object at the mercy of the waves and the weather. The analogy applies to life as a whole; at any moment we are rather like a man in a boat at sea, needing all our skill and knowledge to keep on the course we have chosen. We are only free so long as our knowledge and skill are adequate; once we are beyond the limits of either, we are, to a greater or lesser extent, an object at the mercy of external forces.

Attributes of personality can also limit freedom. Lack of confidence and courage can cut people off from liberating experience. Just before the last war, an important experiment took place in America to see if the entrance examinations to universities were really necessary to secure standards. A number of schools and school systems were given the opportunity to prepare their students for university with the assurance that recommended candidates would be accepted without further examination. Many teachers in the secondary schools responded gratefully to their freedom from imposed curricula, but others hung back, afraid to venture beyond the familiar confines of the academic courses. Freedom cannot be bestowed *in vacuo*. It is the condition in which self-determination is maximized, but the way it is used depends on the personal and moral capacity of the individual. The capacity for freedom is an individual attainment which grows in a climate of choice and responsibility and is the outcome of considerable personal development. When the slaves were set free in America and the West Indies, many were, at first, nonplussed. After the Second World War not a few servicemen needed to be rehabilitated before they could accept without undue anxiety the self-determination of civilian life. The opportunity to be free is a test of how far an individual can use freedom, and some, as Erich Fromm has pointed out, are afraid of it.

Rigidity of mind also limits freedom. The world of the rigid diminishes daily until the area of personal freedom may shrink to the size of a clubroom where views and clichés long forgotten by the world are still exchanged. Thus an adequate flexibility of mind is a condition of freedom. To feel free we need to feel at home. A world that doubles its knowledge every fifteen years can quickly make strangers of those who cease to be contemporary. 'Happy men,' said Carlyle, 'are full of the present.' Part of that happiness is the feeling of being able to manoeuvre personal life successfully in a well-understood environment.

Excessive self-doubt, anxiety, or guilt also inhibits the capacity to be free. One of the earliest casualties in mental ill-health is the ability to make decisions with reasonable equanimity. A decision is a commitment of the self and the last thing a psychologically stressed individual feels strong enough to do is to undertake self-commitment.

Yet another limit on freedom arises from the intrapsychic tyrants – the compulsions. An alcoholic or a drug addict has his personal freedom curtailed to the extent that he is at the mercy of his compulsion. The individual with intense claustrophobic tendencies may find he is not free to travel by Underground or go to cocktail parties. A man who avoids what his brother likes doing because he is unconsciously motivated to prove his independence of his brother is plainly not as free as he might be, nor is the woman who has such a phobia about cats that she refuses all social invitations unless she is quite sure that they come from catless homes. A. J. Ayer makes this contrast: 'A kleptomaniac is not a free agent in respect of his stealing, because he does not go through any process of deciding whether or not to steal. Or rather, if he does go through such a process, it is irrelevant to his behaviour. Whatever he resolved to do, he would steal all the same. And it is this that distinguishes him from the ordinary thief.'

None of us is completely free from compulsive and unconscious

influences upon our actions and decisions, but all schools of psychiatry agree that the ideal is to bring our real motivations as
fully into consciousness as possible. Once again we get the indication that the capacity for freedom is related to personal development. Freedom is not a bonus to be snatched; it is a prize to be
won.

We see, then, that when we examine the nature of personal
freedom we get taken far beyond the simple concept of a life
without any restraint. No such life is possible, and those who
attempt to live as though it were, must, in the nature of things,
end up not free but confused, unrelated, and lost. To live is to
search for ourselves, to influence others, and to be influenced by
them. This dynamic of existence, and all that it entails, is unavoidable in the real world. At critical moments people's lives
can be toppled one way or the other by an apparently trifling
event. Our action may, at any time, be that event. We are never
free to forget how much we are in one another's hands, nor that
the future is at the mercy of the present.

There is one other factor we must consider in this résumé of
the extent and limit of personal freedom. This is the role of
authority in the modern world. The present is an anti-authoritar-
ian age, and a good thing too. Over the years people have had
their bellyful of being pushed around by others who claim
especial rights over them – self-styled representatives of God or
the state or virtue, who proceed to project on to mankind their
ideas of what ought to be, dominance masquerading as dedication.
All this does not ring true any more; people have rumbled it,
and are in revolt. They are tired of picking up the pieces after one
kind of ideological struggle or another. They don't trust the
Big Voices to secure the future of mankind; they don't trust Big
Voices at all.

All to the good. But giving authoritarianism the push does
not mean that you can get on without authority. Authority does
not have to be authoritarian. This is where there is confusion.
Society without authority is possible only in very small and simple
communities. Once you have complexity in a society, you need
organization; once you have this, you need long-range planning

and decision-making; and once you have planning and decision-making, you must have some authority system, and people to make decisions at the time they have to be made. It is possible and desirable to maximize consultation in an organization; it is not possible to eliminate the person who ultimately decides. The point is that you cannot go on consulting and discussing for ever. Someone, sometime, has got to make decisions, and someone has to have the authority to do it.

The solution to the puzzle of how to marry freedom with authority is to regard authority not as a personal *possession*, which some have and others do not, but as a social *role* which some fill on behalf of others. It follows that only those have a right to authority who carry responsibilities that justify the authority. And the authority itself should be regarded as a part of the responsibility – a part of the role rather than the person.

This authority of role may be that of knowing, of doing, or both. Mr Smith queueing for his lunch is an ordinary citizen waiting his turn like everyone else; at the same time he may be a leading authority on snails to whom experts from all over the world defer. As a specialist, he carries the responsibility and authority of his special knowledge; as a person, he is himself and no more. The warden at the crossing is just Mrs Brown at home; on duty she has only to take up her position in the middle of the road and Ministers of the Crown obediently draw to a halt. This is the authority of function pure and simple. Most authority roles combine the authority of knowledge, or skill, with the authority of function. The only other authority we have to take account of in a democracy is authority of prestige, which may be freely accorded for all kinds of reasons but cannot be claimed as a right.

The truth is that we are all under some authority, and part of our freedom lies in understanding and accepting this, while always challenging any extension of authority that oversteps the boundaries of necessity. Particularly we have to guard against the acquisition of authority by those whose motives are limited to self-aggrandizement, or whose ideas have ossified. Such people are incapable of handling authority democratically.

To safeguard the community from the autocrats, every authority system should also be a system of communication, shared responsibility, mutual support, and mutual accountability. Absolute authority corrupts because it isolates, and isolated authority can never learn; it can only forget what it is like to be ordinary. This is why isolated authority ossifies so readily, particularly in a rapidly changing world. But power is not itself corrupting so long as it is 'power *with*', not 'power *over*'. *Power with* is the only kind of personal power tolerable in a democracy – authority directed to fulfilling socially agreed aims, and subject to social control.

To sum up: the contemporary misunderstanding of freedom as the right to do what you like when you like is an understandable excess after the long experience, for most of society, of undignified subordination to those in authority. But it is a serious misconception. We exist as free people through our relationships with others. No man is anything on his own. We grow by interaction, not in isolation. Freedom and responsibility are inseparable. A free society naturally develops essential authority roles. Freedom properly conceived is not exercised at the expense of anyone or anything; it enhances the life of person and society. Personal freedom is not in anybody's gift and it cannot be taken. It has to be worked for, and the entry requirements, if we want the real thing, are high. Such freedom and morality are one.

6

WHAT AM I?

THE very processes that have broken down the authoritarian pattern of earlier forms of society, and set the individual free from its strictures, have also left him very much on his own to make what sense he can of an impersonal, mass society. Hence the identity problem of contemporary man. We are a society of lost people; lonely, as Riesman has pointed out, in the crowd. 'Alienation' is the popular word – the condition of being in society but not of it. 'The alienated person,' says Fromm in *The Sane Society*, 'is out of touch with himself as he is out of touch with any other person.' He is a wanderer in a concrete jungle that seems indifferent to his *personal* existence.

The individual's lack of a sense of identity and involvement touches the very heart of morality in a free society. As abundant evidence shows, isolation, lostness, and a feeling of alienation leave the individual vulnerable to social, psychological, and moral breakdown. The 'loner' is a common figure in both prisons and consulting-rooms. The alienated individual within the social group is the one to look for whenever destructiveness or theft become problems. A whole sector of society may become alienated and grow into a sub-culture in which anti-social attitudes become the pattern of conformity. The member of a sub-culture who is transferred to another group, as when a child finds himself in a new social context when he goes to school, is under special risk of becoming alienated in his new group. Juvenile delinquency and social isolation are very closely related. So are isolation and suicide. Alienated and isolated personalities may just be wretched and apart, or they may fill a variety of anti-social roles. A chip-on-the-shoulder social misfit, gathering around him a group of inadequate and frustrated personalities, is liable to foment all kinds of damage and obstruction to social order.

The relationship between isolation, alienation, and an anti-social or disoriented style of life can be understood without difficulty when we realize how rapidly society has moved on from the static, intimate social groupings of a few decades back to the highly mobile mass conurbation of modern times. This somewhat demoralizing process of urbanization, which has been going on for some time in the West, is today being repeated in areas of rapid technological advance elsewhere in the world. In Africa, for example, the high-spirited but well-behaved type of village boy of thirty years ago, today sometimes assumes the role of gang-leader in a growing town, sustained by his band of followers who, in village life, would have been models of rectitude.

The difference to be noted, in terms of sustaining moral order, is that under conditions of mass society the individuals as persons become the chief depository of moral values, *not the community as a whole*. Mass, mobile society, as distinct from static, intimate society, requires personal thought, moral autonomy, and self-made group involvement as the bases of its moral order. Because we are failing to produce enough of these, we are today caught up in problems of social alienation and personal identity.

Society itself is, of course, at fault by moving too slowly in response to change. It is conducting its affairs with sparse psychological and sociological insight in view of the immense social changes that have occurred. Mass society, impersonal in most of its relationships and unredeemed by sufficiently warm and intimate group structure, is sure to throw up hosts of lost and alienated people and families, whether their reaction to alienation is aggressive resentment or passive defeat. Yet this inevitable outcome of a dehumanized social structure is treated with scant understanding and so is constantly reproduced. The mounting social problems of technological society are the outcome of persisting social errors. The problems will, in the nature of things, continue to accumulate until the errors are put right.

There is a remorseless push in the modern world that threatens to drive the individual into isolation and alienation. As well as the size of modern organization, and its impersonal nature, there is the sheer pressure of day-to-day living, with its ever-mounting distractions and demands. In the end, all but the most robust, or the most involved, are driven into a we-and-they attitude towards this giant, congested, industrial complex which draws millions into its service, as workers and consumers. People are treated as automata to fit job-specifications or to be motivated to buy, while the dearest thing any man has – his unique, yearning, striving self – is totally ignored or grossly, inhumanely undervalued.

People feel manipulated and discounted by the impersonal machinery of modern government. As one example, highly intelligent, highly verbal individuals sit at the centre of things and design forms to control the lives of the rest of us. These forms are scattered throughout the land – indeed the world – and then all of us, including people of poorish intelligence and low verbal capacity, are required to fill in the forms as the means to our personal lives going on at all. The sheer misery and frustration produced annually by forms alone must add up to a mountain of suffering. The owners of small concerns, founded after years of unremitting effort, are sometimes driven to give up by the agony of the endless formalities that strangle the courage out of them. It all adds up to anger and hatred of 'them' – and to dejection, and ulcers, and despair. And all because those whose job it is perpetually to manufacture new controls over private life lack the imagination to feel their way into what it is like to be at the receiving end. 'The form' is only one example of insensitive intrusion. It is the feeling of being at the mercy of manipulators

and meddlers, who are not concerned about an individual's
problems, that drives millions of people into an attitude of in-
furiated alienation towards their own society.

Thus a complex but dissociated and *unimaginative* society
generates the alienation that produces the crime, delinquency,
despair, and neurosis which it then desperately seeks to combat by
the same organizational techniques that produced the original
alienation. This is a vicious circle: the crime rate is threatening,
the delinquency rate is high, suicides are all too common, stress
disorders have become the greatest source of lost man-hours in
industry, and organization is heaped on organization to try to
check it all. There is already a lot of *help* provided in the state and
industrial complex, but it is, in general, still lacking in imaginative
humanity, so the hoped-for improvement eludes the efforts
made to achieve it. The sense of alienation spreads year after year.

But size, pressure, and bureaucracy are by no means the only
forces producing alienation. There are other factors operating
which must also be considered. These take us deep into the changing situation of the individual as the human species continues to
evolve socially. Man is, in part, losing his sense of identity because
he has not adjusted his orientation to fit the facts about his nature
and his situation that science and change have set out before him.
To deal with his identity crisis, modern man has to renovate his
consciousness of himself and his relationships, as well as recon-
structing the political, economic, and organizational framework of
his life.

The first thing that must strike us, once we think about it, is
what a remarkable entity a person is. In all directions around him
for thousands of millions of miles is spread a pulsating, dynamic
universe, of which individual personality is the most remarkable
product. 'One thing is certain,' writes Julian Huxley in *New
Bottles for New Wine*, 'that the well-developed, well-integrated
personality is the highest product of evolution, the fullest realization we know of in the universe.' Every individual is an atom
of consciousness and in his own senses and relationships mirrors
the whole mystery and wonder of existence.

Another dramatic fact is every person's inescapable uniqueness.

Each individual must see himself, if he is to see *himself* at all, not in the mould of others' expectations about him – although, as we have seen, these will influence how he behaves – but in the dynamic condition of personal becoming. No man is definable except in dynamic terms. If the sense of identity shrinks too much it may be that the real personality of the individual is not sufficiently expressed. The individual may be too much submerged in fantasy which ignores both the real world and the potentialities of life; or too much subject to external forces that override and frustrate the personal potential. An individual involved with the world *as himself* is unlikely to suffer much from uncertainty about his own identity.

In *The Integrity of the Personality* Anthony Storr writes:

'No one can tell what sort of person a baby will become; but within it a mysterious process is continuing which will lead to its becoming itself alone; to the emergence of a new, a unique individual. Something within the human ovum determines that it will develop into a human foetus and nothing else; it seems that there is a similar pre-formed organization independent of consciousness which is struggling to emerge and which will ultimately manifest itself as a mature personality.'

(Or, if things go wrong, or to the extent that growth is incomplete, fail to mature.)

Many other psychologists and psychiatrists, notably Alfred Alder and C. G. Jung of early workers, and Gordon Allport, Abraham Maslow, Erich Fromm, and Carl Rogers more recently, have been brought to the conclusion that within every person a process of self-emergence is struggling towards completion, a lifelong process ultimately, since the *emergence* of what Storr calls the 'mature personality' is only the beginning of its development in time.

An individual in the modern world is facing the reality of the struggle to emerge in a more intense form than ever before, because each one of us is now standing alone over against the world, whereas, in the quite recent past, individuals were snugly enmeshed in extended family and intimate group relationships which, while they limited to some extent everyone's free development, also spared each the agonizing self-appraisal of modern man's plaintive search for identity. Today man is facing *himself* in a quite new way. This can be exciting – or devastating. Exciting if he enters into the dynamic of his own emergence with zest and appetite for change; devastating if he fears his own inner nature, or wants an unequivocal answer to his identity conundrum.

The intensified individuality of modern man has to be accepted as a part of his identity crisis. He may sense it as a pressure of external forces that drive him back upon himself. Or he may resist the forces deliberately and take up the position of individuality in revolt, gaining time and opportunity to find out what he really is – which is the way the hippies deal with the modern world. Or he may seek to attain personal individuality in relationship to the world as it is, but without selling out to its pressures and false values.

Nor should this pressure towards greater individualization be regarded as in any way unnatural. It is, as we saw earlier, inherent in the process of evolution itself. 'It seems to me,' writes Leonard Williams in *Samba and the Monkey Mind*, 'that there is an evolution of individuality at work in nature, and with it a development of creative ability that enables animals to rely more on the learning of new techniques and less on instincts that are inborn, a development in fact towards *social culture*, where individuality finds its highest expression, for better or for worse.' That process has carried us to where we are. Through the accumulation of individual creativeness, first civilization itself, and later technological society, were brought into existence. And now, as persons, we have to adjust to the power and immensity of modern society, not by abdication in the face of what we have created, but by an enhancement of individuality in order to control it with thought and humanity, and, when necessary, to transform it.

It is revealing to compare the experience of being an individual as manifest in former or still primitive societies with the experience of individuality in neo-technic man. Primitive man is sheltered from the full impact of his own individuality by the close network of personal relationships that surround him, the routines of social obligations that impose a pattern on each year, and the customary forms of behaviour that make something of a ritual of all encounters. The consequence is that man living in a simple society is less conscious of a separate individuality. For example, a Maori, at one time, did not regard himself as anything but a member of the group. The early administrators in New Zealand came to learn that, if you wanted to get good work from the Maoris, you had to engage at least two of them; an individual Maori employed by himself would be lost and apathetic. As Professor Lambo, working in Nigeria, has shown, this group consciousness can quite quickly give way to modern individualism once life becomes urbanized. It is the townsman, not the country-man, who is brought to ask the question 'What am I?' For the villager, his role and relationships are so obvious that he joins in the common identity without having to seek a clearly defined one of his own.

This shift from group identity to personal identity in the setting of the modern world has important moral implications. The existence of group identity in a primitive society encourages the individual to off-load the responsibility for his own actions. He regards much of what he does and what happens to him as externally controlled. If his crops fail, as we have already noted, he thinks of who the enemy can be who has looked at him with the evil eye, or in what way he has angered his ancestors who are punishing him. In this manner, although the capacity to behave badly is accepted as personal, the causation of the bad action is usually projected on to some external influence. A man who has had a bad day's hunting will not conclude from this that he is a poor hunter, or that he is off form; he will look round for an external explanation. The witch-doctor, if consulted, will reinforce this tendency to project. He will diagnose the ritual omission or the inimical influence.

A modern individual is still considerably caught up in the habit of projecting responsibility for what happens instead of accepting personal responsibility, in so far as it applies in any situation. This might be a harmless get-out if it were not for the fact that, by diminishing his responsibility, a man diminishes himself. Modern man's identity is established by his personal actions and values, and not just by his contribution to the group. He must stand for something, *as himself*, or he will melt into the grey of the universal which, because it is a mass not a community, will swallow him without trace.

We are now in fairly deep water. We shall have to pursue personal identity into unexpected places. Every individual is two entities at once: *Homo sapiens* and a unique person. As *Homo sapiens, only now* is he beginning to recognize what he is: a creature invested with the whole range of possibilities, from tender, self-sacrificing love to hard, egocentric, revengeful hate; from wanton destructiveness to painstaking creation; from utter indolence to dedicated ceaseless effort. *Homo sapiens, qua Homo sapiens*, is bursting with potentialities of every moral shade. From these, personal uniqueness is forged.

This is a rather wild team of horses to get moving in any desired direction, so early man simplified the problem of facing himself by projecting his potentialities for ignoble and noble action in two packets, calling one 'the Devil' (or the equivalent) and the other 'God' (or the equivalent). This 'God', let it be noted, is not the 'God of Creation'. Man had also to face the conundrum of his own existence and called this mystery 'God' also. He then combined his projected capacity for good with his puzzlement about creation into the Christian concept of God. (Modern theologians are at work unscrambling the two since 'evil' is, we have now to accept, in creation, and not, as was once held to be the case, only in man.)

Over the years man has gained enough courage to accept his own evil potentialities. Once he had got reasonably far with this, the concept of the Devil ceased to be necessary as a projection and slipped from the scene. Only fundamentalists now believe in the Devil, and many of those have their tongues in their cheeks. The other projection has proved more durable, but, at last, the 'God' of projected goodness is slowly being replaced by man's rather unwilling acceptance of the fact that he has within him what is noble, golden, and glorious as well as the opposites of all these things. This is a rather startling discovery that carries somewhat frightening responsibilities. Since we are so composed, we really should manage to be reasonably happy and useful instead of glooming away in morose self-doubt. 'Woe is me, for I am a sinful man' begins to sound like an excuse, to which the answer is, 'You're not *only* a sinful man, why not get up and get going?' Man's identity crisis in individual life, and in much modern writing, is only to be solved after man sees himself *whole* as a member of his species and also *unique* as an emergent personality with an immense range of potentialities to draw upon.

Modern man's identity crisis, therefore, does not hinge upon restoring something that has been lost but on his entering into the inheritance of himself fully revealed – a being magnificently endowed with capacities for living that he can bring to fruition by entering, as a person, into relationships with other people and the world. To the extent that he actualizes his unique potentialities, others will recognize him as a person and will hold up for him a mirror in which he can recognize himself. To the extent that man fails to realize his true significance as a person, he is slow to accept his actual responsibilities. When he casts himself, thus, in an inferior role in the surgent evolving modern world, he feels rejected and isolated.

However brash the external world may have become, individuals are still capable of shaping things as persons and as groups provided that they have the courage to be what they are and to enter into the full commitment of being what they are. History is inviting people to do just this. Morality in the modern world is an intensely personal matter. Every day we are expected to declare ourselves in small issues and in great. We say yes or no to options of behaviour, and we take up positions on issues of major importance for the world, like racial conflict, war, reform, and how best to feed the under-nourished millions of the depressed nations. We declare ourselves as *persons* and are expected to do so. The 'don't knows' are tolerated, but rather despised. It is accepted as all right to spend time thinking over a problem, but, in the end, a point of view is expected. At any time a man with a microphone may stop any of us in the street for our personal views on anything in the news and get impatient when there is no ready answer. And if it isn't a man with a microphone, it's our friends or neighbours or business associates.

Such probing is not as trifling as it sometimes seems. It is not only an exploration of what we think, but also of what our values are, of what *we* are. It is a social admission that everyone's opinion counts. By this interaction of person with person, supplemented by propaganda of one kind or another, public opinion is formed, political action influenced, and our lives, or other people's, modified for good or ill. Since no political action is possible in a democracy without a *sufficient* support from public opinion, those of us who live in democracies, however imperfect they may be, are constantly involved in shaping the course of events, by however small a fraction, whether we realize it or not. Not even the 'don't knows' are absolved from this influence. Those who are not able, do not bother, or are not bold enough to think for themselves are sowing indecision and apathy, and preparing the way for other than democratic influences to take over.

In an open society like ours, the moral responsibility of every person is high. Those who jib at the responsibility are, in effect, voting against democracy. Democracy is not an invitation to participate occasionally; it is the expectation and need that every-body shall become continuously involved in thought and action. Those who want the freedom of democracy without the responsi-bility are keeping themselves dry by taking other people's umbrellas. And they lose their chance of full individual identity by stepping aside from *one* important relationship that binds them up with the lives of others. To be known by ourselves, we must become something for others, and to become something we must be committed to something. The uncommitted cannot make more than a superficial impression on others and cannot experience existence at any depth.

Let us now try to answer the question 'What am I?' for modern man. The answer is to be found in the nature of man and in the nature of the modern world. An individual person carries within him both the possibilities of his species and the special uniqueness of being which is himself – something definite, though emerging, never wholly arrived. Society today desperately needs individuals to become more complete as human beings, more *themselves*, because the giant machines of the modern world – mechanical, electronic, organizational, economic – must of their nature move towards the impersonal enslavement of mankind unless they are humanized from within by the calibre and imagination of the people who are moving among them and operating them.

Identity is not to be achieved by withdrawal. Those who refuse to participate in the world as it is, however distasteful they find it, run the risk of ending up in a fantasy world of their own where their personalities will shrink, since contact and commitment, not withdrawal, are the sources of personal growth. The decision to reject society is not sufficient without the commitment to change it. The true nonconformist is not a run-away; he is a revolutionary, even though he avoids violence and seeks to transform society by other means.

A sense of identity springs from an emerging personality interacting productively with the framework of life in which the individual exists. For this to happen there has to be a valid consciousness of self and a realistic perception of the framework. The old framework that served mankind for generations, and was the ground for his sense of individuality, has gone. We are no longer fathered and mothered by clan groups and small intimate communities that used to give people identity just by knowing them well, and to give them significance by needing their contribution to the community life. Again, we can no longer see ourselves as the *dramatis personae* of a struggle between God and the Devil for our souls, a sorry plight perhaps, but a source of significance none the less. We must step out of this historic background into the contemporary setting for our existence where a new kind of identity awaits us – as persons standing alone and very much involved in our own emergence, in association with others, and responsible, as thinking and imaginative individuals, for the present and the future. This kind of commitment is, in the modern world, the source of identity. Noncommitment is an act of non-identity. If, instead of living life, we, as it were, let life live us, we disappear into the formless mass of commercial society and can only demonstrate our existence at all by shouting at our fate, like drowning men calling for help when the storm is raging too fiercely for voices to be heard.

Those who wish to be effective can be effective once they have worked out what they wish to be effective about. Individuals still have influence if they want to use it. The world needs every person's independent voice. So the answer to the modern man's query 'What am I?' turns out to be something like this: 'We are alive. We are unique. We are emerging along with others. With them we are responsible for the present and the future. Our identity is to be found within the dynamic of that situation. We are the dynamic in that situation. So much for the source of identity in the modern environment of man. But identity is not only the outcome of effective individuality; it is also a feeling of uniqueness. This aspect of identity – the inwardness of personal awareness, with its moral implications – we shall review in Chapter Ten.

7

THE PROCESS OF PERSONAL DEVELOPMENT

MORAL maturity is to be attained through growth, like any other maturity. A baby starts out totally egocentric because totally dependent. Twenty years or so later, we hope to find him emerging as a confident young adult, his potentialities blossoming, and well adjusted socially. As we saw in Chapter Four, this road to maturity is, in a primitive, self-perpetuating society, so effectively sign-posted that the young have only to follow the track in order to arrive at respected adulthood. Conformity to age-group norms is anticipated and encouraged; social values are clearly defined and continuously hammered home. At initiation, young people, particularly the young males, are put through a drubbing but self-enhancing experience which simultaneously knocks any over-weening self-assertion out of them and accords them the privileges and status of manhood. It is a system – it still continues in some areas – which maximizes conformity while keeping personal innovation firmly in check.

Young people in societies which have broken out of self-perpetuating moral systems – our modern societies – have a much more adventurous trip to adulthood, with a much more ambitious goal: socially adjusted, self-reliant, morally autonomous individuality. Theirs is a greater struggle than was the case formerly, because they are surrounded by the moral confusion of an open society, while no clear criteria exist whereby they can tell when they have attained the status of adults. Nevertheless, they are members of the species *Homo sapiens*, and therefore social and creative by nature. A young person of the modern world, granted appropriate relationships, information, and experience, is set fair to develop morally through the strugglings and strivings of growth just as he develops in any other aspect of his personality – that is, by a gradual process of learning. In this chapter we shall consider in outline the developmental road an individual traverses in the attainment of maturity.

Two points must be cleared up for a start. One is that the end-product to be sought is *not* a completed perfection. Indeed, the expectation of perfection has, throughout history, been a stumbling-block to moral understanding. Perfection as a state of being is an illusion. There can be a perfect moment; there can be an ideal of perfection as a goal for striving, but never a quite perfect thing, never a perfect continuity: there is always incompleteness and always something beyond. There has, for example, never existed a perfect human body. The attainment of the upright posture in man – an important advance, which freed the hands, improved the range of vision, and stimulated the development of the brain – had to be won at the cost of notable physical imperfections, such as a compromise knee joint, an attenuated and weakened collar bone, and an overloaded lumbar spine. This is the way things go in nature and in growth; every gain involves some loss. Progress is a direction that is never consummated by a final goal. No man can be perfect in body or in mind; no process of growth can be perfect in itself; but the individual, although imperfect and imperfectly endowed, can interact formatively with the experiences provided by his own developmental process so as to advance towards the fulfilment of his own uniqueness – immensely valuable and satisfying, but never, in the nature of things, perfect.

The second danger is that the mere mention of the word

'maturity' should seem to suggest we are concerned with the attainment of a precisely describable state. Maturity is a popular word, but a rather misleading one. It is sometimes used to mean conformity to whatever the establishment of the time thinks to be desirable, although uncritical acceptance of the *status quo* is certainly *not* a mark of maturity. The maturity which we envisage as the end-product of a process of growth is itself a potentiality for further growth. In his Reith Lectures, Professor G. M. Carstairs put it like this:

'I suggest that the mature person shows these attributes: a realistic grasp of his environment, a sense of conviction about his own identity, an ability to cope with his practical tasks, and an ability to establish deep mutual relationships with other people. None of these, obviously, are inborn attributes; they all have to be learned, and they are learned in stages.'

Professor Carstairs's list is, by intention, a minimal one, but it brings out the essential point: that maturity is a preparedness for a continuing advance into experience; it is not to be regarded as an arrival. We should notice at this point that, once we look at human development dynamically, personal maturity and moral maturity are indistinguishable; they together represent a maximized capacity for personal fulfilment in association with others.

Having cleared those two sources of misapprehension out of the way, we are now in a position to review the process by which, stage following stage of development, the individual advances from babyhood to mature adulthood. We shall first consider the untrammelled path of development without investigating the set-backs which inevitably occur, and then look at the effects on development of some of the common blockages which are obstructive enough to distort overall growth.

The baby enters the world as a bundle of potentialities. What he can become nobody knows. There is no built-in information about an individual's capacities. The only way a child can find out what he is is through the experience of living; the only way parents can find out what their child is like is by watching the child as he encounters life, and guiding and encouraging him in his ceaseless explorations. Interaction with the environment and with other people starts at birth. The quality of these experiences is sensed by the child, and through them he acquires an evaluation of himself and others. A warm and loving world assures him that all is well and fosters his self-esteem and courage – the twin roots of thriving personal growth.

Social reactions – smiling, nestling, cuddling – develop early, as also does self-assertion. Quite soon the child has to accommodate himself to the inconvenient fact that those who provide him with love, food, and admiration can, and sometimes do, withhold them, and that other members of the family group sometimes enter into competition with him for what he wants for himself alone. Denial leads to frustration, anger, hatred – and fear of what hatred may bring upon him. This is the first moral crisis of life. It is reduced to manageable proportions – to follow Freud – by the child introjecting the values of society as he experiences them in the behaviour of his parents, and as he interprets them through his childish imagination. This internalized system of 'rights' and 'wrongs' is the rudimentary conscience.

Other morally formative processes are also going on during these early years. The child is discovering himself, other people, and the wider world. He learns to take pleasure in his own body. He learns that other people are there and that he can influence them and challenge them. He finds out that he is weak and small in a world of bigger things, and sets out with indomitable courage to catch up: to walk, to talk, to lift, to carry, to copy and emulate. These strivings lead to all kinds of set-backs and frustrations which the child has to deal with as best he may, encouraged and supported – but not over-controlled – by his parents. His probing questions along the way enable him to come to terms with the problems of his small but expanding personal world: 'Where did I come from?' 'What makes the rain fall?' 'Where does a bird go when it dies?' and so forth.

By the end of a successful infancy, the young child has learnt to interact vigorously and confidently with the world around him. He has learnt to take account of others, to enjoy mixing, and to tolerate sharing. And he has laid down a framework of understanding into which he fits. He feels he is a person in his own right and is constantly experimenting to find out more about this exciting business of being him.

Throughout this first phase of development, the child who is loved, guided, and encouraged aright will receive his first lessons in understanding that a person's area of personal freedom always has limits. For example, the child finds he is free to play in the garden but not on the road. He is free to romp with the animals but not to hurt them. At times he may make as much noise as he chooses; at others he may not. For the child to understand his area of freedom – consistently defined and gradually extended – is an essential moral experience for him. Coming to terms with the realities of the limits, and making use of the freedom within them, teaches him how to accept responsibility for himself and his own actions in an environment where others' needs and wishes must also be respected. Wise guidance also develops his trust in those who are in charge of him. He realizes that they are on his side in his eagerness to grow up, in spite of the control they exert, and in time he learns that co-operation in reasonable demands is a more fruitful way of going on than putting up a life-and-death resistance at every denial of his wishes.

The years between infancy and adolescence serve to carry the child whose opportunities are adequate into ever-widening fields of experience. The normal child of this age is avidly curious and ceaselessly energetic. He is constantly interacting with things, people, and events, and constantly finding out more about himself and his environment as he does so. As his competence extends, so should his area of freedom and self-determination; he can then learn to think for himself and, occasionally, for others. The child of ten is usually a very well-set-up young personality indeed: quick in response, capable within the confines of his understanding, remarkably self-sufficient personally and socially, apart from his periodic need for reinforcement by adult love and reassurance. There are tribes in which boys, from the age of ten, are expected to hunt, kill, and cook their own food, and they manage most of their own maintenance by doing so. Hence, children of this age are capable of carrying real responsibility. But before adolescence, as Piaget and others have shown, moral behaviour is based, not on the understanding of principle, but on example and rule of thumb acquired from earlier experience. Moral insight in the adult sense – weighing situations in terms of principle – is not likely before about twelve years of age, except in particularly advanced children.

The adolescent years, fully experienced, bring an immense advance in personal and moral development. A whole range of new tasks face the adolescent in the struggle to emerge as a person, and, in tackling them and adjusting to them, his understanding of himself, other people, and life broadens and deepens into a new dimension of being that is equally startling for the young person concerned and for the adults around him, or her.

Up to adolescence, the individual's interaction with the world is comparatively limited. At adolescence it opens up in all directions, and particularly socially. This is highly formative morally, because moral insight is gained mainly in social relationships. The home remains an important field of interaction, but beyond it, and of increasing importance, lie other fields: the school (and, later, the place of work), groups of personal friends, other groups, and the world at large with its personal and impersonal influences, including the mass media. The confident adolescent probes and explores all his expanding spheres of contact with a zest and intelligence that make every day a significant experience. Before he reaches his late teens his intellectual powers will be at their maximum and he will turn his sharpened, if still inexperienced, mind on to every situation as it arises. This is why adolescence is such an outstandingly formative phase of life; it is also why the individual who enters adolescence with his curiosity and self-confidence blunted – as many, unfortunately, do today – is at such an appalling disadvantage.

The growth-surge of adolescence has many facets. The range of emotions is extended and their quality is intensified: idealism, sexual feeling, self feeling, and aesthetic wonder all burgeon at the same time, sweeping the adolescent at times into the seventh heaven of ecstasy, and at others precipitating him into a depth of gloom and despair of near-suicidal intensity. This rise and fall of feeling adds to the adolescent's identity problem. To quote from an adolescent discussion: 'I know what I feel like *now*; I don't know what I'll feel like tomorrow.' This flux of feeling causes the adolescent's orientation to life and to others to swirl alarmingly: 'Shall I go forward into uncertainty, or back to what I know?'; and overall the puzzle: 'Which me is me?'

To help him with his conundrum, the adolescent seeks to get a bearing on life by identification with others he admires because they manifest the qualities, achievements, and presence he would like to have. They seem to have the secret of the more abundant life he longs for, and he may copy them in gestures, in dress, in ideas even, in the hope that something of what they are will rub off on to him. Pop stars, the kings of sport, older friends, teachers, and contemporaries will all tempt his emulation. And today we see the interesting development of pop stars, who are themselves identification figures, putting themselves under tutelage to a guru to help them to get their own lives in focus. As Erik Erikson has said, adolescents work through identifications towards identity.

The adolescent's search, with its surgent emotions, brings into being a much intensified inner life. Introspection of any sharpness becomes possible for the first time. This sensing of the self inwardly brings with it a capacity for spiritual loneliness, with disturbing overtones of doubt and guilt. The adolescent's perpetual problem is not only, 'How can I know what I am?' but also, 'How can I share what I am?' And all this, for the most part, takes place in secrecy. Parents, looking through their daughter's school magazine, noticed a poem starting 'I am unwanted and hated'. They wondered who this unfortunate girl could be. At the bottom was their daughter's name.

The challenge of emotional growth is only one of many developmental tasks that the adolescent has to live with, work at, and finally master. Adolescence is also the time when personal independence has to be striven for. Brash bids for recognition will be made. Adult response to these is often critical and condemnatory, which makes the adolescent stiffen into revolt. Head-on collisions can then shatter the tranquillity of the home as adults and adolescents adjust themselves to one another – and all in the ordinary course of growing up with no harm done so long as the parents are sufficiently understanding to meet the adolescent half-way. The clash of purpose between adolescents and their parents, or other adults, can be used to draw adolescents in to discussing and defining the proper limits to their behaviour so that they come to accept the responsibility for their reasonable control. Although always furious at imposed authority – aren't we all? – adolescents are quite capable of seeing what are the different claims of different people in a situation, and are usually willing to adjust their behaviour to meet other people's needs, provided that their own are taken into account.

As the converse of breaking away from the home into wider independence – a necessary but, at times, frightening task – the adolescent seeks the reassurance of closer relationships with other adolescents, and perhaps, also, with adults outside the immediate family circle. This search can be a testing adventure. The individual adolescent is now on his own, making a bid for recognition and appreciation in the wider world. With whom shall I be friends? Who will be friends with me? What can I do which will help me make my mark? Social acceptance brings untold delight; social rejection the utmost misery. For a time the ups and downs of social exploration become all-absorbing.

The existence and challenge of the other sex, and of the inner growth of sexual feeling, add mystery, wonder, yearning, and excitement to this new and enthralling encounter with other people. Along with this comes a deepened self-questioning and uncertainty. Every blemish of body or personality that has been apprehended is moiled over anxiously. Scales are consulted, tape-measures taken out, spots examined, models admired, journals scanned for information and guidance. The hovering question now is, 'Have I got what it takes?' The hard test of experience brings a varying mixture of hope and despair.

During adolescence particularly, the streak of inferiority that, as Alfred Adler pointed out, lurks in all of us, is activated acutely by every set-back so that even the most fortunate adolescent is at times hag-ridden with self-doubt. This he covers over with a thick protective front. Painfully he works at what his value is compared with others, where he fits, and what his status is. Only gradually is a capital of confidence built up, through actual achievement, which allows the adolescent to relax a little on the long road to adulthood.

Unless discouraged about his own powers, the adolescent is also concerned to seek out what he needs to know in order to make sense of his life. He wants to find an outlook and ideas that will give some shape to the apparent confusion and enable him to get oriented. He may turn from one 'solution' to another until he finds something that suits him. During adolescence the 'whys?' of infancy, and the vigorous pragmatic exploration typical of childhood, should mature into a philosophy of life that is convincing and viable for the individual.

Of course, youth is youth, and life offers fun, and the road to adulthood is often gay as well as grim; but the transformation of the self, through courageous experience, from a child into an adult *is* a real struggle, one of the most testing in the whole of life. Its very nature makes it rich with possibilities for moral development. Questions of right and wrong become intensely relevant. Decisions have to be made about the conduct of personal life; principles are sought to help guide the decisions. Under the impact of intensified personal experience, and the search for values inherent in it, the rigid conscience of childhood becomes modified and developed into an organ of moral insight capable of assessing situations as they arise.

Thus, if all goes reasonably well – the rough and smooth totalling up as an advance – individual growth and individual experience combine to form, by the end of adolescence, a young adult, not yet fully matured, but equipped personally and morally to move confidently towards life and the continuing search for fulfilment. He has found out the essentials of what he is and where he fits.

That is, if all goes reasonably well. But sometimes the conditions for the child's development fall short of what is necessary for sound personal and moral growth, and serious immaturity results. The devastating effects of lack of love, warm physical contact, and emotional security in babyhood and infancy are too well known to need stressing. Nothing can undermine a child's confidence and trust so completely as to be unwanted or disregarded, or treated as a thing, however hygienically. But infancy contains other, and less-well-understood pitfalls. A young child needs a stimulating environment to satisfy his insatiable curiosity or he may get dulled by lack of stimulation. He needs contact at quite an early age with other young children or he may become clinging and timid, withdrawn from vitally important social interaction. A child's self-respect and confidence can be undermined by too much criticism, which makes him feel worthless; by too much protection or cossetting, which makes his world formless and threatening; or by extreme inconsistency of treatment, which makes it impossible for the child to differentiate adult standards of right and wrong in any clear way. Also damaging to a child's assurance and self-esteem is the suggestion that his own body and its functions are repugnant to the adults who care for him. From the earliest stages of life a child sees his body as very much himself. To make him ashamed of it, or its excretions, or the pleasure he derives from playing with his body, is to make him ashamed of himself for being what he is – the start of much discouragement, deviousness, and subterfuge, let alone maladjustment and neurosis.

During childhood and adolescence, the essential issue is whether the ups and downs of experience leave the individual with sufficient achievement and confidence to build up his assurance and courage, or whether the outcome is a sense of deep inadequacy. No individual can endure a sense of worthlessness. Everybody wants to be somebody. If, then, at any stage, real life fails to provide sufficient achievement in the struggle to master the tasks of life, the individual, so denied, will turn to some source of compensation to build up his confidence and prestige. Two sources of compensation are readily available. One is to retreat from reality into a fantasy world where dreams can make up for what life has failed to provide. The other is to seek satisfaction by posturing and ostentation of one form or another, from excessive self-display to anti-social violence. Drugs can play a part in both:

they can add intensity to compensatory dreams or give impetus for acts of ostentatious daring to those who have lost hope of success on what Adler called 'the useful side of life'.

For the young man of low attainment, who feels a rejected failure in the struggle for achievement and recognition, compensation through physical toughness is an almost irresistible temptation. For years nobody shows much interest in what he has to offer except to impress upon him that it is not worth much. Then, one day, he finds himself with something that does make people take notice of him – his muscles. Pugnacity and destructiveness put him in the centre of the picture, permit him to get rid of his frustrations, and give him a chance to get his own back on society all in one go. It is hardly surprising that such a young man uses and venerates violence as his means of self-expression. For a girl of low attainment, sex may play a similar role. Sexual maturity offers her a significance far surpassing anything she gained from her meagre past achievements. In consequence, she over-values and over-plays her sexuality. These overt anti-social responses demonstrate the close relationship between personal development and moral immaturity. To neglect the first is to promote the second. Too much dependence on fantasy also undermines personal and moral development.

Fantasy and self-display are aspects of all lives. We use them, at times, to bolster our faltering self-assurance. What happens to the stumbling and inadequate is something different from this; these deeply discouraged young people adopt fantasy and posturing not as occasional palliatives but as styles of life. This isolates them from the mainstream of living because it cuts them off from relationship and growth. They become trapped in a cul-de-sac from which only the most patient and understanding help can extricate them.

We hope to find positive tone – or morale – in an adult's relationship with life. Where this exists, it represents the accumulated effect of a whole series of formative interactions with life which have, on balance, been rewarding. Every interaction is a mixture of satisfaction and frustration which, according to the proportions of each, gives rise to an experience that is rewarding or the reverse. Where, in any experience, the satisfaction is, over time, reasonably high and the frustration reasonably low, the resulting feeling tone will be positive and the tendency to return to that experience will be reinforced.

Children and adolescents who are helped to gain rewarding experiences through useful endeavour will be kept moving towards reality and maturity. But if all we can offer is experience which leads to high frustration and low satisfaction, the young people will lose heart and look elsewhere. The low attainer who has felt humiliated by his lack of success at school, with girls, or whatever it may be, may find a brawl – in which he can make an impression with his muscular strength – a much more satisfying experience than any sort of orderly effort he knows of.

R. D. Laing believes that a schizophrenic individual turns to insanity as a, for him, logical way out of an intolerable social situation. Similarly we may surmise that a withdrawn or anti-social individual is seeking to satisfy legitimate human aspirations in unfortunate ways because these have been urged upon him through his lack of attainment in approved outlets. The way to raise the level of moral maturity in the nation would seem, then, to be through greater care in helping children and adolescents to surmount their developmental tasks, and in rehabilitating the attitudes and self-esteem of children who come to school already damaged.

Two further points remain to be cleared up in this outline sketch of the individual's path from birth to adulthood. First, to take a little farther the distinction already mentioned between moral maturity and social conformity. Some writers treat socialization as the process by which an individual learns to conform to the mores of his society. In fact, social maturity should go some way beyond this. It is natural that a mature person should be co-operative and, therefore, willing to go along with his culture to the extent possible for him. But maturity implies moral insight, and the effort to apply principles that have been tested in experience and found to be valid. Wherever the be-haviour of society falls short of these personal principles, it is plainly the part of a morally mature person to attack as vigorously as he is able what, in society, he judges to be wrong. The socially mature person will not be afraid to be a nonconformist when the situation warrants it. This is the creative aspect of social maturity.

Secondly, for the sake of simplicity this chapter has been written as if people ended up either thoroughly socialized or thoroughly desocialized. The truth, rather, is that we are all mixtures. Each one of us is unique as a person and experiences uniquely his own environment and relationships. The resulting experiences sometimes help and sometimes hinder. The path of life for no one is totally positive and for no one totally negative. Each one of us has to strive to make something of what he is and what he experiences. In the process we shall all get mauled and scarred somewhat and bear the marks of it. Life is a struggle, and a search, to complete and integrate ourselves. Every decade of it – every year – faces us with new problems. The criterion of satisfactory personal development at any stage of life is not the absence of frailty in ourselves but the ability to produce something of value from our strivings, and to deal well enough with the present to be equipped to take on the future.

This chapter has dealt primarily with infancy and adolescence because they are the two great formative phases of personal and moral development. But development is a task for life, and it only stops when people become so set in their ways that no further change is possible. This, however, need never happen. As people get older the world around them changes, and so long as a lively interaction with the changing world continues, so does development. Life never lets up on us. Being married is different from being single; having a family is different from being childless; when the children grow up, parents are precipitated into a new pattern of relationship – together and on their own again, but now much older. Divorce or a death may cut across existence and call for rapid readjustments. Retirement brings its own problems. To face all the tasks of living as they come, not as affronts but as challenges, calls for an ever-deepening insight into life and values. The whole of life is an adventure in discovery, and, at the end of it, what lies behind is not only a life lived but also a hundred other lives that could have been lived. Such is the richness of the personal potential in each one of us.

Every day – every waking hour, every waking minute – sights, sounds, feelings, incidents, relationships are impinging upon us, and, even in sleep, this rich and formative interchange between ourselves and the world is being run over again in the depths of the mind, and parts of it played out symbolically in the dream-life, itself an important balance to the urgencies and demands of existence. Every day, too, there are choices and decisions, temptations to be weak, challenges to show our strength, demands upon our capacity for self-control, set-backs, achievements, reassessments. Within all this turmoil of being, values are forged into principles, tested, confirmed, or rejected. Such is the process of attaining moral maturity. It is a part of the rich stuff of living itself. Three aspects of this will come in for more detailed attention in the following chapters: man's encounter with sex, violence, and the inner life of man.

8

SEXUAL MORALITY

In a consideration of personal morality, sex is a special issue in western society. It is, as always, an influence with which everyone has to come to terms; it is a powerful personal drive which is directed towards others; but it has been hedged in by taboos instead of being left free to develop its own regulators and values within human experience. Sexual morality has, in consequence, remained in a very rudimentary state over the generations. For these and other reasons, sex has become a thing apart, an object of fascination but laden with apprehensions, embarrassment, perversions, and guilt, so that, even today, for many people the word morality means, primarily, sexual behaviour.

In fact, the morality of sex is no different from any other sort of morality. Moral values arise from creative relationships and the creative use of the self. They are, that is, developmental principles. In sex, as in the rest of life, the key principles are self-respect, respect for others, consideration and concern for one another, responsibility, courage, and a right balance of spontaneity and control. Man's encounter with sex, so often regarded as inimical to everything of moral value, provides an area of

8

intense experience within which principles for living can be
particularly clearly revealed and reinforced. This is an unfamiliar
idea for some people but it is all of a piece with the reorientation
in thought which man's ever-expanding understanding of his
nature, and the nature of reality, is bringing about.

The reversal of viewpoint about sex is part of a widespread
shift of perspective. In this century much old thinking is being
turned topsy-turvy. Ideas that have carried conviction for generations are having to be discarded in favour of others, some of them
the reverse of the original ideas. Particularly interesting is the way
that ideas formerly thought to be poles apart are being brought
together in a single dynamic concept. For example, energy was
for centuries regarded as noble and spiritual in essence, as against
matter, which was thought to be gross and evil. We now know
that matter and energy are the equivalent of one another. Einstein's
$E = mc^2$ wiped out at one blow volumes of false philosophy.

The mind–body dichotomy has also had to go. Old-world
thinking considered mind as exalted and the body as base. No
such difference exists. The two are intimately related in a single
dynamic. Similarly with intellect and emotion. The first was
formerly regarded as noble, over against the second, which was
denigrated as an unreliable and inferior function – something to
be expunged if possible. We now realize that the mainsprings of
human activity, including thinking, are emotional, and that the
best creative edge for human achievement is given by reason and
emotion operating together.

The body–soul contrast is equally false. The 'soul' of man – his
sense of personal being at its highest level of awareness – is the
product of a harmony in which his total personality is involved:
reason, feelings, body, intuition. . . .

As Browning wrote:

> All good things
> Are ours, nor soul helps flesh more, now, than flesh helps soul.

Man's traditionally jaundiced attitude to sex was in part
related to his erroneous views on matter, flesh, and emotion, so
it is not surprising that earlier assumptions about sex are now

being turned inside out too. Earlier thinking led to the view that, because sex was exciting, absorbing, and often distracting, you would be able, to the extent that you cut it out, to intensify intellectual, altruistic, and spiritual power. There was also the moralistic angle: human personality must be 'purified' from sex in order to achieve its highest development. All this is untrue. Creativity, effective energy, social purpose, and a full and rewarding sex-life are often found in combination.

We have now in prospect – though still to be attained – the richest and most wholesome era of human sexuality in history, founded in sex that has been personalized, accepted, understood, properly valued, and properly controlled by the principles of its own full fruition. It has taken a long time to get to this point of promise, and the reason for the blockage needs to be appreciated in order that the responsible freedom of human sexuality may be brought into perspective.

Our tradition has been anti-sex mainly because, until very recently, the powerful resources of organized Christianity have maintained the image of sex as a kind of naughty indulgence to be gratified only under conditions ecclesiastically laid down and, even then, suspect, and certainly sinful if passion and pleasure entered into it. It is a sad story of misinterpretation. To the writers of Leviticus and Deuteronomy, semen, menstruation, mating, and childbirth were unclean things. Woman was regarded as the vessel of uncleanness.

'If a woman have conceived seed and born a man child: then she shall be unclean seven days; according to the days of the separation for her infirmity shall she be unclean. . . . And she shall then continue in the blood of her purifying three and thirty days; she shall touch no hallowed thing, nor come into the sanctuary, until the days of her purifying be fulfilled. But if she bear a maid child, then she shall be unclean two weeks . . . and she shall continue in the blood of her purifying threescore and six days' (Leviticus 12: 2–5, Authorized version).

The ideas coming in from the other tradition – the pagan side – were only a degree or two better. In the pagan world of Ancient

Greece, sex was valued as a source of joy and the body admired, but woman was held to be an inferior mortal, for the most part incapable of intelligent companionship; and matter, including flesh, was thought of as cloddish and evil compared with the realm of thought and reason, which was 'pure'.

The leaders of the Christian Church, from St Paul onwards, inherited the worst of both worlds so far as ideas about sex were concerned. Paul, a guilt-ridden genius, felt gently towards women but regarded them, nevertheless, as second-class citizens – after all, he believed that God had made man first and then woman from man. Paul also thought sex to be a threat to spiritual life and the body a snare.

He, and the other leaders of the early Church, struggled cease-lessly in the torment of trying to resolve the conflict between their bodies crying out for fulfilment and their duty – as they saw it – to reject that same flesh, believing that only that was pure and holy which was untouched by the senses. 'Who shall deliver me from the body of this death?' pleaded St Paul. St Augustine, a towering intellect of early Christianity, troubled himself with the thought: 'If I be *conceived in iniquity and my mother nourished me, even within the womb, in sin,* where I beseech thee, O my God, where, O my Lord, was I thy servant, or at what time was I ever innocent?' (St Augustine's italics.)

St Francis, in a later age, is said to have found himself beset by visions of naked women in his struggle to abnegate his flesh, and thought them to be temptations sent by the Devil. Poor Origen, a greatly gifted Christian teacher and writer of the third century, castrated himself in his attempt to silence for ever the yearning of his body to be used for love.

We can understand the conflicts and confusion which made these men see things as they did, and sympathize with their un-necessary efforts to defeat in their own persons the forces of crea-tion that had produced them, and yet we cannot but be amazed that their erroneous ideas should have served to blight the course of human sexuality throughout twenty centuries. The modifica-tion of the Church's negative and prudish attitude towards sex is of *very* recent origin. Just before the last war it was possible for the novelist and dramatist, Charles Morgan, to write in the preface to his at-that-time sophisticated play, *The Flashing Stream*: '*I differ from many of my contemporaries* in believing that the sexual act is an act of consequence, and, at the same time, that *it is not in itself evil.*' (My italics.)

So sex has had a bad start in our history and only now is the evil of anti-sex losing its grip on our society. The sexual confusion of the present – which blatantly exists – is to be compared with what happens in the playground when the bell for the start of break rings in an old-fashioned school. The released children rush around the playground in frantic activity, disorderly not because they are free but because they have been cooped up for so long. Yet out of the wildness following the long-postponed defeat of prudery and inhibition – with its meaningless promiscuity, the sleep-ins, the exotic experiments in extreme nonconformity, the obsession with abnormality and perversion – a new attitude to sex is emerging. At long last, sex is becoming a positive value of life, a creative influence in the human search for wholeness, fulfilment, and mutuality, a human relationship amenable to human values.

How, it may be asked, are we to control a function like sex, usually considered as something quite ungovernable except by rigid restriction, through such values as respect and consideration for one another? Can one repulse a tiger with a fly-whisk? This is a fair question to ask in a society in which the development of sexuality is still regarded with embarrassment and in which the individual is faced with the alternatives of either putting the function aside until marriage or of furtive use. The result is a tense attitude to sex in place of acceptance within a context of personal responsibility.

Sex has got a reputation for being uncontrollable, *because* it has been submerged in guilt and sin. Nothing has done greater disservice to sexual morality than the way moralists have set it on one side as a thing apart – an 'it' to be snatched at under conditions laid down by black-or-white taboos. You cannot, in the same area of life, have taboos *and* personal responsibility. If you impose the one you dispel the other. Which is why sex, in our society, is still at such a deplorably low state of development. By inhibiting sex within a fence of taboos, instead of accepting it within the control of responsible human relationships, man has made – and often continues to make – human sexuality sub-human. Deprived of physical love, the male reduces himself to the condition of a sex-starved stallion that snorts from its stable and mounts the nearest mare, all grace and selectivity gone – a mode of behaviour not found among horses under natural conditions. Indeed, the behaviour of males in sexually inhibited Europe is sometimes worse than sub-human; it is sub-animal, since many animals conduct their mating with considerable charm and delicacy. It has become, to quote John MacMurray, 'a vulgarity and a scandal'.

We have failed to civilize sex not because it cannot be civilized but because it has been repressed and, thereby, rendered liable to every variety of perverted outlet. The magnificence and power of human sexuality, its beauty, challenge, and enchantment, have been lost in an underworld of fear, guilt, and perversion, with the Church both generating the guilt and offering means to its alleviation. The whole situation has been degrading, and man has been degraded by it, and the degradation will take some time to work out. That man is not doomed to be crucified by his own sexuality is amply proved by what happens in those societies where the *attitude* to sex is uninhibited, and control is left to an agreed pattern of good manners which gives sexual relations grace and charm without emasculating them.

Such societies accept sex as a delightful and important fact of life, not as an embarrassment to be shuffled around shamefacedly. Regulations exist, but these are to control sexual behaviour, not to repress it. Among the Kikuyu of Kenya, for example, precise rules are laid down for the proper conduct of adolescent love, but it is freely accepted as desirable and healthy for all young people. Love-making is so arranged that it includes orgasm but not penetration, in order to eliminate the risk of illegitimate births. This is achieved by the girl wearing during love-making a little protective skirt with thongs that tie between the legs. In *Facing Mount Kenya*, Jomo Kenyatta explains: 'This form of intimate contact between young people is considered right and proper and the very foundation stone upon which to build a race morally, physically, and mentally sound. For it safeguards the youth from nervous and psychic maladjustment.'

Many other African societies follow – or traditionally followed – a similar system of controlled sexual expression, with the young people themselves versed in the prescribed limits and responsible for maintaining them. In such societies rape is rare or unknown, and other serious perversions also – until the intrusion of western inhibitions, along with the disruption of the established moral order, brings in the whole sorry crop. In his classic, *The Zulu People*, Dr A. T. Bryant, a missionary who spent sixty years with the Zulus, writes:

'UkuHlobonga [external sexual intercourse between the unmarried] is universally practised among the Zulus without any qualms of conscience. It is practised only by free and mutual consent on both sides, and only within certain lawful bounds. Even among lovers an "undeliberate" impregnation of a girl was, in former times, a transgression hardly less grave than was that of rape itself. Incredible as it may seem, prior to the White-man's coming, both these offences were in Zululand virtually unheard of; they were so rare. Though we personally dwelt for many long years amidst thousands of Zulu Natives, all of them heathens, and while the country was still purely Native territory, we can recall not more than a single case of rape, and not one of illegitimacy.'

The same point was brought out in a recent paper by Professor Philip Mayer, who, with his wife, has been studying the rural Red Xhosa, where traditional custom still obtains. He has been in a position to compare the village girls with the christianized girls at school and the urban Xhosa girls. The rural Xhosa girls have sexual freedom, within the limits of accepted behaviour as organized by the young people themselves, but have far fewer premarital pregnancies than the other girls.

The combination of freedom from inhibition with responsibility and good manners in sex is found in many unsophisticated communities. If we, in our society, seem to have a section of people who are irredeemably crude in their sex lives, it is because we have made them so, through the inhibited attitudes still prevalent in society. These are passed on to young people as unnecessary guilt and shame about sex with all the ugly consequences.

The point is not that we could, or should, copy some primitive system of control as the solution to the sexual development of our young people. We are now, as has already been stated, in an open society and cannot revert to the tidy moral order of earlier stages of social development. But we can learn important principles, nevertheless, from the success of these control systems. The most important of them is this. *Values and control develop through the use of a natural function, not through its rejection.* One learns to swim in the water, not on the bank.

A central absurdity of traditional sexual morality in western society is that it attempts to put sexual development in cold storage at the very time when it can be a profound influence in emotional, personal, and moral development. In his late teens and early twenties, the young male is at his maximum virility. When natural love relationships are denied him, he is forced to turn to a substitute outlet. In more than nine cases out of ten this is masturbation, often supplemented by fantasies for which an unlimited supply of 'girlie' periodicals, transparencies, and so forth provide abundant raw material. So the healthy young male, living according to the expectations of the establishment, develops a schizoid emotional attitude to physical love, partly comprised of real friendships with real girls, evocative but chaste, and partly comprised of a sequence of lonely masturbatory acts, nourished by fantasies to which there is no limit. From this distortion of experience, a mature, sensitive lover is somehow supposed to emerge in time for marriage.

The difficulties the female encounters in a sexually inhibited society, in developing a mature capacity for physical love, are of a somewhat different order from those experienced by the male. For women the experience of love, delayed too long, and denied the means to its own growth, is often quite unable to contain the expectations that have been heaped upon it; it may also lack relaxation and warmth. The result, when the time for marriage is reached, is often an anticlimax which, at one sharp stroke, can wreck past dreams and future hopes of fulfilment through love. Hence a couple on honeymoon, at a time when they need all their resources to meet the new intimate propinquity they have embarked upon, are liable to be thrown up against a fumbling confusion in their sex-life. Young people caught in this vortex of uncertainty are told by the writers of books on sex and marriage to 'be patient'. Which is about as helpful as throwing two non-swimmers into the middle of a river and telling them to rescue one another.

It may justly be argued that a marriage in which neither partner has had any previous experience is today a rarity. Be that as it may, the marriage of two virgins is what traditional morality continues to hold up as the ideal, and as the best possible foundation for future marital happiness. If a young man, who has been training himself in masturbation and fantasy for several years, gets into bed with a young woman, who has been training herself on dreams, and possibly masturbation also, it is presumed that the union will be blessed in heaven, provided that a marriage certificate has been collected on the way. Unfortunately it all too often leads to marital disaster on earth and a collapse of values in lost esteem, resentment, recrimination, and despair. Even if one – or both – of the partners has had experience, the attitude of inhibition and guilt, caught in the individual's own past, can impede the sensitivity, tenderness, and passion of relaxed sexual love. People fit for marriage need to be free from sexual inhibition *in their feelings*. In their actions, there must always be consideration and sensitivity. This subtle combination comes from experience, not from denial.

The extraordinary position is that the Christian moralists – as distinct from the liberal Christians – declare that the monstrous mutilation of emotional development produced by sexual inhibition before marriage must be tolerated because it is 'the will of God'. What kind of God does this point of view put before us? A God, presumably, who has created young people to reach puberty at thirteen to fifteen on average, and who then wishes them to leave their new function unused for years, even though the young male reaches his highest virility during his late teens and early twenties. To call this 'right' is to mock the wisdom of the Creator whom the moralists claim to serve.

These same moralists come back with the argument: 'Ah, but the natural function of sex is to produce children.' They are wrong here also. The natural function of sex is not *only* to produce children. As Dr Desmond Morris and others have pointed out, were this the case human beings would not be prepared for mating the whole year through, but would be seasonal, like animals; nor would the body be so splendidly equipped for love that it invites a lingering tenderness of caress and passion instead of the quick act of copulation that suffices for animal procreation. In man, sex is a powerful force in relationships and personal development. It is an important social and binding activity, rich in mutual delight. Procreation is only one of its biological functions. This can now be controlled. Hence, we are in a position to pay proper regard to the important developmental aspects of physical love, so that young people may grow towards marriage and be ready for it in their feelings, and in their bodies, when it comes. This is often not so today. Not a few marriages fail to survive the honeymoon, because of sexual ignorance, inhibition, and clumsiness.

We have to make a fresh start. To evaluate sex aright we must arrive at some general conclusion about what we wish sex to become for human beings, and then consider the developmental stages by which sexuality as a potential may be fostered through the kind of growth that makes the mature experience possible.

Mature, passionate sexuality is a central component in happy marriage. It gives to marriage a warmth, depth, and mutuality which spreads beyond the mated pair to invest the whole home with love and cheerfulness and fun. It is a vital source of reinforcement to the bond between the couple – the more successful the love, the stronger the bond. It carries the partners to ever greater depths of self and mutual discovery. For a writer such as Suzanne Lilar, the transforming power of mutual physical passion is such as to warrant the name of 'sacred' in its own right. The consummation of physical love in shared enchantment is, thus, not only the means to procreation itself, but the source of happiness and self-discovery which makes the home a loving, stimulating, gay, and companionable place for the children to grow up in. Such is the positive power of sex, rightly valued and rightly used.

But, of course, a few minutes at the altar, or the registrar's desk, does not magically confer upon the young couple the maturity of emotional and sexual sensitivity and awareness which is needed from the inception of marriage. If the marriage partners are to be ready enough to make a good start, with good prospects of enduring happiness together, then the previous years should have been years of growth leading to that level of development.

Three facets of experience are especially important. Mature sexuality involves the trusting gift of one's own body to another. If this gift is to be happy and uninhibited, then the partners must have learnt to accept and delight in their own bodies as a source of pleasure. Secondly, the feeling tone should be one of uninhibited warmth and desire. Thirdly, respect for one's own body, as well as for one's own self, should be such as to make giving it to another highly selective.

All three facets are influenced right from the start of life. Children can be brought up to take pleasure in their own bodies or to be half-ashamed of them, or more likely, ashamed of half of them:

> But to the girdle do the Gods inherit,
> Beneath is all the fiend's.

Children can be taught to trust their bodies and to be bold in opportunities of using them, or they can be, as one African described it, 'afraid to dance'. Children can catch warmth from the relationships around them, and themselves grow up warm in their approach to others, or they may be frozen in a domestic climate where there is, to use Ian Suttie's phrase, 'a taboo on tenderness'. Self-respect may be fostered or numbed. Which of the possibilities is a child's lot, or the combination that is his lot, will influence, to a greater or lesser extent, his readiness for the flowering of personal sexuality during adolescence.

The great role of sexuality in personal and moral development throughout adolescence is that it breaks into the intense self-absorption of the adolescent and pulls him or her into a confront-ation with another person that stimulates care and concern. The young adolescent girl of twelve or thirteen finds herself longing to love. At first almost any available person will do because love at this stage is more a projected fantasy than a relationship. The girl may feel herself to be in love with a boy she has not even spoken to or with a pop singer she cannot hope to meet. All the same, she is learning to direct her feelings towards another person with total dedication. When one member of a fan club was asked how she felt about her hero she replied: 'I would like to die for him.' Unrealistic certainly, but a movement away from the egocentricity of childhood nevertheless.

More realistic relationships soon intervene and with them the longing to be perfect for the loved one. Acceptance provokes a whole range of aspiration; rebuff leads to self-examination. Whichever way it goes, the consideration, 'What am I to others?' begins to play a part in awareness. Soon relationships of deep, realistic mutual concern and support are formed, such as are revealed in this letter written to the advice column of a girls' periodical:

'I am fifteen years old. My boy-friend who is 15½ is shortly moving with his family to another city. We have gone out together for quite some time now, long enough for me to know that this is not a passing infatuation. I have been out with other boys but never felt the same way about them. I love and respect and trust him very much. He says the same about me and shows his affection by doing so many warm-hearted things, that are not just superficial politeness, which only I notice. He has already promised to write to me from his new home. But if I constantly receive letters, surely they will remind me more and more of him.

'Should I break off our friendship now before he goes and not go out with him again? I cannot help seeing him because we attend the same school.

'Please tell me what to do for the best. I cannot imagine what I will do without him, for he seems almost to have become part of me. He never talks about other girls and won't even look at them, because he loves me.

'Do you think I am making a mountain out of a molehill and letting self-pity overrun me? I am working hard at school for G.C.E. but I never seem to think of anything else but Pete's going away.'

Early sexual feeling is tentative, gentle, and tender, full of loneliness and yearning, and longing for the presence of the other. When hopes are dashed, real suffering ensues. This is true for both sexes. 'Boys cry,' as the pop record had it, 'when their hearts are broken.' Boys often play it tough because they think they are expected to do so, but underneath is gentleness as well as uncertainty. Responsibility for one another grows and a sense of social responsibility also. A pretty girl of seventeen, asked how she felt when men first turned their heads to look at her, replied: 'Excited, then humble, because it made me feel responsible.' Boys become fiercely loyal and protective towards the girls they love, and their feelings bubble over into altruism.

Research into the attitudes of adolescents has shown that casual, shallow, promiscuous playing at love does not represent the typical sexual behaviour of adolescents; it is characteristic of a poorly adjusted fringe of young people who are turning to sex to fill a gap in love or security, or of suggestible young people who follow those who talk big for the sake of reassuring themselves.

As pairing-off becomes more permanent and relationships deepen, the young people grow more realistically aware of one another. They also begin to smooth off each other's corners by friendly mutual criticism. Still bitterly resentful of adult criticism, they are nevertheless prepared to take it from one another. Sex love thus becomes formative at two levels: as mutual caring and as mutual guidance.

Here also we have something to learn from less sophisticated societies. The impact of girls on boys, in the relationship of friendship and love, is a civilizing one. Knowledge of this is part of the folk wisdom of sexually uninhibited societies. Talking of the traditional sex life of the young people in his community, a Matabele explained: 'It's not just the sex; the girls knock the rough corners off the boys' characters.'

As the trust grows between a young couple, so does the total relationship until the young people are fully ready for the consummation of their relationship in complete physical love. At this stage, some will become engaged, others will pair off unofficially. Sometimes a partnership will last, sometimes it will not, but the experience of any sincere relationship brings some self-understanding and sharpens sensitivity towards the other. Adolescents themselves, certain extreme fringes excepted, regard sincerity as the *sine qua non* of love. They very much feel they should be *fair* to one another. In the research conducted by E. M. and M. Eppel, reported in *Adolescents and Morality*, the young people of the sample were asked to complete the sentence 'It's wrong to . . .' . The largest number of responses fell into the category 'Unfairness to People'.

Contrary to the gloomy predictions of the anti-sex moralists, young people in partnership, including the partnership of living together, are not distracted from other tasks by their sex life. Rather is the reverse true. It is, for example, the lonely student at university, not the one who is partnered or married, who is liable to be ineffective. Conversely, there are on record some outstanding examples of young married students achieving high honours at universities. As Logan and Goldberg found in their sample of eighteen-year-old boys in a London suburb, maturity in sexual behaviour often goes along with other criteria of maturity. The frequent suggestion that young people who have premarital sexual relationships are morally inferior to chaste ones is not supported by the evidence. What is important is not whether or not sexual relationships take place, but the quality of the relationships. And quality can only grow in experience. It is through the drive of sex that the adolescent learns to love, and to think of others with deep concern.

A rich experience of partnership and love in adolescence

makes a good selection of marriage partners more likely. Even among animals a notable decline in their selectivity is to be observed when sexual deprivation is imposed. While accepting that what happens among animals is not necessarily applicable to man, it seems reasonable to suppose that a condition of sexual starvation is not a good one from which to select a marriage partner.

There remains the vexed problem of possible illegitimacy if young people are set free from the taboos on premarital relationships so that they may grow in emotional depth and sensitivity ready for the commitment of marriage and founding a home. Three points are worth making here. The first is that the girls who get into trouble are not usually the pretty and relaxed ones but the plain and tense ones. It is their hunger for love not their unbridled passion that leads them to take unnecessary risks. This suggests a solution through personal and social education rather than through inhibition. Secondly, if the values of mutual concern are developed through accepting adolescent sexuality instead of seeking to repress it, both girls and boys can more clearly understand that their duty is to make sure that any child of theirs has the best possible chance of happiness – which means a happy home. Within a climate of mutual responsibility, warmth, and trust, this is a much more powerful incentive to take precautions against an illegitimate birth than if sex is regarded as a forbidden fruit to be snatched when a chance comes.

In the third place, the facts of contraception should be made available in good time as well as the means to it. Young people prepared with the truth, and free from the strain of secrecy and pretence, are no more likely than anyone else to get carried away. The morality of inhibition promotes the conditions for risk and illegitimacy whereas the morality of freedom and responsibility encourages intelligent care. It is much easier, within a climate free from sexual inhibition, to impress on young people that a limit on their sexual freedom is that no children shall be conceived. This limit is often found, as we have noted, in uninhibited societies. And it is respected.

The central theme of this chapter is that we have, in our era, to reconstruct the whole basis of sexual morality so that it may be transformed from the grotesque and irresponsible patterns produced by inhibition into the creative and civilizing forms of responsible human sexuality. This is both a personal and a social question. Sex exists as a powerful force and the need for its control is obvious. The problem before us today is how to establish controls so that human sexuality may be free to express itself within appropriate limits. The attempt to control sex by taboo cannot work in an age that has outgrown confidence in authoritarian absolutes, and, in any case, the outcome of such control manifestly discredits it.

The morality of freedom in sex depends on the secure establishment within personal life and society of values of responsibility and mutual concern through which each situation, as it impinges on personal life, may be given its most creative, compassionate, and formative expression. It is in such terms that many young people are already conducting their relationships, including their sexual relationships. These young people represent the shape of things to come, but, if the significant values are to be effective in guiding and controlling sex-life within society as a whole, then these values must be so manifest in education and in life that those who are confused may be helped to discover the true meaning in what has become formless and grasping in their lives.

Before closing this chapter, we must take a look at one more common anxiety about sex. Right from the earliest times, sexual *licence* and the decline of civilization have been linked in people's minds with the ominous idea that sexual *liberty* causes a civilization to decline. Is this true? Obviously it isn't. As has already been mentioned, great upsurges in civilization have taken place along with increased sexual emancipation. However, sexual *licence* and decline may well go together, and for an obvious reason. A civilization that has lost its way also becomes bored. A bored civilization tries to squeeze excitement out of anything available. Sex is always available and, in conditions of boredom, gets distorted for use as a mere source of thrills. Our civilization is rather bored with itself and sex is being corrupted to appease that boredom. The antidote to this is not inhibition, which only leads to greater perversity, but a restoration of social purpose based on contemporary possibilities and responsibilities. What is involved in this takes us beyond the range of this chapter. Suffice it to say that the struggle against the meaningless and the sordid in life could be greatly helped by raising the quality of sex, through freeing human sexuality to find its happy and responsible fulfilment in right use. To quote John MacMurray again – he was referring to the whole life of the emotions: 'only a faculty that is free to exercise itself can ever be educated'.

In this chapter the morality of man's encounter with sex, and its developmental correlates, has been taken only to the threshold of marriage. Adult sexuality will be discussed further in a later chapter.

9

THE CONTROL OF VIOLENCE

HUMAN history is a record not only of a great creativity but also of great violence: bloody wars, burning cities, massacres, the screams of the tortured, judicial executions. The modern age has added its own monstrous destroyers: nuclear explosives, napalm, defoliants, nerve gases, and bacteriological killers. To find out what accounts for this violence and destruction we have to look into the dynamics of human nature and the human condition. We also have to consider how violent propensities, in individuals and groups, may be controlled. This is a moral issue of the greatest importance.

For a start, we should not be afraid of aggressiveness as such. Life is a robust business. Abundant energy is developed in healthy people. With this they tackle living, establish themselves, and meet their needs. One of the forms that applied human energy takes is self-assertion: in part a positive drive to actualize individual uniqueness; in part a compensation for a sense of personal inadequacy. Without this, the emerging, unique individual would be swamped by the social forces making for standardization and conformity. Through the aggressive drive to assert and actualize the self – manifest almost from birth – each individual develops as a person, and also makes possible the evolution of society, which is the product of the persons who compose it.

At the opening session of the First International Congress on Mental Health (London, 1948) Dr Frederick Allen summed up the subtle balance between self-assertion and social relatedness in the growth of the individual:

'Out of the dynamic interaction between living related individuals, activated by the early reaching out of the infant, sustained and influenced by the responses and feelings he arouses in others, emerge the child's potentialities for constructive or destructive aggressive action and feeling. This process determines how the child can become an individual, separate and unique in himself, while at the same time relinquishing part of his individuality in order to become a member of a group. This is the ever-recurring drama of human growth . . . a process uniquely individual and yet always social.'

The individual urge to gain a place in the group is found in both animal and human societies. But within this widespread biological dynamic there are dangers. An individual does not only strive for recognition; he also requires confirmation that he has attained it. This makes him eager for social prestige, or status, and extremely touchy about loss of face. The search for, and defence of, individual fulfilment and prestige means competition, so that all social animals are caught up in a conflict between competitive and co-operative incentives, both of which play a part in life and have played a part in evolutionary advance. According to circumstances, an individual can feel helped and supported by others or challenged by them. Challenges to the individual – to his wants, to his beliefs, or to his status – are never far away in life. The natural response to such threats is the aggressive opposition of personal will. Such aggression can, quite easily, be provoked to the point of violence.

Group aggressiveness has similar roots. Those who feel themselves to be denied or threatened – the comparatively powerless ones within society – demand the security and place in the sun that others are enjoying and, sooner or later, turn on those who are holding them down. The ones in power seek to retain it. Each group sees the other as its enemy and aggression mounts. The sense of thwarting is touched off not only by denial of material things and opportunity, but by any pressure that is felt as purposelessly limiting and restrictive. Bureaucracy is hated for this reason. Man will always resent and oppose, overtly or covertly, whatever threatens his right to self-determination. This has been, and will continue to be, one of the great transforming forces in history. It can easily lead to bloodshed and destruction, when what is seen as justice is denied.

A complication in the pattern of human violence is that aggression is not always directed against the source of threat but can be displaced on to a substitute object. Slamming the door, smashing something, a rick deliberately burnt down, are examples of violence displaced from the actual cause of resentment. Redirected aggression can be observed in almost any group of people. Father, feeling tetchy from a bad day, criticizes mother; mother snaps at little Anne, and the child shoves the cat off its favourite chair. The same process can be seen in a monkey troop, when a cuff from the big boss may be passed from one to another down the social hierarchy.

But why should a minor irritant like the weather, or the coffee being cold, or something equally trivial, have the effect of increasing human aggression in the same way that a restriction or sense of injustice does? The answer would seem to be that any thwarting or frustration is interpreted as a threat to the self by our automatic response mechanisms and we react accordingly. A purely intra-psychic event, like an anxiety, can set adrenalin pouring into our bloodstream and start off other reactions of the vegetative nervous system which prepare us for 'fight or flight', although neither is appropriate in the circumstances. Similarly, the feeling of being thwarted can trigger off a surge of aggressiveness. Life is full of thwarting pin-pricks and other frustrations to the free operation of our will so that we all carry within us a store of unused aggression, ready to find expression through any convenient object. Fatigue and stress can lessen our self-control, and then any little thing may set us off. Women are liable to be more irritable – and more criminal! – in the days immediately preceding menstruation.

The risks of violence deepen when we add to these facts the possibility that the struggle for self-actualization may itself prove abortive and become a source of intense frustration that penetrates to the very roots of the individual psyche. A person's striving may produce no satisfying status or significance; the outcome of living may be experienced mainly as discouragement, failure, and rejection; and the good flavour of life turn into a bitterness, resentment, and hate which seek any object on which to vent themselves. Erich Fromm sums up this condition in *Man For Himself*:

'It would seem that the degree of destructiveness is proportionate to the degree to which the unfolding of a person's capacities is blocked. I am not referring here to occasional frustrations of this or that desire but to the blockage of spontaneous expression of man's sensory, emotional, physical and intellectual capacities, to the thwarting of his productive potentialities. If life's tendency to grow, to be lived, is thwarted, the energy thus blocked undergoes a process of change and is transformed into life-destructive energy. *Destructiveness is the outcome of unlived life.*'

Anthony Storr, too, has stressed, in *Human Aggression* and elsewhere, that denial of self-realization provokes anti-social aggression.

Humanity's quest for power and dominance must also be understood as a key feature in his behaviour. Man has advanced to the point he has reached by learning to control both his environment and himself sufficiently to achieve his ends. Man's urge to control, combined with his striving for personal prestige and superiority, accounts for his hunger for power. Power offers control, status, and significance at one go. We can add to this, for extra measure, the male's concern about physical potency, which any source of power can symbolize. This taste for power can be a positive element in man's creative drive; misdirected, it can do fearful damage. It depends, as we have seen, whether the power sought is power *with* others or power *over* others.

Another factor we need to take account of in writing the formula for the destructive human potential is that individuals can easily project their need for significance and prestige so that they readily identify with group action that symbolizes power and status. Military music and marching men always attract a crowd. A soccer victory for the home side can set a whole town rejoicing. 'England in danger' say the vendors' placards when some opposing bowler has taken three for twenty. People can also readily project fear as a group threat to group life. Projection and identification account for the readiness with which individual aggressiveness can become focused as group violence. This is the dangerous aspect of group loyalty, as Koestler has pointed out in *The Ghost in the Machine*.

The triple incentives to group violence are frustration (of needs or hopes), threat, and the lure of power and status. When the Nazis emerged in Germany, all three were operating together. Economic failure had generated intense frustration; Germany felt threatened by the armaments of other nations, and Hitler held out the promise of power and status, not only as a possibility for a resurgent Germany but as the right of a superior people to dominate others. Any war in history, including civil wars, can be analysed as a varying combination of these three elements.

We see, then, that human aggressiveness is a necessary part of man's creative potentialities. But aggressiveness can run amok with disastrous results. The moral problem is not how to eliminate the propensities that produce human aggressiveness, but how to educate and control them in the interests of social and international order, and the fulfilment of personal and social life. This involves finding out what we can from our animal ancestry, looking at society as it is, and looking ahead to the future.

The fighting behaviour of a wide range of creatures – from sticklebacks to giant carnivores – has come under review in recent years. The outcome of all this work, rather to everyone's surprise, is that nature is nothing like as red in tooth and claw as she was hitherto supposed to be. Man, by comparison, stands out as particularly bloodthirsty. What fighting goes on within an animal species is limited to mating disputes, securing territorial rights, and establishing the individual's place in the group hier-archy. Fighting is not inaugurated for its own sake, nor is it, as a rule, to the death. In the animal kingdom a dispute between members of a species is taken as settled once one or other of the contestants admits defeat by demonstrating that he has had enough. A furious combat between two dog wolves is swiftly terminated if one throws in the sponge by offering his unprotected throat to the other's attack. This switches off the fighting response, honour is satisfied, mutual status is established, but no serious harm done.

Our nearest cousins, the primates, are markedly peaceable creatures. This turns out to be true even of the gorillas, whose reputation among early travellers was quite otherwise. Schaller, in his fascinating book *The Year of the Gorilla*, describes how he became acquainted, by his frequent near presence, with several groups of mountain gorillas of the Congo. He found them benign, well behaved, and rather lazy. Apart from a little chest-beating to see if the stranger could be intimidated into flight, or perhaps to ascertain whether or not he regarded himself as a rival male, the gorillas left Schaller alone and, in due course, took his presence for granted.

Other work done with primates – Jane Goodall with her chimpanzees, Hall and DeVore with baboons, Phyllis Jay with langurs, and many others – has told the same story. Plenty of showing-off takes place, and some scowling, snarling, and buffet-ing, but, under natural conditions, the primates are well con-ducted socially. Even when two roving groups clash, territorial rights are established without bloodshed. Carpenter, writing about the howlers of Barro Colorado Island, in the Isthmus of Panama, tells us: 'Howlers do not defend *boundaries* or whole territories; *they defend the place where they are* . . . typically by interchanges of roaring at approaching or approached animals.' It is a case of yell it out, not fight it out.

Even the powerfully armed and irascible baboon usually settles inter-group and individual rivalries by threat rather than fight. When a dominant male is provoked into actual attack, he lets his victim off with a good trouncing instead of killing him, which it would be easy for him to do. But things do not often get to the stage of contact; a scowl and a thump on the ground with a paw are usually enough on the part of a dominant male to quell any sign of obstreperous rivalry or lack of respect. In their report on 'Baboon Social Behaviour' (in *Primate Behaviour*), Hall and DeVore state: 'In *all* the episodes observed, no-contact threat was a far more frequent culmination than physical attack.' Primate species, in fact, have built-in controls that prevent their doing serious damage to one another.

Studying these controls gives us useful clues through which to explore the control of human violence. Three factors seem to secure the low level of violence in primate communities. One is the relationship between the number of individuals and the space occupied by the collective. Primates, as well as liking to live in contact with others – in families, groups, or troops – need elbow-room. Over-congestion produces a pressure to spread wider. This control is self-operating in natural conditions, where space is plentiful. An expansion of population merely involves taking over extended foraging grounds well before the point at which overcrowding leads to aggression. However, enforced over-congestion, as may happen in captivity, leads to vicious squabbling – a point we should take note of.

A second factor in controlling primate aggression is the establishment of a status hierarchy. The play of the youngsters and the challenge and tussle of young adults lead to a clear recognition of who comes where in individual prestige within the primate community. During the growth period, each animal gets to know just how strong he is *vis-à-vis* others. By the time he is full grown, he knows precisely to whom he must defer and who should defer to him. Once the network of prestige has been worked out, an occasional scowl or snarl or show of strength is all that is required to maintain it. Members of the primate troop, like members of a tennis or golf club, can, at any time, challenge another member to a show of strength, but the handicaps of the contestants do not vary wildly, and the matter is soon settled as to who is on top – usually by an intimidation contest, without dangerous biting.

A third factor has only recently been put forward, but it offers the best explanation so far of why man, although coming from respectable animal stock, has turned out to be so violent in settling the disputes of his kind. We owe this insight to Konrad Lorenz. In his book *On Aggression*, he shows that all creatures seem to have appropriate built-in behavioural responses that inhibit them from destroying members of their own species. The carnivores, armed as they are with lethal teeth and claws, have a powerful inhibitory system to match. The primates, comparatively lightly armed, or unarmed, also are inhibited against fighting one another damagingly, but only in accordance with their relatively insignificant weapons. But the system breaks down in human society because man, the creative primate, has invented all kinds of weapons to supplement his natural fighting power.

The invention of weapons started as a necessity of survival. Man's ancestors left the forests to hunt in the plains. The change brought them into competition with the heavily armed carnivores. Early men had to contrive weapons with which to compete for food and with which to defend themselves from their powerful rivals. Inevitably, in course of time, men turned their hunting tools to use in the personal and group status struggles and territorial rivalries that were also a part of life. Thus, man found himself armed with deadlier weapons than any animal – but he still retained an inhibitory system appropriate only to the community life of comparatively harmless apes. Hence arises, according to Lorenz, the gap between man's 'rich endowment of social instincts' and his murderous propensities.

A further point made by Lorenz, as well as by Desmond Morris in *The Naked Ape*, is that man's ability to kill at a distance renders even his quite weak inhibitory mechanisms less effective. Would a bomb-aimer ever let loose his second stick of bombs if he could see, close up, the bloody consequences of his first? To quote Lorenz: 'If moral responsibility and unwillingness to kill have indubitably increased, the ease and emotional impunity of killing have increased at the same rate.'

To expose the causes of violence is to open up the opportunity to control them. This is the heartening feature of the present.

But before we investigate how controls on human aggression may be refurbished to deal with the contemporary risk of explosive outbreaks of violence taking over and wrecking societies and the world, we must face yet one more reason why the most intelligent primate has also been the most bloodthirsty.

Because man has an intelligence and an imagination, he struggles for dominance and territory not only in terms of power but in terms of ideas and in terms of symbols. He identifies with causes and ideologies and defends them as zealously as if he were defending himself. For the same reason, man cannot, as an animal does, accept victory and stop the fight once his opponent has made the right gesture of defeat. An idea is not destroyed by an act of physical submission. To destroy an idea for certain, it is necessary to kill the individual or brain-wash him into the desired way of thinking; at very least to reduce him to social impotence so that what he stands for will count for nothing. Hence man's ruthlessness to his enemies; hence why ideological wars are the bitterest of all, and why wars, whatever reason they are fought for, are always given an ideological dressing to make the annihil-ation of the enemy seem wholly desirable. It is when we see others as symbols of what we fear that we treat them inhumanely.

It is plain that the control of violence is not going to be a simple matter. But now we know the shape of the task we can make a start with creating the social, national, and international order that will permit individuals and groups to dispose of their aggressive energies in constructive, or at least harmless, ways. Provoked but unexpressed aggression is the raw material of war.

Young males must be our particular concern in this replanning because they are possessed of superabundant energy and an urgent need for status and significance. To civilize and socialize its young males, other things being equal, is the biggest contri-bution any society can make to internal and international amity; to neglect to do so, equally certainly, will lead to recurrent hooliganism and violence, and a mood of belligerency that can readily be excited to group violence, including racialism.

In the control of violence, as in the control of sex, we have a good deal to learn from the experience of simpler societies, even though the techniques they use may not be directly transferable to our own social scene. In primitive societies we often find controlled outlets for the violent tendencies of young males, combined with opportunities for the exploration of status and the exercise of responsibility. These outlets and opportunities are supplemented by a challenging but satisfying system of initiation into adulthood. The whole gives the young men a start in life far better related to what young males need than what we, in general, offer to our young males in western society.

For example, the herd-boy phase in the life of young males in many parts of rural Africa provides, or used to provide, an excellent outlet for physical robustness under group control. At the same time status relationships were sorted out. Fighting was commonplace, sometimes between individuals, sometimes between groups – over rivalry for a stretch of pasture, for instance, or the first use of a water-hole. Plenty of blows were exchanged, with fists or sticks, but serious damage to one another was not condoned. The older boys supervised the younger boys and the adults of the community held the older boys and group leaders responsible for keeping extreme violence in check. These encounters enabled the boys and youths to get the measure of one another in terms of courage or cowardice, swiftness or slowness, cleverness in strategy or unimaginative leadership. All this mutual evaluation carried through into adult life just as it does in the old-boy or fraternity network in England or America. But, in primitive societies, *everyone* has a place in the status network.

Professor and Mrs Mayer's report on the Red Xhosa, already mentioned, is particularly valuable for what it has to teach about the control of aggression in rural Xhosa society at the present time. The youths of thirteen to twenty carry sticks and frequently engage in cudgel games. As they grow older they advance in status and authority and take the responsibility for supervising and training those younger than themselves. Senior members often travel considerable distances, joining in dances and sometimes taking part in group contests with their sticks. All the activity of these young people – including love-making – is self-regulating: the developing status network is also a responsibility network. The adults take an interest in what goes on, but from a distance. The fighting is kept within reasonable bounds by the good sense of the youthful leaders and the conventions of the contests – including the right of anyone getting the worst of it to call a halt. Only very occasionally is anyone seriously hurt.

The pay-off to the system comes with initiation and the official acceptance of the young men into full manhood. At this point all the young men put aside their fighting-sticks as a sign that they will settle their disputes in future with words, not blows. To argue, and use the tribal law, with intelligence and skill is considered a mark of manhood. Only boys 'settle things by the stick'.

The system of the Red Xhosa is psychologically and morally brilliant. It uses the pugnacity and sexuality of the young males as the motivations through which responsibility, self-control, and status relationships are developed. It provides all young people with a challenging, exciting, and eventful adolescence. And it rounds off the adolescent phase for the young men with an initiation ritual that confers personal prestige and adult responsibility in a single package. Thus, robust play and adventure, sexual love and relationships, and the attainment of status, are intimately associated with the extension of self-control in the experience of growing up. The energies of youth are liberated in a context of socialization. Among the reported consequences are that illegitimacy and senseless violence are very rare among the Red Xhosa.

By comparison the young males of western civilization are poorly provided for. The most able, academically or physically, are put into sharp competition and get from this some opportunity of acquiring a sense of value about themselves and one another in terms of socially admired goals. But much of this is on the basis of individual competitiveness, so that the elements of group cohesiveness and responsibility and status, in the business of living and growing up – so much needed and valued by adolescents – are largely lost. The less able – the low attainers – are in a very much weaker position. They have no place in the status hierarchy of the meritocracy race and get left in a confused muddle at the bottom of the heap, where they scrap and jostle, gang up, show off, and become a nuisance in an effort to work out a status pattern among themselves. Since the status values of the meritocracy race are beyond their reach they have to elaborate their own value system.

A so-called sub-culture is precisely this – a sector of society driven from the mainstream and forced to create a status system of its own: a frustrating situation, because it carries a sense of rejection, which readily leads to senseless violence and destructiveness among its young men as they make bids for status and significance. The members of a tough gang know where each stands in relation to toughness as accurately as members of a science sixth know where each stands in mathematics or physics. But the science students can see their relationship to the mainstream of success; the tough boys cannot. Evidence from animal communities suggests that an individual who does not know his status level in the group is driven to search for it. This search, for the less able young men in our society, may take curious forms, including raising hell at a football game, slashing the seats of railway carriages, or doing a ton along the main road. It is, of course, from the low attainers, caught up in status uncertainty, that most of the trouble comes. This is to be expected because every society is a status system and a society that cannot assure a satisfying status for all its members will reap a whirlwind of resentment from those it rejects.

There is room to mention here only two more aspects of the denial of the needs of youth in our society. One is that the adult community is still niggardly in extending responsibility to young people, as F. Musgrove pointed out in *Youth and the Social Order*, and as a variety of student revolts has brought out. A sense of responsibility can be gained only by exercising responsibility. Few adolescents are given much chance of this. Whenever an uneducated sense of social responsibility is combined with status uncertainty in an individual, violent outbursts are highly probable.

The other point is that young people need occasional opportunities for letting off steam in a big way. Where, in our culture, do they find opportunities for this except in forms regarded as reprehensible by society? People talk as though the permissive society lives with its hair permanently down. In fact, although we have shaken off a good deal of prudery and convention, we have never been more well behaved as a society than we are today. As a schoolboy complained in a discussion: 'We're supposed to be well behaved on the bus coming to school; we're supposed to be well behaved at school; we're supposed to be well behaved going home; we're supposed to be well behaved in the park, quiet in the library, and careful on the roads. Where *can* we stir it up a bit?'

The need for a periodic explosive display, or 'triumph ceremony', is found among the primates. Adrian Kortlandt in *Chimpanzees in the Wild* describes such an occasion in a clearing of the eastern Congo:

'The adult males were often the first to appear, their arrival always heralded by their cries, which grew in intensity as they approached. When they were quite close to the clearing, they would fall silent, and a broad black face would peep out cautiously through the leaves. Then one by one the males would emerge; usually each of them carefully looked and listened before he stepped out from behind the bushes and trees. Most of the time at least one of them walked upright for a while in order to get a better view of the open ground. Once they decided they were safe, the large males broke out into a wild and deafening display. They chased one another, shrieking and screaming. They stamped the ground with hands and feet and smacked tree trunks with one open hand. Sometimes they pulled down half-grown papaw trees. Occasionally one of them would grab a branch and brandish or throw it while running full tilt through the group.'

Jane Goodall has also described similar noisy ape saturnalia.

Perhaps we would all benefit as a society from occasionally letting off steam more robustly than is possible at an evening's dancing or through vicarious adventure on the big or little screen. Perhaps we need some new ceremonial days that make up for our lost fairs and the debilitation of our festivals. Europeans who have participated through the carnival in Trinidad describe themselves at its close as 'empty but happy' – the 'calm of mind; all passion spent'.

How, then, are we to control violence in the modern world? We may deduce from what has already been said that a community where violence is a problem internally is one that is mismanaged in terms of human needs. Perhaps it is unfair to minorities and provokes revolt; perhaps it leaves groups of its people feeling rejected and resentful; perhaps it frustrates the energies and aspirations of youth; perhaps it overcrowds people too much; perhaps it falls short in promoting a sense of purpose in which people can share, enhancing thereby their feeling of personal value and prestige. Whatever the causes, they are controllable. It is the duty of modern government to plan how to open the way to fulfilment for *all* its people. It is the duty of the citizens of a modern community to see that the government does so. The control of violence in a community is, basically, no more and no less difficult than the control of disease. It is a matter of providing the conditions for healthy life and growth.

The control of violence internationally, in the present and the future, depends upon some major, but obvious, reorientation of thought: collaboration in place of antagonism. This change is, fortunately, beginning to take place. In every field we are passing out of the age of competition into the era of co-operation. Superficially competitiveness may seem to be intensifying, but techniques of collaboration are everywhere being sought for. Already transport, communications, medical standards and surveillance, scientific knowledge, and the suppression of crime have been internationalized. Within the next few decades, population control, food production, conservation of natural resources, and development programmes are likely to be high on the international agenda. In the end, even the production of consumer goods will have to be organized as an international programme instead of purely competitively. The mergers taking place, the setting up of consortia to undertake big schemes, the struggle to attain a viable economic system for the world, the development of state enterprises, and state support for private enterprises are all signs of this trend

A collaborating world will produce disagreements and conflicts in plenty, but war between nations will not make sense, any more than it now makes sense for England to go to war with Scotland, although in the fourteenth century the two countries were constantly fighting and even today are in conflict on a number of points. Acts of the crassest folly and negligence – such as refusal to attend to the population explosion and world food shortage – could, of course, prevent a consciously interdependent world from emerging, but the interaction of knowledge and ideas throughout the modern world is likely to secure enough feed-back to promote necessary action before the ultimate disaster of world starvation overtakes us. Always provided, of course, that enough of us care.

Human frustration will continue, human aggression mount, and violence break out from time to time, but less and less as war, provided that life is made robust and satisfying enough for enough people. It is fortunate that the props of war are themselves giving way. For example, the war-mongering technique of painting the enemy and his ideas as diabolical, in order to focus unused aggression, is becoming less effective now that we are beginning to know more about each other as human beings. Also in decline is the claim to absolute rightness with its assumption that those who do not agree represent a threat that must be destroyed. We are coming to see all knowledge and ideas as partial, so that we benefit most not from destroying the other man but from finding out his point of view and learning something from it. Finally, young men no longer regard war as a source of glory and achievement; it seems messy and meaningless to them.

Man's faulty inhibitory equipment will not be remedied by these changes, but, in man, ideas can control the direction of primitive drives. If the other person, the other nation, is not seen as primarily a threat, but primarily as a collaborator, the stimulus to attack is removed. The way the modern world is going makes co-operation a matter of common sense. The values of co-operation are slowly but surely becoming the dominant ideas. In this is the hope for the future control of international aggressiveness.

Denied the old scapegoats, where can man's personal self-assertion and unresolved aggression find an outlet? Partly in creative recreations, robust adventure, vigorous social rituals and competitive play; partly in the struggle for personal fulfilment as such; and partly in working constructively on the problems and conflicts of group action. To draw people into active participation provides a continuing outlet for the originality, vitality, and drive of each individual. Wherever we find individuals absorbed into collaboration in achieving something they regard as worth-while, there, too, we find fulfilment and friendliness. The greatest single contribution to personal fulfilment and the constructive control of violence would be the establishment throughout society of systems and organizations that give everyone a place, a role, and a chance to have a personal share in decision-making and solving group problems. At the present time participant democracy is slowly struggling its way in. This new social order, which will also, inevitably, be a new moral order, is beginning to take shape.

A truly democratic society needs to exclude nothing of what is human – certainly not conflict – but instead can offer outlets, within reasonable limits and controls, so that the powers of individuals may come to a focus in fulfilment that is both highly personal and highly social. The control of violence in ourselves and socially ultimately depends upon the establishment of such societies as the normal habitat of modern man.

10

THE INNER WORLD

CHANGING the idiom in the middle of a book should be avoided. In this book, however, for this chapter at least, a change of idiom is inevitable. Man uses two main modes of discourse: one is the objective discourse of information, explanation, and practical evaluation; the other is the discourse of feeling and experience. The consideration of individual morality spans both discourses because it has to do with both inner and outer worlds. Morality is something that can be studied objectively, but the heart of the matter is in feeling. In this chapter, feeling and experience are central and the discourse must change in tone.

The roots of an individual's moral feeling are in his unique inner world, which, in its turn, determines how he sees himself, how he sees life, and how he relates to the outer world – all elements in the developmental dynamic, the principles of which are, we have seen, identical with moral principles.

The inner world is the subjective arena where we seek to make sense of life, and are aware of moral struggle. It is here that we experience the conflict of idea with idea, of motive with motive, of weakness with strength, of will with apathy, of clarity with confusion, of love and hate. Guilt and despair lurk here; the residues of past failures stay to mock; anxiety, conflict, and suffering are endured. Here experience is metamorphosed into personal understanding; insight enlightens suddenly in the darkness; hope revives; aspiration springs and yearns for actualization. The tone of inwardness at any moment fills the mind, ranging from ecstasy to despondency. Sometimes inwardness is in turmoil; at others comes a deep satisfying sense of peace. Somehow this inwardness grows and changes so that, catching an echo of a past self, we realize something has been at work reshaping us in the unseen quiet of our own depths. Things happen in this silence.

This active inwardness is the secret drama of being, mirroring the other drama of our outward actions in the world and interactions with the world, but more acutely felt because it is the enduring, though changing, substance of ourselves. An interaction with the world can reach a crescendo of intensity which mounts and dies away, while its formative influence upon our inwardness will be enduring, a part of the experience by which we become what we are. But this inwardness is more than a depository of experience and a recording system, though it is both of these; it is dynamic and creative in its own right; it is our very selves at work bringing our wholeness into being, into effectiveness, and into relationship, intensely personal, unpredictable, mysterious. As Matthew Arnold put it:

> We cannot kindle when we will
> The fire that in the heart resides.
> The spirit bloweth and is still,
> In mystery the soul abides:
> But tasks in hours of insight willed
> Can be through hours of gloom fulfilled.

Thus far, in this book, we have been looking at the principles of living mainly from the outside – as they explain, affect, and guide people and society. We do not, however, live only 'here' and 'out there'. We are also conscious of this inwardness, this core of private being, which we can never wholly share with others, although we get near to this when we begin really to understand one another, and especially in the relationship of love, where mutual acceptance is itself a source of deep experience.

For the present, inwardness is too inaccessible a theme for science to handle with precision. Models can be offered which account for our sense of depth. Our brain is the outcome of long evolution during which layer upon layer of neurological structure has been built up. The sense of depth may arise from this physiological complexity. Another possible model is the computer model with its memory stores and processing systems. Such models are useful and important, but they do not tell the whole story. Those who enter their own inner worlds find there a nature of experience that transcends the mechanisms of experience. No concept so far framed – the ego, the self, and self-concept, the psyche, the soul – quite fits the reality as we know it.

Psychology is painstakingly searching out and putting together the components and mechanisms of mental life, but has not yet adequately explained the nature of the amalgam of feeling, thought, and judgement we call personal experience. This intimate self-awareness is the point where the variety of the universe, the complexities of experience and our own nature interact to form the 'Ultimate I' – the very core of self-feeling. If we attempt to watch it, or hold it down, it disappears; yet it is always there as the sounding-board of experience, digesting what happens, responding, evaluating, being. Our inner world is, in essence, the continuing experience of ourselves within the context of the universe. The quality of that experience is our final verdict on life. If we feel free, we are free; if we feel bound, we are bound; if life feels good, it is good; if we feel desperate, we are in despair; if life seems futile, it is futile; if life feels significant, it is significant.

But the privacy of this inner world – its subjective quality – does not imply separateness from the outer world. It is the outer world personally possessed as inner meaning, reality transmuted by the inward vision. The personal psyche is a microcosm of humanity and each awakened individual experiences and suffers for all mankind. We are all infinitely different and all infinitely one. Our common humanity makes us one, in experience or in imagination, so that we can immediately enter into the splendour of a Haydn concerto composed nearly two centuries ago, respond to the moods of Shakespeare who was writing two centuries farther back still, share without difficulty the yearning in an Anglo-Saxon lyric at the start of our island history, or recapture the excitement of the hunters who gave art its birth on the walls of their caves long before the first civilization appeared on earth.

The 'Ultimate I' seems to have two routes of communication: outwards into the world, with its range from the gigantic to the infinitesimal, and inwards into depth. At the fringe of both our outward and inward worlds is the unknown. At present we can only be perplexed by the seeming endlessness of the array of the universe around us; to probe, at the other extreme of the outward, into the patterns of energy that underlie the atomic nucleus, brings man into a world of puzzlingly swift and protean change that is itself influenced by the very act of observation. The subjective inward route leads also to the inexplicable – experience within experience within experience – until we reach the source of the scientist's leap of intuition, the artist's vision of reality, and the mystic's moments of transcendental awareness, and can explain none of them. We sense a deep significance beneath the everyday syntax of affairs, an underlying reality that eludes us but in which we have a share.

To see oneself in this context is, by tradition, religious. It is to accept ourselves as in a state of struggle, and of search, and of being, within a mystery. That this is the condition of man is undeniable, but the moment one uses the word 'religious' people are liable to presume that one is throwing in one's lot with a set of institutionalized ideas. This is by no means the only possible outcome, and to think it so is to miss the real nature of man's religious striving. One of the great needs of the present is for men to be free to explore their personal being in all its mystery without feeling themselves consigned thereby to being pigeon-holed. Those who want a label and a home are free to choose, but it is possible to know the force of man's utmost quest and to share in it without feeling able to settle down in any of the available religious systems. The central realities are the depth of personal experience and the nature of life as a search. It is possible to accept these, and the struggle implied, without commitment to any formula. The commitment can be to life, to humanity, to reality as we perceive it, without the mediation of a set of ideas that is, at best, a compromise with what we feel to be true.

Indeed, a notable feature of contemporary life is the number of people who cling to one or other of the organized religions for comfort and community, while privately holding reservations about what they are supposed to believe. Each frames his personal metaphysic. The time is plainly on its way when, instead of herding under different umbrellas, we shall share – person to person, in continuous dialogue and relationship – the search into the mystery which enfolds us, not least the mystery of our own being and the immense significance that it has for us.

An indwelling longing of the 'Ultimate I' is for inward harmony and for a sense of unity with the whole. Both are of profound moral significance because they are self-transcending experiences. The sense of inner harmony is intensely personal, and also in some way of universal quality. So, too, the moments of unified experience, released perhaps by beauty or wonder inwardly perceived, extend both the sense of being, and of being-at-one with some partially apprehended whole. We are held for a moment amid the urgency of living and feel timeless. Thus Keats:

> Then on the shore
> Of the wide world I stand alone and think,
> Till Love and Fame to nothingness do sink.

Some call this experience being in communion with God. We have to be a little careful of what we mean before we put it so, remembering that men in simple times held thought and dreams to be direct communion with God: 'And the Lord said unto Noah . . .' 'And God spoke unto Abraham and said . . .'. Most people now regard dreams and thought as aspects of personal life. This is equally true of the transcendental experiences. The longing for harmony and unity – and for understanding – springs from within the psyche, and the experiences of them are human. They may well take us into another order of apprehending, and what is apprehended may well be something of the universe not yet understood, but it is unnecessary to draw on the supernatural to explain such experience. Extraordinary as it is, it is no more remarkable than that patterns of electro-neuronic impulses travelling along our optic nerves end up as our vision of the world to the limit of perceived beauty, whereas other sets of similar impulses travelling to our centres of hearing give us the universe of sound, the whole way from the fall of a pin to Beethoven's Ninth Symphony. The natural as we now know it is itself so mysterious, it is no longer necessary to bring in concepts of the supernatural. As Professor A. H. Maslow puts it: 'The spiritual life is part of our biological life. It is the "highest" part of it, but yet part of it. The spiritual life is part of the human essence. It is a defining-characteristic of human nature, without which human nature is not full human nature. It is part of the real self, of one's identity, of one's inner core, or one's specieshood, of full-humanness.'

Any great work of art is astounding, if you think about it. It marries time and eternity in a single statement. Yet great art is not usually regarded as supernatural. The position is that the ordinary and extraordinary in nature open up such vistas of possibility that we do not necessarily have to go beyond them for explanations of any human experience.

It may well be, therefore, that these transcendental experiences and perceptions people call 'God' will, in the end, turn out to be a part of nature, as much a part of nature as beauty and man's joy in beauty. It took man a long time to grasp that he is part of nature; now he perhaps has to expand farther his ideas of what nature embraces. The real difference of view between deists, agnostics, and atheists is not about whether self-transcendence and higher moral qualities – man's spiritual nature in total – exist, but whether or not they are considered as part of nature or as an intrusion from outside nature. The gap constantly gets narrower as scientists appreciate the complexity of reality, and theologians realize how fundamentally they have to modify their ideas to match up with modern knowledge.

The modern theologians themselves are beginning to reject the supernatural God. To say, 'God is the ground of our being,' is to do just this. For it is equally true to say, 'The universe is the ground of our being.' People talk about 'the death of God'. What they mean is that the supernatural God of earlier thinking is dead. But the mystery of existence itself remains and what we shall discover as we search farther no one can say.

The world of the modern scientists is far more mysterious than the world of the early Christians. For the early Christians there was a place for everything and everything was in its place. For us nature is a multi-dimensional, multi-faceted jigsaw puzzle that eludes ultimate solution, although patches here and patches there are getting filled in. We are in on something far more extraordinary than our forefathers ever dreamed of.

And in the midst of it all is each individual – an inwardness felt within a personal organism, itself occupying only a few cubic feet of the vast universe, and yet with a mind and imagination capable of reaching out to an apprehension of the whole. Thus, Henry Vaughan, the contemporary of Newton:

> I saw Eternity the other night,
> Like a great ring of pure and endless light,
> As calm, as it was bright;
> And round beneath it, Time in hours, days, years,
> Driv'n by the spheres
> Like a vast shadow moved; in which the world
> And all her train were hurled.

This was, for Vaughan, a vision of enlightenment, an exalted perception in which he was both lost and made whole. For a moment the inner and outer mysteries seemed unified. Such moments of heightened awareness come to everyone at times and are treasured. Their scale is from the mystic's moment of illumination to the glimpse of glory caught in the peace and beauty of a June evening. The positive incentive to take drugs is to create or recapture these heightened states of awareness, but the flaw here is that this particular road to perception is artificially induced – not arising from the personality but imposed upon it – so that the drug-taker may be left with a devastating habit while the perception fades into unrecapturable remoteness.

Morally and developmentally our concern must be about the growth and condition of the inner world and the nature of its relatedness to what is outside itself, accepting that it may relate itself to the universal either by exploring outwards or searching inwards. And indeed some seem to be much happier doing one than the other, though all people travel by both roads to some extent, and need to do so, for the security and uniqueness of the Self depends upon the closeness of its relationships with the not-Self. The lament of the person too much cut off is, 'I don't exist.' Isolation is starvation to personal development, which is one reason why it is experienced as acute pain. The goal, always, must be to maximize inner growth and to extend relatedness; the two are, in fact, part of a single dynamic. We should, as Jung has pointed out, feel indissolubly united with the world of men and objects, yet also be able to transmute this wealth of experience into a personal consciousness which brings together self-knowledge and a vision of the whole. Our personal perspective is our means of relationship with reality.

We are now at a point at which we find the artist, the scientist, and the mystic all engaged towards the same end. They are all searching for harmony, form, significance. They are using human perception at its most intense in order to understand more clearly the nature of man and his situation. Success in this search brings self-transcending experience so convincing and satisfying that those who receive it are goaded on ceaselessly to further exploration. Their work is their life and they must think and feel and strive towards ever-greater clarification of what they want to communicate until time ultimately defeats them. They feel called and driven. This is the highest order of human functioning. Such people are the path-finders for mankind. In them the inner world and outer reality become one in acts of creation that add new dimensions to human experience. Each starts with an act of faith – that there is order to be found. Each ends with a new conviction about the nature of that order. These path-finders give form to confusion and the experience is deeply satisfying, for themselves and for those they help to see more clearly.

Lesser mortals in their simpler ways are engaged on a like

quest. All men seek wholeness and harmony and understanding. The attraction of institutionalized religion for some people is that it *appears* to offer ready-made answers to these yearnings. But to arrive vicariously is not to reach the destination at all, as the great religious teachers have always emphasized. Wholeness and harmony, they taught, are to be won through living and striving towards fulfilment and enlightenment. He who would save his life must be prepared to lose it. With which modern psychology is in accord: an analysis is a kind of Pilgrim's Progress – through despondency to hope; through confusion to clarity; a painful reliving of not-sufficiently-lived experience. In a way all life is a self-analysis which throws out challenges through which the unlived in us rises up again and again until it is faced and drawn into harmony within our inner world through experience or imaginative acceptance. Gradually, painfully, the inner world is brought nearer wholeness (or integration or fulfilment) by replacing with the reality of experience what has not been lived and is fantasy. There are some short cuts. Intuition, imagination, and the insights gained through the arts can, *to some extent*, stand in for actual experience.

Suffering has its own special significance in this context. Brute suffering – crude denial of needs or inflicted pain – is brutalizing or overwhelming. But suffering met in the course of living, accepted and survived, deepens and unifies the inner life. Suffering is a mode of intense experience and is, therefore, formative. Indeed, there can be no intense experience without suffering. To strive is to suffer, for we shall often fail or fall short; to love is to suffer, because our concern for those we love will carry us into suffering; to care is to suffer, for there is always suffering at hand; to live is to suffer, because if we go out into life we shall certainly get hurt in one way or another. Through suffering, if in no other way, we are committed to life. John MacMurray sums this up:

'The capacity for joy is also the capacity for pain. We soon find that any increase in our sensitiveness to what is lovely in the world increases also our capacity for being hurt. That is the dilemma in which life has placed us. We must choose between a life that is thin and narrow, uncreative and mechanical, with the assurance that even if it is not very exciting it will not be intolerably painful; and a life in which the increase in its fullness and creativeness brings a vast increase in delight, but also in pain and hurt.'

Wholeness, harmony, and understanding may be attained at two levels: at one level by resigning one's own identity and taking over someone else's predigested system – whether religious or political or philosophical – or, at a deeper level, by embarking upon the perils of discovery for oneself, in dialogue with others, past and present, who have dared the search. The first is apparently the safer, but may well turn out to be a more brittle solution. Because it is not sufficiently rooted in personal experience and self-understanding, it may give way under the stresses of life or as a result of extension in human knowledge. The second is more durable, because more resilient, but involves risks in its attainment:

> For none can tell to what red hell
> His sightless soul may stray.

It is sometimes assumed that people who have obviously arrived at wholeness and harmony have always been models of tranquillity and virtue. Not so. Many great moral teachers, for example, came to quietude and meditation after many years of robust living. Did they achieve their tranquillity in spite of their early wildness or because of it? Commitment to life is the strength of inwardness so that a wild life can lead ultimately to fulfilment if it is deeply and sincerely experienced. Tennyson knew this, as all poets must, and in prudish Victorian England dared to write in *In Memoriam*:

> And dare we to this fancy give,
> That had the wild oat not been sown,
> The soil, left barren, scarce had grown
> The grain by which a man may live.

The point is that life-affirmation is the supreme positive attitude since the movement of the creative process throughout has been towards the development and enrichment of life, including the inward life. If we reject life as good in itself, we reject the universe, we reject evolution, we reject ourselves. Shallowness and triviality are the great enemies of wholeness, not experience, which is the road by which it is reached.

If all men seek wholeness, harmony, and understanding, why is it so difficult to attain? Mainly because of disruption and confusion of the inner world. Man becomes estranged from himself and his situation – alienated, to use the popular word. This blocks the harmony, clouds the perception, and impoverishes inner life. Alienation in the modern world is a complex matter involving self-rejection on the one hand and distaste for society as it is on the other. Today both elements are much in evidence, which is the reason why alienation is endemic in our society. Many are hanging back from involvement in discouraged noncommitment; others, assured enough in themselves for commitment, regard with distaste the superficiality and brashness of commercialist society and refuse to sell themselves to it. Many, also, find competitive internationalism repugnant at a time when the world needs care and concern and co-operation, not force. The Flower People are one outward and visible sign of this growing spiritual withdrawal.

Self-alienation has many sources. One is the 'bad image' of man already discussed in Chapter Three. The very fact that this exists in society and is often reinforced tempts people to measure themselves by it, find themselves wanting, and reject themselves, when what they need most in these stressful times is to be enheartened about their own humanity.

Another source is the expectation of perfection in oneself, which is partly a reaction to the bad image and partly the result of ideas foisted on children in their formative years. Instead of seeing themselves as incomplete, striving, and potentially significant, young people are encouraged to see themselves as falling short of others' ambitions for them. This leaves them with a feeling of worthlessness, of being a sham, which may persist into adulthood in spite of obvious achievement. Gilbert Harding expressed this when he said that his greatest fear was his fear of being found out. Few of us are free from this kind of self-rejecting over-expectation about ourselves, but, if it looms too large in the psyche, it can become disrupting, incapacitating self-hate.

The aftermath of anti-sex in society must also be playing its part in promoting self-alienation. Man is a sexual animal, and to be told that sex is something unclean, is to be told that *he* is unclean. The mania for engulfing young people in guilt about masturbation, described by Alex Comfort in *The Anxiety Makers*, must have driven hosts of boys and girls into habits of self-disgust which will have survived into adult life and been passed on to their children. The attitude to sex in society as a whole is still that sex is somehow indecent, which attitude denies dignity to human love, and therefore constantly reinforces feelings of self-alienation.

Self-rejection may also arise from seeing other people too superficially and accepting them at their face value to our own discredit. We know a good deal about our own imperfections, but each puts on the best front he can manage with which to face the world – our 'persona', as Jung called it. The consequence of this may be that we are excessively aware of our own inadequacies, while others appear to us comparatively strong, knowledgeable, and competent. If we do not realize that this harmless, and socially necessary, game of bluff is going on, we may feel more inferior than we need and lose heart that way.

Self-alienation may be summed up in a word – guilt – a word with which both religion and psychiatry are closely involved. Guilt intrudes one way or another. Hence the cure for much self-alienation is the purging of guilt. This is the object of divine forgiveness in the Christian religion. An alternative is to share ourselves and our failures more frankly with each other, to forgive one another and – which is more difficult – to forgive ourselves. Before this is possible we have to be prepared to admit in ourselves what is weak and mean. Vanity may prevent this. Vanity then becomes the root of self-alienation. Why so much self-protection? Presumably because we do not trust each other enough to admit ourselves to one another. Some are prepared to confess to God what they will not admit to their neighbour. This does not bring them any nearer to their neighbour. Thus, alienation leads to alienation and we stay too much apart from one another to be at peace inwardly. All of which has been said time and time again by the great moral innovators, such as Jesus and Buddha, and by the mystics, such as the Sufis of Islam, but we can now more clearly see what they were talking about. They were seeking to tell us how to plumb the depths of ourselves, find inner harmony and understanding, and, by dispelling what is negative, release the positive forces for more abundant life, within ourselves and in relationships.

The lesson is that we escape from guilty self-incarceration by drawing nearer to others in mutual understanding and compassion. We have to accept that there is nothing in any human being that is not a possibility in ourselves also, and nothing in ourselves that is not echoed in the experience and behaviour of the entire human race. Our uniqueness is in the pattern of what we are, and in our particular personal potentiality, not in any single item of ourselves. We are in others and others are in us and by living in that truth we simultaneously learn more about others and more about ourselves and so deepen our self-knowledge and set ourselves free to share our inwardness with others without apprehension. We should share our inwardness frankly in the communion of shared humanity. It is the encounter of person with person that is fruitful, not the impact of mask on mask.

There is a pattern running through the insights of psychology, the arts, and religion which tells us on what the health, and moral strength, of our inner world depends. We have to know ourselves, accept ourselves, admit ourselves, and share ourselves. Once more we are taken back to the principles of living and living together we have found in other contexts. The principles of human association and interaction are fundamental to growth at every level of being. To live confidently in the truth of what we are, in valid relationships with others, is to move towards wholeness, harmony, and inner freedom. And, once we are free, within ourselves, we cease to be under a compulsion to enslave others. Such inner freedom is the goal of our becoming.

Part Three

REASSESSMENTS

11

THE NEW COSMOLOGY

In the first two parts of this book the case has been made that man is a moral animal who builds a moral order as a necessary framework for living in society. It has also been put forward that man has now to replace the static moral order of earlier times, based on tradition and conformity, by a dynamic moral order founded in discovered principles of living. In this third part of the book, we shall take up three particular aspects of a contemporary moral outlook – the changing perspective on the universe, on our traditional religious beliefs, and on the meaning of life. These are all pertinent to individual morality because what we believe affects how we behave. A modern morality derives, in part, from a modern perspective. We will start with the cosmological outlook of man and its implications for man's interpretation of himself and his situation.

One great contrast between the present and the past is that, over the centuries, we have gradually lost a highly personalized universe and find ourselves now in one that, ourselves apart, seems to operate impersonally. For pre-civilized and early civilized man, the cosmos, to quote Professor Redfield, was 'personal and humanlike'. The sun and moon were thought to be persons, or in the charge of persons; the Egyptians gave the Nile personal attributes. Storms and epidemics were seen as the whims of gods. A good harvest was a personal gift from a divine source. The relationship of individuals to such a universe was almost all the time personal. Furthermore, everyone felt over-watched – by the gods, or God, or the ancestors, or the spirits of the tribe. The prime moral duty was to live up to the expecta-tions of the watchers and swift retribution was anticipated for the negligent or disobedient.

In these earlier times, responsibility for what happened on earth was not regarded as primarily man's responsibility; his duty was to obey, not to think or to be creative. As recently as Newton's day, the influence of spiritual beings in affairs was still a dominant idea. In the two and a half centuries since then, the rule of the 'laws of nature' – the most precise description we can manage of what is actually going on – has entirely taken over from the idea that the personal behaviour of divinities and spirits lies behind events. About almost everything, we now ask 'Why?' not 'Who?', and expect to find an answer in terms of the action and interaction of impersonal forces. If such a universe seems cold by comparison with the moody, personalized universe of primitive thought, it also raises the significance of man as the being who discovers and uses these forces.

Another vast change in perspective has come with our gradually awakening understanding of the size of the universe. The early Greeks thought the earth was flat and a few thousand miles in extent. By 350 B.C., the Greeks had established that the earth was a sphere. Two hundred years later, Hipparchus correctly cal-culated the distance of the moon. The picture of the universe then commonly held was of a huge hollow rotating sphere in which the stars were fixed, with the earth and moon at the centre of it. This model dominated human thought for centuries. To quote Isaac Asimov (*The Universe*): 'For 1,800 years after Hip-parchus man's understanding of the dimensions of the Universe proceeded no further.' After that, came a gradually accelerating extension of knowledge until the amazing vista of modern astronomy was opened up. And what a vista!

Our earth, it turns out, is a medium-sized planet, orbiting around a medium-sized star on one of the arms of an enormous spiral galaxy which contains 100,000 million stars. But our own huge galaxy is only a tiny fraction of the whole. During the past 300 years, man has been looking deeper and deeper into space as he has made more and more powerful implements for doing so: first optical telescopes, up to the instrument at Mount Palomar with its 200-inch reflector, and, more recently, radio telescopes. We have discovered a vastness hitherto undreamed of.

Astronomers, of course, do not measure in miles but in light years, a light year being the distance travelled by light in one year – that is 5,880,000,000,000 miles. The range of modern telescopes, optical and radio, permits man to probe out into space to distances of thousands of millions of light years. In whatever direction the astronomer looks, he sees galaxies beyond galaxies, beyond galaxies. There are 100,000 million of them within the visible universe, and we do not know how many more farther away still. The huge number of stars in galaxies, and of galaxies in the universe, does not mean that the universe is in any way overcrowded. Vast distances separate star from star and galaxy from galaxy. Our sun is 25,000,000,000,000 miles from its nearest neighbour, while galaxies are about two million *light years* apart.

This new perspective is *very* new. We have learnt more about our place in the universe in the past twenty-five years than in all the rest of human history put together. We are now a very long way away from the man-centred universe of earlier times. This brings a corresponding shift in perspective and outlook: our 'world view' must affect our thinking.

When people became aware of the immensity of space, the first reaction was one of loss. The comforting centralness had gone, to be replaced by a feeling of insignificance. The vastness appeared alien to man. Life itself looked like a lonely accident. This feeling of rejection, almost of being an intruder, no longer makes sense. The new immensity, while taking away our former assurance of unique significance, also brings us the comfort of company. In our galaxy alone, there are, according to Professor Philip Morrison, probably 200 million other stars around which planets are orbiting that provide the necessary conditions for life to evolve. On some of these, at least, intelligent life will almost certainly have developed. One may assume that some of this intelligent life will be ahead of ours and some behind. In the other galaxies, of course, similar numbers of inhabitable planets are likely. Our significance is not brushed aside but takes on a new appearance. Intelligence and personality are high-order systems of dynamic organization in a universe of which dynamism and energy are the universal characteristics. Conscious life is special, and self-conscious life is extra special. Each one of us is a custodian in his own being of this special awareness.

Today we find ourselves challenged by the very fact of our existence to actualize ourselves to the limits of our capability. We are the eyes, the ears, the feelings, the imagination, and the conscious creativity of the universe. This is true, however we regard the universe – whether as a mysterious process working itself out or as the will of God operating through a mysterious process.

If we believe in the value of life, whatever its origins, the value is here and now, on this earth. And the responsibility, the vital choice, is ours: to make something of life – life on the planet as a whole as well as personal life – or to trample the pearl of life into the mud of indifference. The only indifference in the universe is the indifference of intelligent beings opting out of concern. The forces of nature are not indifferent; they are impersonal, which is not the same thing; and since they have produced us they cannot be regarded as against us. We are the inheritors of the highest that the creative process on this planet has so far achieved, and, as conscious beings, we have now ourselves become capable of immense powers for creation or destruction. That is the situation of man as the new cosmology reveals it.

The new knowledge affects perspective in other ways also. Until very recently the common way of regarding the world was as an assembly of a large number of discrete items and creatures, each specifically made for its own purpose. In place of this view, scientific man has gradually uncovered something much more exciting: a universal dynamism in which a small number of basic units and a few energies and forces, interacting with one another, result in the evolution of a great range of materials and living forms.

The fundamental is energy. Energy organized and stabilized in certain ways takes on the aspect and properties of matter. Every atom of matter is, we have discovered, a special arrangement of only three major components: the electron, the proton, and the neutron, each a minute energy system on its own account. So the material world we know, in all its variety, is founded on the patterning and repatterning of three minute systems of energy – in the form of atoms, of which there are about a hundred, or as bonded atoms, or molecules, of which there are an almost unlimited number.

If we go up a step in the order of things – to living matter – we again find endless variety produced from the permutations and combinations of a comparatively few basic entities. The chemical unit of life is the protein molecule – a complicated affair, mainly composed of four common atoms: carbon, hydrogen, oxygen, and nitrogen. Thus the staggering wealth of life arises from an equally staggering fundamental simplicity. A giraffe eating a leaf, the tick-bird on its neck, the tick the bird is eating, and the leaf being nibbled by the giraffe are all mainly the outcome of different complex arrangements of carbon, hydrogen, oxygen, and nitrogen atoms, plus calcium for the harder parts, a little iron, and traces of a few other minerals. How does the life get into the system of atoms? It does not have to. Life is no longer regarded as a mysterious addition to matter. 'Life is,' quotes W. J. Harris in his prize essay on the origin of life, 'one of the countless properties of carbon.' It is the way matter behaves when atoms are strung together in certain complicated ways and other conditions are right.

Everything in the universe is the product of pattern and relationship. New patterns and relationships emerge when conditions are right. That is the kind of universe we live in. We, too, are a special kind of pattern and become what we do become by

virtue of our existence and the creative potential of our relationships with what is around us. In us, also, the new emerges when
conditions are right – at any level of our being. But, being conscious, we have the advantage that we can ourselves create the
potentially fruitful conditions for ourselves and one another –
once we know what the conditions are.

Another extraordinary and evocative fact about our universe
is that an incredible latent capacity for change exists in things.
The wide range of materials we call plastics is an example of
man's developing latent possibilities in inorganic substances.
The development of potentialities hidden in living things has
been even more remarkable. The many varieties of dog have
been produced by selective breeding from a few natural species.
Large, sweet, succulent apples, such as Cox's Orange Pippin and
Grannie Smith, have been obtained by cross-fertilization and
grafting techniques from the tiny, hard, bitter crab apple. All
the elegant garden roses have the humble dog-rose as their
ancestor – horticulturists have worked the miracle by drawing
out the possibilities within the wild rose.

In nature, genetic potentialities are developed by the forces of
natural selection – changes in environmental conditions – and
by chance changes in inheritance. Man, to fulfil an aim he
fancies, can provide plants and creatures with the breeding
conditions that bring out the variation he wants. Given time
and intention, it would be possible to produce a dog as big as a
pony or a pony as small as a collie, and many other oddities as
well. There are some limits: for example, a very large insect is
not possible because the way an insect breathes sets a restriction
on the size of its body. Such limits apart, however, life is extra-
ordinarily versatile, and man can draw on this versatility to shape
nature to his needs. He can, of course, make mistakes too, and
does. But his knowledge grows through both success and failure.

This accumulating knowledge puts man in a new position on
the world stage. He can now tap for his own purposes the basic
energies of the creative process. Every person, we have seen, is a
focus of creative dynamism within a vast system of energy,
manifest as all the kaleidoscopic content of the universe. Man is

influenced by what is not himself and can influence it. His powers are, therefore, potentially unlimited. As he learns to understand the dynamic of which he is himself a part, more and more of it falls within his area of control. He is at the present entering yet another area; he is reaching out towards manipulating the chemistry of life itself. Living things, we noted, are composed mainly of protein molecules. The protein architecture determines what a creature is like. The code controlling the architecture, which ensures that any species reproduces itself, is a chemical message contained in the nucleus of every living cell. As one might expect from what we observe elsewhere in nature, this code is an example of simple units elaborated to produce complex results. The information built into living cells, which controls growth so that all the varieties of living creatures, visible and invisible, can exist and reproduce themselves is spelt out by variations on only four chemical letters. This genetic code, as everybody knows, is now being cracked. Here we seem to be on the threshold of an ultimate. Man can go no farther biologically than the understanding and control of the life process itself.

Nothing of man's new situation is more surprising than his nearness, now, to controlling the ultimate in physical and biological reality. The basic energy of the material universe arises from the fusion of hydrogen into helium – the energy of the sun itself. Scientists are today grappling with the final technical problems which at present stand between man and the control of this energy. The gap between man and the ultimate control of biological forces is wider, but, as we have seen, we are already glimpsing the far side. As Donald Gould said in a recent broadcast, the 'biological Hiroshima' is upon us – the equivalent in biology of the discovery of atomic energy.

This does not turn men into gods, because men are themselves products of the creative process. They control the forces of nature by patiently learning how to do so, not by producing the forces for themselves. But the new situation does face man with the responsibility of using well the sources of power coming into his hands. The greater the power, the greater the responsibility.

Before considering further how the new cosmology affects

some of man's ancient presuppositions, we have one more novelty of the new orientation to consider. The universe, as now revealed, appears as a continuum, seething everywhere with energy, but varying in concentration. Most of the universe is extremely tenuous (space), but in comparatively rare places it is more massive (stars, planets, etc.). This continuum runs the gamut of temperature from extremely hot to extremely cold – and at either extreme extraordinary things begin to happen: in intense heat the components of atoms separate to form a plasma of wildly moving free electrons and protons; in intense cold metals become superconductors. Within this continuum there is no such thing as empty space. The vast interstellar and intergalactic spaces are sparsely occupied with hydrogen atoms and dust, and are interlaced with electromagnetic waves, cosmic rays, and other kinds of energy and movement. Dynamic space is the ground of a dynamic universe, the whole an immense unity of interrelated parts and forces.

How does this extraordinary new perspective on the universe alter man's old preconceptions about the nature of things and of himself? As we have seen, his ideas of dependent centralness have to be replaced by ideas of creative responsibility. He now sees himself not as the sole example of intelligent life, but as an active partner in the intelligence and personality that is, almost certainly, scattered throughout the universe. He also sees himself not as an entity outside nature, but as the product of natural forces, made of the very stuff of the universe and shaped by the long span of the evolutionary process. This leaves, particularly, two ancient preconceptions to be considered: the hope of immortality, and belief in God.

Personal survival, from the facts at present known to science, can neither be proved nor disproved. Nevertheless, the new cosmology itself leads us on to a question of its own about the possibility of survival. The universe can be considered qualitatively as a system of developmental stages. At the base is the infinite spread of space, itself a matrix of forces and stresses. At the next stage up comes the simplest atom – the hydrogen atom. Hydrogen accounts for 90 per cent of the matter in the universe, but we do not yet know how it comes into existence. It may arise, at a guess, as a kind of crystallization into an enduring form of more elementary, more transitory, units of energy, of which many are now known. It may emerge, as other things do, when conditions are right. The next stage is the elaboration of hydrogen into more complex atoms within the cauldrons of the stars. The next stage is the bonding together of atoms into molecules. The next arises from the complication of the molecule until we reach living matter. Then comes the elaboration of living matter into organisms. Then the increase in size, complexity, sensitivity, and intelligence of organisms. And, from this stage, man, and his self-organization into societies.

Each major stage of complexity may be regarded as the outcome of the preceding stage. From a lot of space arises a comparatively small amount of matter. From a lot of matter emerges a comparatively small amount of life. From a lot of life arises a comparatively small amount of intelligent self-conscious life – man. The question inevitably arises, 'How can we tell that, in man, we have reached the top of the hierarchy?' Is it not possible that personality as we know it underlies something else which we have no means of understanding? It is, of course, possible, but at this point we enter the realm of speculation and personal choice. We can neither prove nor disprove it one way or the other. But we may notice this is a different question from the old one about personal survival, which is also unanswerable.

And God? Of course, belief or non-belief in God is not decided solely on man's perspective on the universe, but there is obviously a relationship between the two, so we can ask what the new outlook has to tell us about the concept of God. The new cosmology leads us to speak of a creative process. This brings us face to face with the question, 'Could so much have been achieved with so little if an intelligence was not constantly at work on its design?' The extraordinary thing is that the answer, against all the expectations of common sense, appears to be, 'Yes, it could.' Whereas we see everywhere objects and creatures that seem to bear the marks of deliberate design, they turn out, in fact, to be the result of the interaction of natural forces. The universe contains limitless energy and limitless potential. Granted these, plus chance interactions within varying situations, and the creative process goes on its way productively. There is no evidence of anything in the creative process over and above the interaction of natural forces during the millions of years of evolution prior to man. The concept of Providence has ceased to be tenable. It is for this reason that many scientists are atheists or agnostics, and not because they are unpleasant fellows with no hearts, imagination, or high consciousness.

This is the conundrum facing modern man. And, in the end, every individual is left to solve it for himself. Creation is a process. A Creator? But, if a Creator, why is the creative potential of the universe self-sufficient? God as the first cause to start it all off? Then is this God outside the universe? And is God supposed suddenly to have returned to his creation with the arrival of man, after millions of years of somewhat haphazard evolution? And what about those presumed millions of other inhabited planets? How may the ultimate be interpreted on them? The mystery remains and deepens. We are even now struggling to find some new perspective on the whole which will make sense of it in a way that the old concepts did, but do no more. It is a tormenting problem. The atheists find it difficult to explain why a creative process exists at all, yet – as Teilhard de Chardin and others have shown – there is a positive direction in evolution. The theists are nonplussed at the undeniable revelation of a self-actuating, self-transforming universe. Modern man is here left without any certainty.

Curiously enough, during the very years when some theologians and clergymen have come to feel that their God is disappearing into the mists, some scientists have been turning their minds to framing a tenable concept of God. For example, here is J. B. S. Haldane, quoted by W. H. Thorpe in *Science, Man and Morals*: 'It seems to me that everywhere ethical experience testifies to a super-individual reality of some kind. The good life, if not necessarily self-denial, is always self-transcendence.' Such, and similar, statements arise because there is an equal dissatisfaction with arbitrary definitions of God and with the categorical denial of any possibility of consciousness extending beyond the person. There is a nagging feeling that something is missing somewhere. As *nothing but* the outcome of energy and probability, the universe, including human consciousness as a part of it, seems too remarkable to be true. But no concept of a God to fill the gap has so far succeeded in explaining the mystery of existence, a mystery which does not grow less but deepens as man adds to his knowledge. The mystery, let us notice, lies in the nature of Nature itself, with ourselves as part of it; not in the supernatural. Modern knowledge is constantly extending our wonder about Nature while rendering concepts of the supernatural ever more vague and empty.

The more we know the more we are challenged to search further. The great teacher is the quest for truth, and the ultimate faith that everything is part of a discoverable order. The new cosmology gives us many new insights about ourselves and the universe. For the first time we see ourselves in our true status as responsible creators within a creative process. The perspective appropriate to this new role is stirring and challenging, but it cannot, from its very nature, give us certainty. We live in the presence of mystery, and probably always shall, since every frontier reached opens up new territory beyond it. The answers to the ultimate questions – indeed, to all questions – must remain open-ended. Our role is to explore, to use, to develop; our act of faith to believe that it is all worth-while; our reward, the joy of effectiveness, fulfilment, and wholeness of being; our frustration, that we have to settle for uncertainty about the ultimate questions. The warmth and excitement come from sharing in the mystery and the search.

CHRISTIAN CONUNDRUM

A LITTLE over a hundred years ago, there was some apprehension among nervous individuals in case a comet predicted to appear in 1858 should collide with our planet. James Gilbert, a publisher of scholarly treatises at 49 Paternoster Row, sought to allay anxieties with a pamphlet entitled *Will the Great Comet, Now Rapidly Approaching, Strike the Earth?* The argument the writer uses to prove that it will not is of some interest.

He calculates that, of the 967 million people in the world, only 396 million were Christians. Hence, '565 millions are ignorant of the True God'. Since the Millennium, according to the Bible, 'must be before the end', the writer argues that immediate destruction is impossible. He concludes: 'We may therefore be sure in the Sacred Word of Truth, that though the world may deserve chastisement at the hand of the Almighty, the time is not yet come for "the end of things"; and that our Earth will roll safely – perhaps for countless ages – in the realms of space.'

In that argument we can see many elements in traditional Christian thought that, a hundred years later, make a good deal of traditional Christian thought unacceptable, even to many Christians. There is the assumption that only Christianity is a worthy religion – six million Jews are classed among those 'ignorant of the True God'. There is an unquestioning belief in prophecy and the literal truth of the Bible, and there is the concept of God as a harsh judge, displeased with man. The argument is of the same order as that used against Galileo in the seventeenth century; his ideas about the universe could not be true because they were 'expressly contrary to Holy Scripture'.

Therein lies the conundrum of the Christian Church today. Christianity has made an immense contribution to western civilization, in humanity, in art, in architecture, in learning, in education. This is true, even when we take full account of its bad patches: religious wars and massacres, the Inquisition, feuding, witch-hunting, bigotry, and prudery. But it now finds much of its traditional attitude an encumbrance. A great religion, like a great work of art, can carry new insight to succeeding ages of mankind by bringing out new facets and depths of itself. During the recent past, however, thought and theology have got badly out of step. The Church has tried to keep its doctrines firm over the last three hundred years, in spite of social changes and the advance of human knowledge. It has moved by inches, whereas human knowledge has moved forward with great strides, particularly in the past century. Consequently orthodox Christianity is no longer a good fit to society.

Christianity is 'our' religion in western civilization, but today many people cannot feel it as 'for me'. Our situation is analogous to that of the intellectuals of Plato's time, who, finding belief in the gods of Olympus impossible, did not quite know what to do for the best. Since Christian thought has played a central role in the past in sustaining the moral order of our society, we shall have to look into the contemporary position in some detail. What, as we move towards the twenty-first century, is happening to 'our' religion?

One thing that is happening is confusion. Some churches have moved in their ideas; some have not. Under the title 'Christianity' one can find almost the entire range of human social behaviour and outlook, from authoritarianism to democracy, from Communism to the extreme right wing, from humanism to transcendentalism, from pro-life attitudes and convictions to anti-life attitudes and convictions.

What accounts for this disparity in thought, now grown so extreme that a pacifist and a fire-eating general – a dove and a hawk – may both belong to the same congregation and justify their diametrically opposed outlooks in terms of the same faith? The root cause is a wholesome and hopeful freedom for Christians to think about Christianity as not permitted formerly. The process by which this position has been reached gives the clue to the present uncertain position of 'our' religion. Early Christianity existed as a fellowship of small groups of ordinary people, united by a new vision of God, life, and one another. Later it grew into a state religion, created its own power hierarchy, and laid down a dogma of faith to maintain its unity; it became authoritarian. Over the centuries ecclesiastical authoritarianism was overtaken by the Renaissance and civil democracy so that it ceased to be easy to sustain religious conformity by force or authority. And now the Church, speaking generally, does not know whether to hold itself together by a system of required belief (which is the Roman Catholic approach) or to encourage people to think for themselves and take up different positions (the Protestant tradition). The result is that individual Christians, whatever their selected church, represent a wide spectrum of view. This is a robust state of affairs, but leaves in question what, in fact, the common ground is.

From early in the Christian era, the ecclesiastical powers saw the danger to the Church's authority of allowing ordinary people to think for themselves about Christianity. The translation and publication of the Bible were ruthlessly opposed. Tyndale's promise, in the sixteenth century, that he would make it possible for 'a boy that driveth the plough' to read the scriptures struck horror into the heart of Cuthbert Tunstall, the then Bishop of London. Later, when Tyndale's magnificent translation of the New Testament had been printed, Bishop Tunstall collected all the copies he could lay hands on and had them publicly burnt. Tyndale was forced to take refuge in Antwerp, where he continued his work until he was captured by his enemies, imprisoned for sixteen months, and then burnt at the stake. It is said that, out of admiration and regard, the executioner strangled him first to save him the agony of the flames. So, for centuries, the Sacred Book of Christianity was regarded as unsafe in other than priestly hands.

The apprehension of the Church authorities was well founded in view of their aim to keep the tenets of Christian belief immune from criticism. They were intelligent men and well aware of the inconsistencies and anomalies to be found in the Bible. Once let the Bible become available to every literate person, and it was plain it would not be long before Christian dogma itself came under investigation. But questioning began early, and has continued to the present. In the fourteenth century Wycliff, himself an early translator of the New Testament, 'assailed the central dogma of transubstantiation'. His Lollard movement was suppressed with the execution of Oldcastle in 1417 'as heretic and traitor'. It continued as an underground movement, however, and ran schools for 'unlettered men' where manuscript versions of Wycliff's translation of the New Testament were studied and learnt by heart. The backwash of this early essay in free thought, adding to the shake-up of the Reformation, led, in 1563, to the promulgation of the Articles of Religion by the Church of England 'for the avoiding of Diversities of Opinions, and for the establishing of Consent touching true Religion'. After 1571 there were thirty-nine articles – a blueprint for comformity with which, until the present century, priests of the Church of England had to swear agreement at ordination. In the nineteenth and twentieth centuries the Thirty-Nine Articles were overtaken by modern biblical scholarship, which brought all kinds of new light to the New Testament narrative and undermined earlier presuppositions that the Bible should be regarded as an immaculate text of pure truth. This searching inquiry did not affect the Bible's status as a document of immense historical and literary importance; it for ever removed the claim that it should be immune from the insights of human criticism. Freedom of thought won through and as a result the dogmatic certainty of earlier Christian belief fell apart. This is the new situation with which the Church is now struggling. It is fruitful in new ideas but makes any absolute claims extremely difficult to sustain.

In 1922, the Archbishops of Canterbury and York, disturbed by the resulting doubt, set up a commission to sort things out. Its Report appeared in 1938, under the title of *Doctrine in the Church of England*. It was an attempt to restore some sort of order to the growing confusion created by the continuing clash between dogma and the questioning of dogma.

The Report shows that much that was formerly considered central and sacrosanct had already given way under the pressure of critical thought. It conceded that the miracles recorded in the New Testament might well have been the results of legends attached to the record of Jesus, as is a common occurrence in the stories of great religious leaders. Of the Virgin Birth it says: 'The historical evidence by itself cannot be other than inconclusive.' The concept of 'original sin' is watered down. Even the Resurrection is subject to doubts: 'The connexion made in the New Testament between the emptiness of the tomb and the appearances of the Risen Lord belongs rather to the sphere of religious symbolism than to that of historical fact.' The Report was an honest and courageous attempt to admit the eclipse of a number of orthodox beliefs, while seeking to clarify what remained intact.

And now, thirty years later, much of what seemed still acceptable to the archbishops' commission is becoming harder and harder for intelligent people to believe. Yet the struggle to rescue the remains of Christian orthodoxy still goes on. A whole range of attempts is being made to bridge the gap between dogma and modern knowledge. The spectrum runs from the non-rational approach of Barth – you must have faith and believe – to the 'Christian humanist' view which tells us that, if we consider biblical truth as allegorical and symbolic instead of factual, things will fall into place.

The argument by faith can hardly be expected to help, because the gap between dogma and knowledge is growing steadily wider and those who cling blindly to a fundamentalist position will ultimately end up in a schizoid relationship to life, whether as

Animal 'altruism'

Courage:
a crowned plover protects
her nest

b Friendship:
cat and duck

c Tolerance:
owl and budgerigar

2 Children are naturally indomitable

a

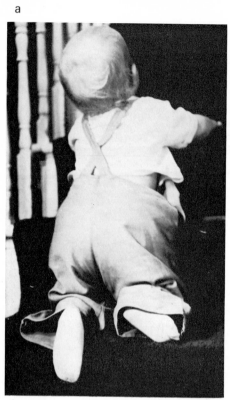

b

c

Sacred symbol of origin and survival:

juringa stone of Australian aborigines

Signpost in the wrong direction:

Articles of Religion.

Original sin standeth not in the following of Adam, (as the Pelagians do vainly talk) but it is the fault and corruption of the nature of every man, that naturally is ingendred of the off-spring of Adam, whereby man is very far gone from original righteousnes, and is of his own nature inclined to evil, so that the flesh lusteth alwayes contrary to the spirit, and therefore in every person born into this world, it deserveth Gods wrath and damnation. And this infection of nature doth remain, yea, in them that are regenerated, whereby the lust of the flesh, called in Greek φρόνημα σαρκός, which some do expound the wisdom, some sensuality, some the affection, some the desire of the flesh, is not subject to the law of God. And although there is no condemnation for them that believe and are baptized, yet the Apostle doth confes, that concupiscence and lust hath of it self the nature of sin.

The IXth Article of Religion, 1562–3, 'for the avoiding of Diversities of Opinions, and for the establishing of consent touching true Religion'

5 The defeat of prudery

a Ann Packer wins
  the 800 metres Gold
  Medal, Tokyo, 1964,
  in 2 minutes, 1.1
  seconds

b Unidentified lady
  athlete clears
  approximately 2
  feet 6 inches at the
  London Olympic
  Games, 1908

Individual and group striving:

a–b Channel swimmer; learner climbers

Friendly rivalry:

c   Frank Tyson bowls a fast one

Creative self-expression

a Joseph Herman at work
in his studio

b A sculptor models a
portrait bust

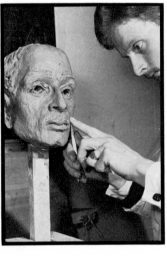

Involved participation
Student concern

a Mothers at Edmonton demand a pedestrian crossing

b An early starter asleep on the job

Ritual
The celebration of summer, an annual May Day ceremony at Padstow, Cornwall

11 Marriage

a Adventuring together–

b or one another's jailers?

"Bang! Bang! Bang!"

individuals or as sub-groups defending themselves desperately against the expansion of human knowledge.

The argument about the allegorical and symbolic interpretation of belief has more substance. Much of belief held formerly to be factual rings true, as allegory, with what we know about man's evolution, man's nature, and man's striving. To start at the beginning, the Garden of Eden story offers a good example of allegorical truth. To eat of the fruit of the tree of knowledge was to lose the innocence of the animal. At that point individual independence was born, and with it the potential for creativity, and self-doubt, and responsibility – and, therefore, the sense of failure and of sin. Somewhere along the evolutionary ladder, not in a moment but over time, rudimentary man must have passed through that phase: instead of having instinct as a guide, he became aware of choices, and so of the need to sort out right from wrong.

So far so good. But the Eden allegory is anything but tidy by modern standards. Why was man's advance to self-consciousness presented as against the will of God? Why was a woman chosen as the implement of Satan? Why was man made first and woman from one of his ribs? Why were Adam and Eve ashamed of their nakedness after they had gained knowledge of good and evil? It is perhaps mean to quibble about such offshoots of the old chronicler's brave intuition, but those who argue for allegory cannot set aside the fact that some of the ideas accruing no longer accord with man's concept of himself. All the same, the allegorical approach to Old Testament belief is illuminating, though incomplete.

But when allegorical explanations are applied to New Testament belief, the result is greater confusion rather than clarity. Take, for example, the dogma of the resurrection of the body. A number of modern Christians interpret this as an allegory for the survival of individual identity after death in some coherent form. But the gospel accounts, and traditional Christianity, make great play upon the fact that the *body* of Jesus arose, and lives eternally. It is reported that Jesus deliberately demonstrated this to the disciples: 'Touch me and see; no ghost has flesh and bones as you

can see that I have.' Jesus then asked the disciples if they had with
them anything to eat. 'They offered him a piece of fish they had
cooked, which he took and ate before their eyes.' (Luke 24: 39, 41,
New English Bible.)

Those who regard the resurrection of the body as symbolic
have to regard this part of the New Testament as an interpolation.
But if major beliefs of Christianity in the past were based on what
some now suspect were interpolations, what is left of the claims to
absolute truth of Christian dogma as a whole? Many Christians no
longer seek to make claims to absolute truth, but others do. This
is yet another aspect of the conundrum: is Christianity an
absolutist faith or is it not?

Deeper problems still face the Church. One of them is whether
the concept of a God who intervenes is any longer tenable.
Another is how far the character of Jesus, as revealed in the
gospels, is consistent with the nature of 'the God of evolution'.
Both questions are brought up by the existence of physical
suffering. All the aspects of physical suffering – pain, agony,
disease, slow death – were in the world millions of years before
man appeared on the evolutionary scene, although original doctrine held that suffering came into the world through man's
sinfulness, through his evil use of free will. Jesus, it is recorded,
did not only tell men how to live; he also cured sickness and alle-
viated suffering wherever he found it; and his message was that
all men should do so. 'Inasmuch as ye have done it unto one of
the least of these my brethren ye have done it unto me' (Matthew
25: 40, Authorized Version). And yet the lepers, whom Jesus
cured, to take only one example, were dying by inches because
of a micro-organism which is as much a created thing as an ele-
phant – the responsibility of God himself since He was 'Maker
of heaven and earth, and of all things visible and invisible'.
This creates a curious situation in which Jesus is reported as
struggling against the direct outcome in suffering of the very
handiwork of God.

There is no way out along the lines that God in his wisdom
permits suffering because suffering can bring out the best in
people. Unnecessary suffering, as from natural disaster, may

destroy to no purpose. Yet God, if supposed to be a God who intervenes at will, must be held responsible for much useless suffering, whereas the gospel records tell us that Jesus helped all suffering that came his way. Hence the inconsistency. Can one imagine for a moment that a man of Jesus's acute sensitivity and quick sympathy would condone, for example, the deliberate withholding of rain, in a drought, which brings thousands of animals, wild and domestic, to slow, miserable death and wipes out, year after year, the subsistence crops of starving people? The 'evil' in nature prior to man, the devastations of disease in history, and the hurt and suffering arising from 'Acts of God' face Christian orthodoxy with a conundrum it cannot solve.

Another difficulty, already touched on earlier, is that the course of biological evolution prior to man – about 2,000 million years – does not give us evidence of a steady movement towards higher forms, but of an uncertain zigzag course marked by false starts, dead ends, and, sometimes, vast annihilations. The idea of an all-loving and almighty Creator is inconsistent with this evidence. The only rationally tolerable concept would be of a struggling, exploring, experimenting Creator. Such a concept of God would be consistent with the facts. But this is not the Christian concept.

One response to these difficulties on the part of theologians has been a vigorous attempt to modify the image of God into a form more acceptable to modern man. The evolution of a god-concept is, of course, quite normal in the history of a religion. The God of Isaiah is different from the God of Abraham, and the Father God of Jesus is different again. But what is quite unusual is the proliferation of different god-concepts at the same time, such as we find among Christian thinkers today. A great range of presentations now exists simultaneously. The God of John Robinson's *Honest to God* bears few resemblances to the God offered us in Billy Graham's *Peace With God*. The God of Teilhard de Chardin is somewhat different again. Bultmann and Bonhoeffer offer still other viewpoints about the nature of God. Nor is that the end: *quot theologici, tot dei*. Almost every decade a refurbished theology finds print. This is proof of lively thought and dialogue, but is obviously inconsistent with claims to absolute truth.

Variation in interpretation is equally marked among the rank-and-file. Within a group of fifth-form girls and boys attending the same grammar school the following variations appeared, with others, to the question: 'What is your idea of God?'

'A spirit.'

'Some kind of spirit.'

'A person.'

'God is not a person, but he is there in some form.'

'I imagine God as an immense power in the form of an aged man who is wise.'

'I imagine God as the power of creation, personified by goodness and love.'

'My idea of God is that it is all the good things in people, and everything beautiful on earth.'

'Like a second father, who I feel can always help when anything goes wrong.'

'God is an impersonal perfection.'

'I can't imagine God.'

'I don't know what God is like or even if there is one.'

'I don't know that there is a god.'

'I don't believe in god.'

Such personalized interpretation is characteristic of society today. One would expect things to be thus in a democracy. Significantly, a series of essays published in 1967 entitled *The God I Want*, and covering a range of religious standpoints, is dedicated, like the altar of the Athenians, 'To the Unknown God'. Difference and controversy are the outcome of freedom to think. But they mark the end of founding moral order on precise tenets of belief. Such a foundation *requires* rigidity. It is not possible to sustain a moral order of this kind, with any force, on the basis of *dubitable* dogma.

The solution of the conundrum can arise only from a fresh start. Christianity, to thrive anew, must turn back once again to the teachings of the man on whom Christianity was originally founded. In Jesus, Christianity has a person of incomparable moral genius; whereas orthodoxy cracks under the impact of history, genius does not. The churches would be wise to stop trying to salvage dogma and to concentrate instead on the task of reinterpreting the genius of Jesus for modern man. An unknown number of Christians are themselves coming to see that the future of Christianity lies here. The Rev. A. Stephan Hopkinson, in an essay in *The God I Want*, writes:

'Whether or no the gospels be taken as "gospel truth", no Christian doubts that they contain a vivid and substantially accurate account of the impression made by their subject's life and teaching. We need to return to that teaching and to focus all our attention upon it, rather than to accept at secondhand what others appear to have found in it – or what, from other sources, they have contrived to associate with it.'

Unfortunately, here too there is a serious stumbling-block, because there are two kinds of message emanating from the gospels. One – the message of St John's Gospel – is full of a sense of man's unworthiness and focuses its attention on the Second Coming and eternal life. The other – coming from Matthew, Mark, and Luke – is much more concerned with how to live here and now. The other-worldliness of Christianity stems primarily from John's gospel. So does the emphasis on sin and repentance. The idea of Jesus as 'the Lamb of God' who 'takes away the sin of the world' is from John. In the first three gospels the emphasis is on the forgiveness of sins – the removal of human guilt, that is; in John the emphasis is on man as a sinner.

John does not entirely neglect life in this world. It is he who reports Jesus as saying: 'I am come that they might have life, and that they might have it more abundantly' (John 10: 10, Authorized Version). Yet, with John, you can never be sure whether he is talking about the present or the hereafter, so wrapped up is he in his concept of Jesus as the Son of God, and in the inheritance of eternal life through belief in Jesus as the Son

of God. In the other gospels the stress is the other way round –
on living now, on building the Kingdom of God on earth.
And in these three gospels Jesus refers to himself constantly as
the Son of Man.

We are left then to choose between John and the other three
evangelists in deciding whether Jesus was chiefly concerned with
transforming life on earth or primarily concerned with life
eternal. Which was right? Now, whereas John's honesty, integrity, zeal, and brilliance cannot for a moment be in doubt, his
validity is suspect for two reasons. The evidence suggests that his
gospel was written last – some seventy years, perhaps, after the
death of Jesus. Much more serious is the fact that he builds his case
on public 'signs' of Jesus's divinity – spectacular miracles against
which Jesus is reported in the other gospels as having taken a
definite stand. For example, in Mark: 'Why does this generation
ask for a sign? I tell you this: no sign shall be given to this generation' (Mark 8: 12, New English Bible). But in the second chapter
of John, we read: 'This deed at Cana-in-Galilee is the first of the
signs by which Jesus revealed his glory and led his disciples to
believe in him' (John 2: 11, New English Bible). What was this
sign? It was the turning of water into wine at the wedding feast,
exactly the kind of conjuring trick that Jesus had stated he wanted
to have nothing to do with. This miracle is not reported in
Matthew, Mark, or Luke.

Another of the spectacular signs reported in John is the raising
of Lazarus after he had been four days in the tomb. Such an
amazing feat, if it ever occurred, must have swept around the
miracle-loving world of Jesus's day. Yet it, again, is not reported
in the earlier records of Matthew, Mark, and Luke. Other anomalies also appear in John, as, for example, a completely different
account of the healing of the man sick with a palsy, and – more
notable – the Sermon on the Mount is omitted. In view of this,
it is hard to trust John's gospel as a *record*, in spite of its quality as
literature. One is left with the feeling that John had a conviction
about Jesus to which he directed all the force of his powerful writing, drawing on any material, checked or unchecked, that would
help to substantiate what *he* felt to be the right point of view.

The other gospels give us a very different picture: a teacher full of life-affirmation, with a vision of how transformed the world could be if only men lived their lives by new principles. Jesus believed in God and in eternal life, but his great drive, as shown in the first three gospels, was towards transforming life on earth through releasing in action the power of love he knew to be inherent in man.

The Church has been particularly attracted to John's viewpoint, so that it has imposed upon itself an image which is life-denying and obsessed with sin. This has been almost fatal. Nothing could be more alien to a modern mind than the otherworldliness of John. Modern man is not much concerned about saving his soul for eternity; he sees fulfilment as something to be striven for in life. This aim can draw insight and inspiration from the teachings of the first three gospels – the authentic teachings of Jesus, it would seem – much more than from the passionate, but misleading, writings of John.

What, more precisely, was the authentic message? The first thing to strike a modern mind about the teaching of Jesus as it emerges from the first three gospels must be the huge problem of communication Jesus was up against. Much as one would like to know what the conversation was like when Jesus held a private discussion with the occasional *friendly* Pharisee, there is reported in the gospels only what he said when speaking in the presence of ordinary people. He had to make his points in language they could understand.

This was a difficult task. Jesus was speaking to a resentful subject people, yet he sought to convince them that the whole fullness of life could be theirs if they drew upon what they had within themselves. The Jews had to promote an intense sense of nationalism in order to survive as a people, but Jesus wanted them to accept that non-Jews were valuable human beings too. The Jewish community was organized under its ecclesiastical oligarchy who administered the ancient Law; Jesus sought to put the needs of man first and the Law second. The people of Jesus's days were used to accepting whatever was offered by authority; Jesus told them to seek for themselves: 'Ask, and it shall be given you; seek, and ye shall find; knock, and it shall be opened unto you' (Luke 11: 9, Authorized Version).

Faced with this intimidating task of communication, Jesus worked away constantly at trying to reshape people's ideas, sometimes addressing large audiences, sometimes speaking to individuals, and sometimes speaking intimately to his chosen twelve. In the end the message got home and stuck long enough for it to be recorded. Its influence has been incalculable because the insight of Jesus was that of a moral genius who intuitively grasped the truth about the nature of man and of the right relationships between men.

Looking back at what Jesus said and when he said it, one can only be astounded. 'Blessed are the meek for they shall inherit the earth.' How preposterous amidst all the power of Rome! A hundred years ago it seemed almost as absurd. But the world today is alive with the activity of emerging 'humble' people.

'Judge not that ye be not judged' was another penetrating insight which we now know to be true. It is those who condemn too readily who draw condemnation upon themselves. Better to forgive 'unto seventy times seven', for we all have in us that which is in need of forgiveness. In the short prayer Jesus framed for his disciples, he reduced this idea to ultimate simplicity – we can expect to be forgiven to the extent that we forgive.

Trying approach after approach, Jesus sought to convey what he meant by 'The Kingdom of God'. It was within men; it was around men; it was like a growing seed, like yeast, like treasure hidden in the ground. It was the potentialities of people waiting to be brought to full fruition. In the parables of the sower and the talents, Jesus told men to strive for their fulfilment. *Use* your powers, Jesus urged, trust life, cast out fear and guilt, live *now* and deal with tomorrow when it comes, but do all this so that you care for your neighbour's well-being as much as you care for your own: 'Treat others as you would like them to treat you.' Don't hang on to things if they are holding you back from wholeness and life; get rid of them and live. Lose yourself in life so that you may find what you really are. Don't think that symbols of significance – money, power, position – can ever serve in the place of wholeness and abundant life: 'What does a man gain by winning the whole world at the cost of his true self?' (Mark 8: 36, New English Bible).

Out the message poured, unimpeachable wisdom, framed in language that anyone could understand – insights centuries ahead of their time. Not all as original as was at one time supposed, but reshaped and reinterpreted into teaching of great penetration, which has new meaning for each new age.

What of the vexed question of the divinity of Jesus? Others readily made this claim for him, but, in the first three gospels, he always seems loth to make it for himself. No doubt he was uncertain, just as he also seems to have been uncertain about when the Kingdom of God would come. Sometimes he seems to have thought, like St Paul, that it was 'at hand'; at other times he seems less clear about it. It must have been difficult for Jesus to interpret and evaluate his own genius in the world he was living in. 'Call not thou me good,' he once said, and an agonizing failure of expectation must have lain behind that terrible cry from the cross: 'My God! My God! Why hast thou forsaken me?'

Jesus, however great, was a man of his time, and must have been caught up in many of the beliefs of his time. He sought to reinterpret the whole theology of the Jews, but he must have known that, in doing so, it was vital not to outrage the expectations of his simple followers too far. He had to go along with many of their concepts and we shall never know exactly how he would have described his ideas of God and heaven and other things if he had been speaking to someone approaching the same calibre as himself. His message was essentially to people about people. He only entered the thorny area of theological discussion when provoked. Whatever he gave to the children after he said, 'Suffer the little children to come unto me, and forbid them not, for of such is the Kingdom of Heaven,' it was certainly not an R.I. lesson. 'I tell you,' Jesus added, 'that whoever does not accept the Kingdom of God like a child will never enter it.' He loved the eager zest for life of children. He loved *life*. His message was everywhere life-affirming and whenever it has been interpreted so as to become life-denying we can be sure it has been distorted.

In Jesus and his work is a man vital enough, a life remarkable enough, and a teaching penetrating enough, to contribute profoundly to the thought and moral ideas of the modern world. The churches can live by the truth of Christianity so long as they have the strength and courage to follow the teachings of Jesus in their challenging simplicity.

And the flogging, the crown of thorns, the terrible death for which we are all supposed to be guilty, the blood which is said to have redeemed us? The tragic death was all too horribly inevitable. The two recorded instances of Jesus getting really angry are when he drove the cheating money-lenders out of the temple, and when he told the scribes and pharisees what he thought of them. The invective on this latter occasion was sharp and bold. To take a selection from Matthew 23: 'Woe unto you, scribes and Pharisees, hypocrites! You shut up the kingdom against men for you neither go in yourselves neither do you allow those who are entering to go in. . . . You devour widows' houses and for a pretence make long prayer: therefore you shall receive the greater damnation. You fools. You blind guides which strain at a gnat and swallow a camel. You are like unto whited sepulchres, which indeed appear beautiful outward but are within full of dead men's bones of all uncleanness. You serpents. You generation of vipers. How can you escape the damnation of hell?'

This is most unparliamentary language, and few people, even today, would dare to attack the rich and powerful so fiercely in public. To speak like that of the Establishment in the first century A.D. was suicidal. There was a 'This man must go' campaign in high places, and after that it was a matter of a squalid little conspiracy to pin something on Jesus that would warrant his execution.

The death of Jesus was a story of personal courage and offended affluence that has, alas, been repeated scores of times in human history. We feel saddened by the pity of it all, uplifted by the courage of Jesus, and appalled at the kind of awful waste that so often destroys what is precious because it is interpreted as a threat to what is gross. All that, yes, and more, but modern men cannot feel personally guilty for this precise event, even though we may freely admit that we, too, are capable of insensitivity and enormity. At Golgotha on that fateful Friday a great man died bravely for what he believed to be right. The glory is that men are made of such stuff that the best of them behave like this if the ultimate challenge comes.

So far as the social philosophy of Jesus is concerned, the principles he enunciated have not only been rediscovered in our gradually extending knowledge of man and society but they have become today not ideals only, but the practical values of personal, social, national and international life without which we cannot survive, let alone advance. Disentangled from their accretion of rigid, often life-denying, dogma, they stand out as essential principles of a contemporary moral order.

Whether the churches have the vigour and courage to reassess their thinking so that their active service for mankind is matched by tenable beliefs remains to be seen. Will the ecumenical movement seek to grow by the reduction of dogma, or by spreading agreed dogmatic authoritarianism more widely, or will it founder at the first real clash?

The common ground for the churches is an acceptable perspective on the universe, and active effort in establishing a social and moral order for the modern world. The task of the churches in a mass technological society is, supremely, to humanize, to challenge material values and sectional interests, to help build and sustain community life, to free from fear, to bring compassion, to support, at need to rescue, to help make whole. The churches will thrive through deeds, not through dogmas, as the best Christians always have done, and always do. It is hard to see how there can be any other future. As Julian Huxley has stressed in *Religion Without Revelation*, the religious institutions of the future – if there are to be any at all – will be based on human experience in its totality, not based on ideas of supernatural revelation.

In any religion of the future there will be reverence for the transcendental and the spiritual. Man's mind and imagination carry him into the transcendental and spiritual, which exist as aspects of reality. The milieu of men is a vast mysterious universe of unlimited potentiality. It is to this that man strives to relate himself at all levels of his being. The conscious element in creation – the element of knowing and feeling, of awareness and wonder – remains one of its deepest mysteries, but it is, nevertheless, a part of nature. The religious quest will continue not as accommodation with ancient myth but as encounter with present mystery, as veneration and faith in the creative within nature and within ourselves, as yearning towards the wisest and noblest and kindest that can be, as hope of triumphing over all that shackles and limits the liberation of the human spirit.

The religious need is a profound emotional need for relationship and commitment. It is experienced in different forms by different people. But people are also rational and, as Margaret Isherwood, for one, has recently pointed out, need beliefs that square with the facts as we know them. The conundrum of Christianity is how to close the gap between feeling and fact. Many, today, find themselves in the position of the professor who said: 'I cannot believe that I have to purchase eternal life at the price of my intellect.'

13

THE MEANING OF LIFE

To question the meaning of life is an aspect of free thought in the open society. When society was closed and authoritarian, acceptance and obedience ruled most people's lives and the meaning of life was embedded in this situation. The majority of people thought what they were told to think, did as they were told, and looked for their reward in heaven. There were few chinks left for doubt or uncertainty; if any appeared, efforts were quickly made to stop them up.

People are still unused to the new climate of openness and freedom, and many, while enjoying the feeling of freedom and denouncing authoritarian systems, nevertheless yearn for the clear-cut meaning to life that only autocracy can provide. What is the exact meaning of a single free hour, let alone a lifetime, if one man spends it gossiping, another cleaning his car, a third visiting a sick friend, a fourth playing snooker, a fifth reading philosophy, and so on? If all five were marching to a rally singing in unison 'Ruritania Rules the World', they would find it much easier to feel that life had *a* meaning.

Things *don't* have *a* meaning. What, for example, is the

meaning of 'water'? This is an unanswerable question. All we can say in reply is what we have experienced water to be. The word conjures up a score of impressions: cool drinks, limpid pools, washing, rain, a storm at sea, reflected lights, experiments in the laboratory, making tea, boiling eggs, fishing. . . . The meaning of water for us arises from the relationships we have personally established with water in our lives. It has no other meaning. So it is with life. Its meaning for us lies in the relationships we have established with it. If life seems to have lost its meaning, this is to be accounted for by any combination of three possibilities: we may be nostalgic for a certainty that cannot co-exist with freedom of thought; we may, through some personal difficulty, lack significant relations with what is outside ourselves; or we may so much dislike society as it is that we can find no satisfaction in relating to it.

'But,' someone may complain, 'it all adds up to nothing unless I can see a purpose in life.' This is a much simpler problem. The purpose in life could not be clearer. We can watch the unfolding of life for millions of years and its impact is to enrich and enhance the quality of life. We cannot, of course, say that self-improvement is the *intention* of life, but it is certainly the direction in which life has continuously moved – from simplicity to complexity, from insensitivity to sensitivity, from instinct to conscious aims, from organic automaton to personality. Whether any particular individual regards evolution as a mysterious process, or as God in action, the picture it presents is the same and its 'goal' is the same – ever higher manifestations of life. Whatever our religious–philosophical standpoint, this, unquestionably, is what life is moving towards. We can all share in this movement.

The very fact that people ask persistently about the meaning of life shows that they want to feel themselves involved in something over and above their own lives and their own personal interests, however rich in satisfaction these may be. Man needs a self-transcending purpose and is only really happy when he finds one. Fullness of experience lies beyond egocentric aims. This is one reason why nobody spends much time worrying about the meaning of life when society is unified in striving for a common purpose, as in times of war. When not at war, a society hunts for its moral equivalent. It usually fails, because any particular trumpet call carries conviction only for a minority.

How, then, is the individual to find meaning – which means self-fulfilment that is also self-transcendent – in an open society in which ideas and purposes fragment into bewildering variety and in which much of living is repetitious, unsatisfying, empty?

Meaning comes from relationship, and relationship of any depth involves commitment. Without relationships and commitment man becomes a thing blown about by the chances of circumstance, tomorrow no different from yesterday, through the weeks, months, and years of living. An individual is not a thing but a person, so that to live like a thing brings accumulating frustration. Man avoids the responsibilities of relationship and commitment only by becoming sub-human and, therefore, self-frustrating – denying the deep creative aspects of the self that await actualization.

Organizations, also, can impose sub-humanity upon people by paying no regard to them as persons. The industry that treats its employees as 'hands' is of this kind. It generates so much frustration that an explosion of resentment is, all the time, only just below the surface. Modern industrial psychology is not concerned only with fitting the right individuals to the right jobs, but with seeing that all employees are treated as people in the relationships that tie in each person to the main organization. A factory, a school, a university, an office, a hospital that brings this kind of organization into being, not as a sop to the participants, but because those in authority believe in it, will create a self-social dynamic in its mode of being which draws people together within its warmth and purpose. Working in such an institution has more satisfaction for the participants, and therefore more meaning.

Some people will be content to find meaning at the level of immediate relationships. If their relationships, both their social relationships and working relationships, are happy, and they can see a modest fulfilment ahead for themselves and those they love, then life will be satisfying and significant. A grandmother whose three children are happily married and who feels welcome and able to contribute in all their homes, and who can share and enjoy life with a loved and companionable husband, is unlikely to spend much time inquiring about the meaning of life. To feel loved and wanted, and to have others to care for, is sufficient.

But some people need to extend their relatedness and sense of value beyond the immediate intimate circle of family, friends, and personal objectives. They need, also, the commitment to more extensive purposes. They want to know about, become involved in, and influence the wider concerns of mankind. They think and feel in terms of long-range aims, not all the time but part of the time, and need the assurance that their own lives contribute to the fulfilment of these aims. Membership of groups often indicates the direction of people's long-term aspirations. The active member of a church wants that church to prosper and is prepared to work and make sacrifices for it. A sociologist may join a particular organization because he is deeply concerned with the future well-being of society as well as with knowing and manipulating facts about society. The keen trade-unionist hopes that his union, and unionism as a whole, will thrive, not only that his own wage-packet may be fatter but in order that social justice shall be done. The Flower People want gentleness and humanity to replace commercial and national competitiveness. For each, the meaning of life is extended by the relationships and commitments in which they are involved.

For the first group of people – those completely satisfied with intimate relationships – the meaning in life remains intact so long as the relationships, from which the meaning comes, exist or remain secure. But supposing the grandmother mentioned just now is isolated because her children go abroad, or because she is too dominant in bearing, or because she is out of sympathy with younger people; then she will quickly be reduced to feeling that life is pointless. Isolation can rub out all significance from the experience of living.

For the second group of people, life has a meaning so long as the long-term aim keeps its validity for the individual, and so long as the individual feels he has a contribution to make to the aim. But supposing, for example, that the ardent Conservative or Labour man comes to the conclusion that those at the top are not really concerned with *his* aims at all; that they only really want his work and his vote in order that they may achieve *their* aims. Not only will his enthusiasm slump, but his sense of commitment will go, and with it an element of significance from his own life. And so for all similar situations.

This leads us into the heart of the search for meaning in contemporary times. The social fragmentation and mobility of the modern world makes it easier for people to become unrelated to their immediate society and to feel insignificant accordingly. For those who seek a wider relationship, it is no longer clear what, if anything, warrants personal commitment. People are sick to death of inflated pretensions and absurd rivalries. What is the point of making sacrifices in order that your country may be 'strong' if strength seems merely to encourage people to bully one another or blow one another up? What is the point of making sacrifices in order that one's country may be strong economically, if all that seems to offer is the right to a higher power to consume in return for a more rabid rat race than ever? People are looking for fulfilment for themselves and one another. They want an end to wasting the substance of their lives in order to fulfil someone else's expectations. They will not commit themselves to the old sad round of rivalries; they want something with the purpose and excitement of the positive about it. They want co-operation for betterment, not meaningless conflict.

How may relatedness, and commitment, and therefore meaning, be brought back into the lives of individuals who are prepared for creative involvement but cannot see anything they trust enough to commit themselves to? The answer would seem to be that we have to find deeper roots. Our primary commitment is not to the Communist party, or the Roman Catholic Church, or the Liberals, or the Quakers, or the Humanists, or the T.G.W.U. or the Confederation of British Industry, or what else we may choose, but to life and to one another. This should be the first commitment of everyone and everyone needs to work out for himself exactly what this commitment entails. After that we can sort ourselves into groups that suit us, *not in rivalry but in fellowship*.

None of us is entirely right, and none of us so far wrong that there are not large areas of common ground between us. In this age, for the first time in history, people are turning from sharpened rivalries as the sources of identification and commitment, and are looking instead for patterns of collaboration that will retain all the interest and value of different viewpoints, while drawing satisfaction not from ridiculous posturings of unique and total rightness, but from the exploration and elaboration of the common ground. They value dialogue above dispute.

There is a deadness and despair in international affairs, and in many aspects of national affairs also, because many of those in power are unaware of this changing attitude, which is spreading among ordinary people as the appropriate attitude with which to deal with life, now that we have the means to create the conditions for the good life for all – not a ready-made cake but an extension of opportunity – and need only intelligent collaboration to bring man this further step forward in his development on this planet. When shortage was *inevitable* in the world, there was a terrible logic in making sure that your nation did not go without. The guns were brought out to save the butter. Shortage is no longer inevitable. World planning of population and of food production could solve the malnutrition problem in a few decades. Co-operation can solve *any* practical problem now facing mankind.

People sense the truth of this in their bones – that rivalry is out and co-operation in. They are sickened by the futility of continuing rivalry. What fantastic nonsense it is, they feel, that the U.S.A. and the U.S.S.R. should impoverish their people to a noticeable extent by having a race for the moon when collaboration would be cheaper and safer and quicker. The achievement of a base on the moon should be scored up as a *human* achievement, not as a boost to the vanity of Washington or Moscow. Modern man will recover a sense of meaning in life only when he is convinced that co-operation in the common interest is getting the edge over competition.

This can be demonstrated on a small scale in any human

organization. If the top management of a firm is a united team, sharing common purposes and free from acute personal rivalries, this is felt throughout the entire organization. Other things being equal, morale is then very much higher than when the opposite obtains – splits, rivalries, and lack of singleness of aim at the top. A change of management, in the wrong direction, will quickly reduce a happy firm, formerly with abundant energy flowing productively, into a state of depression and irritation in which everyone is getting on everyone else's nerves. The reverse is true also.

What is true for a single institution is true for a country, or for the world. The purposes of the management should be clear and the rivalries of members of the team not too intense. In the world at large today neither condition is fulfilled. Few countries trust their own governments, let alone one another's, while the rivalries between the nations, or blocs, are acute.

People distrust this situation and find themselves hesitant to participate. In the past, governments could get away with enormities and still be regarded as having the best interests of the people at heart, because information was slow to get around and could be tailored to preserve the governmental image. Today information travels literally as fast as light and, one way or another, the skeletons are found in the cupboards and the cats let out of the bags almost as soon as they have been concealed. The princes of power have lost their clothes and nobody hesitates to announce that they look naked. This does not mean that we are held up as a world while waiting for saints to enter politics; it does mean that the façade of immaculate authority, whether governmental, academic, or ecclesiastical, has been breached, and that problems of mankind will have to be tackled and resolved in the future by co-operation and participation up and down the line, and not by arbitrary decisions from élite cadres at the top, laying down the law over the heads of their underlings. Honesty and force can be brought into politics, not only via individual politicians of integrity and energy, but also by a widespread sharing in all the difficulties that a modern state and a modern world give rise to.

This is a crucial point in generating meaning in life. There is

much in the modern commercial society and the kind of government it produces that the disillusioned intelligentsia, not to mention the rank and file of the community, react to with boredom
and disgust. This is understandable but misguided, because
among all the rubble of the past, and the confusion of the present,
the future is beginning to emerge. The brash irresponsibility and
pressure of commercialism at its worst make any sensitive person
shrink away, but there are, nevertheless, within the industrial
complex, firms and enterprises that are models of co-operative
human endeavour and happy purposeful relationships, where
profits are to the fore but not necessarily first, so that people feel
cared for and valued as people. Such firms, incidentally, are
often doing extremely well commercially because, within them,
human energies are liberated to achieve the common aim, and
nobody feels he will be discarded at the first error or thrown
aside at the first sound of economic alarm.

In government, also, the future is here in the present. Beneath
the errors that get the headlines, a lot of good law gets enacted,
and, day in day out, hosts of conscientious and dedicated people
work hours that would surprise many commuters in order to
shape such laws and put them through. To write government
off as a dishonest mess is unfair, even though there is dishonesty
and mess to be remedied.

It is also true that, if enough people care enough, the government machine can be brought to respond, not immediately, but
soon enough to catch the tide of change, in putting wrongs right
and bringing the future to birth. The new humane laws on capital
punishment, homosexuality, and abortion were brought to the
point of enactment by ordinary people showing their concern.
Governments cannot be expected to espouse legislation until
support for it has been proved. In any case, most humane issues,
like divorce reform or the abolition of blood sports, are non-
party issues – even if one party or the other shows a bias pro or
contra – and a free vote of the House is the most satisfactory way
of getting such reforms through.

We have not, therefore, been disinherited from our political
influence as much as many suppose. The monolithic might of the

modern state can be shared by ordinary people who know how to work with the great machine. For those who seek to reshape society, including reshaping government, there is, on any issue, a way forward. The first stage is to stir concern latent in the community. When interest is aroused, the organs of mass communication begin to join in with their powerful informational force – a new and important factor. Soon afterwards comes change.

For modern man, then, commitment takes a rather novel form. In earlier days those who sought to be effective joined organizations offering panaceas and battled on towards their various brands of Utopia. Today the only rewarding commitment is commitment to the future, and together we can bring a worth-while future into being, not by setting Utopia against Utopia but by sharing the common problems of our common humanity, working out what needs to be done, and using the means available to promote change in order to achieve it. The party we have to join in order to be effective is the human race. Those not prepared to join humanity in its difficulties, either at the private or the public level, are isolates or parasites, for neither of whom can life have any depth of meaning, because isolation and parasitism cripple relationship. For the rest, to join the creative struggle as one's own very self is to find meaning. The bored touchliners of the modern world fail to understand what the modern world is really like, and what the possibilities are in it for individuals who seek to promote effective change.

Social commitment with a first loyalty direct to life and its improvement, with choice of group as a second priority, also keys in with the modern trend which is inevitably narrowing the ideological distinction between party and party. Every country today is facing a situation created by its position in an increasingly interdependent world. The facts of the case are such that, if they are at all clearly apprehended, the range of choices in general policy is limited. On more and more issues a common ground of purpose is unavoidable. All political parties must have such similar aims as securing good health, good housing, good education, and economic prosperity. Methods of achieving these aims vary, but often only marginally. Parties in opposition are finding it harder to draw up alternative programmes that are markedly different from the programmes being followed by their rivals in office. In the end, all any party can claim is to do the same things better, and change emphasis and priorities somewhat, for the situation itself dictates what the aims must be.

Because we are one world facing one set of basic problems, however varied in local application, even the extremes of ideological conflict, as between the American way of life and Communism, lose their sharp distinctions. The head of a huge combine finds himself tackling very similar problems of planning and human motivation, whether the profits of the enterprise go into the national exchequer or into private pockets. And where private monopoly is in the saddle, more and more money has to be drained off by taxes into the national exchequer, because the government of a modern community must spend ever-increasing sums on national maintenance and development, whatever social philosophy it is wedded to. In this context, too, we see the new patterns taking shape. There is a situation, there are problems, and there are people whose integrity, co-operation, and creative effort can solve these problems. To take part in this is commitment and from commitment comes meaning.

The re-creation of meaning in life is the result of a person relating himself to his world at as many points and in as many ways as he needs to fulfil himself, and of finding happy associations while doing so. Every relatedness is a point of interaction and every point of interaction is an opportunity for fulfilment and satisfaction and growth. There is meaning for us in the use of our powers. Each individual will build his own pattern in his own way, but the pattern must be built one way or another if life is to be experienced as significant. The individual's task is to search out the pattern that satisfies him while being sensitively awake to the needs of others. The range of his commitment measures his range as a person. To be overcommitted is frustrating and exhausting; to be undercommitted is frustrating and boring. To be fully committed in accord with what one is – in love, in friendship, in work, in participation, in social effectiveness, in enjoyment, in ideas, in purpose, in perspective – is to get from life the fullness of its meaning as an experience and as an on-going concern.

We must now turn to two questions that the satisfactions of relatedness and commitment cannot answer; one is where it is all going – the ultimate future; the other is death. To these questions there is no answer, but there are a few points to be made all the same.

The three possible futures for man are:

(1) Self-destruction arising from his inability to turn quickly enough from competition to co-operation as the way of running the world.

(2) A continuing, if uneven, advance into an ever more penetrating understanding of nature, and man as a part of nature, with the opening up of new possibilities for human development and the enrichment of human experience.

(3) The exploitation of the resources of the world through expanding scientific know-how, and the expansion of population, until the world is raped empty and stamped bare.

Which of these futures we get depends on the decisions we and our governments make now. For those who accept their responsibilities as custodians of this planet, the second is the only possible choice, and their thinking and action should be directed to bringing it about. Our purpose must be to raise the quality of living so that every person, wherever he or she may live, is assured of the opportunity for a full life. This means that we must be wary of all quantity that threatens quality: quantity of people, quantity of towns, quantity of roads, quantity of aeroplanes. We have to decide where the margin comes between quantity and quality. If we do not, we shall rapidly get into the third of the possible futures, in which, wherever anyone goes that is worth going, he will find as much congestion and as much noise as the noise and congestion left behind. For proper growth man needs space and quiet and natural beauty and peace, not all the time, but for it to be attainable. These will be early casualties of the future if determination to achieve (2) is not made a dominant purpose for mankind.

By farming the sea, factory farming, converting open land for plough and pasture, and by other means, the present, or an increased, world population could be maintained for a time, *at a price*. Food expansion must, in any case, be achieved in order to bring the existing world population up to good standards of nutrition. But even while this is being attained, ultimate quality control must be envisaged. The grace and dignity of human life – of all life – are under threat. We have to decide whether we want to be human ants, rushed to work and back on monorails, toiling inside sound-proofed rooms to keep out the sonic bangs, fed efficiently on vitamin-fortified synthetic foods, and entertained without limit in the evenings, or whether we want to be human beings.

Assuming that the choice is (2), perhaps only come to after spending a dangerously long time blundering towards (3),what then? No one can possibly say. Man has within him untold reserves at present barely touched. A learned gathering at the Royal Society, the audience at an opera, the crowd at a students' gathering, or the group in the local are the same kind of men and women, endowed with the same kinds of personal power, as the Stone Age peoples with skins for clothing, flint implements for tools, and caves for homes. The difference lies in the difference in opportunity. Take another stride into the future, as great as the stride from then to now, take another stride as great, and ten more still, and where shall we be? It is quite impossible to predict. in man's incredible brain with its twelve million cells there is ample margin for development. We have to take on trust the unknown future which man will enter as the years pass, and enter only to leave again on further explorations of the possible. Our task is to be sure that we do nothing now to damage the future for our descendants. We hope that they may look back on us as people who helped to prepare for their lives, not as short-sighted, selfish squanderers of the human inheritance.

Finally, we cannot leave the subject of meaning in life without considering death. Man, it has been said, is the only animal that knows it must die. This is, of course, true, and not really remark-able. Once man developed intelligence and imagination he was in a position when the fact of his own inevitable death became clear to him. This is a factor in being self-conscious at all. Man reacts to this knowledge in various ways. Some people believe in personal continuance after death. Some accept this life as the total of human experience and seek to make the most of it by searching for personal fulfilment. Others, again, take the view that, if there is no immortality there is no use in bothering, and see the logic of life as having as good a time as they can, regardless of others.

In the practice of living, there is little difference between the first and second views. If immortality were an established fact, the best way to spend temporal life would be as much in an effort of self-discovery and fulfilment as if this life were regarded as all there is. The third view is just erroneous – the aim to 'have a good time for myself' as a first priority is too self-centred to lead to a fruitful and satisfying outcome because individuals cannot live happily of themselves but only in co-operative relationships with others. As Wordsworth said: 'The man whose eye is ever on himself doth look on one, the least of nature's works.' By this he meant that the excessively self-centred person shrivels up in his own egocentricity. Which is, as we have seen earlier, a fact of life which cannot be ignored without self-destruction.

In the face of death, whether we are Christians or not, we are left with an act of faith: for the Christians, their faith in immortality; for the Humanists, their faith that the enhancement of life in individual and society is a value worth striving for in itself. Both have to accept the fact that but for the cycle of life and death, through which evolutionary advance is possible, the human species would never have emerged at all. Is it not also true that we live with more passion because we know we must die?

And in life, the meaning comes in living, as wholly as we can, as abundantly as we can, as bravely as we can, here and now, sharing the experience with others, caring for others as we care for ourselves, and accepting our responsibility for leaving the world better than we found it. There is meaning enough in this to last a lifetime. The old man who enjoys the open air while planting a tree for his great-grandchildren to play under goes to bed content, and rounds off his good day with quiet sleep.

Part Four

PROSPECTIVE

14

MORAL EDUCATION

The continuity of a culture – which, as we have seen, is always based on a moral order – depends upon the values and knowledge of one generation being passed on to the next. Among animals the 'culture' of behaviour survives because almost all of it is built into genetical inheritance. In simple self-perpetuating cultures – the social milieu of man for most of his existence as a species – the values and knowledge of the parents were transferred to the children by interlocking systems of education and inculcation described earlier. The whole weight of the culture made an integrated impact upon the coming generation, the members of which imbibed the traditional values and knowledge without any sense of compulsion or violation, rather as we accept without question the eating rituals of our community – cooking techniques, three meals a day, knives, spoons, and forks, and so forth.

The new situation facing us is that we are now culturally fragmented – in outlook, ideas, beliefs, attitudes, behaviour, dress – and yet must succeed in transmitting, along with knowledge, the values upon which our society depends if it is not to cease to be itself and either move sharply towards autocracy – always a grave risk for any democracy – or slump into a structure-less chaos in which important values may be eroded away without their gradual disappearance being observed. Along with social values, we have to foster those values upon which self-development and self-fulfilment depend. As we saw in Chapter Four, the values of self and social growth complement one another in a democracy. But we must succeed in handing them on to each new generation if democratic society is to flourish and grow.

The exciting thing about the open, exploratory present is that, although it could degenerate into cultural chaos, it can equally well be the ground of a new freedom, a hitherto unattained emancipation of the human spirit, burgeoning from the encouragement of individual and group creativity. As we have seen, for most of history most individuals have been forced to accept their society and to conform; nowadays the pressure of innovation breaks up the structure and opens a way for both nonconformity and creative self-determination. Commercial interests accelerate the process by cashing in on innovation, but they do not themselves, as a rule, inaugurate the originality that produces the change. They have not created modern man's taste for change; they have only exploited it. In Communist countries, as well as in capitalist ones, the pull of the new is powerful.

We are now, inescapably, living in an innovating world, in which an increasing number of people enjoy change instead of fearing and resisting it. An aspect of this open, exploratory world is that it stimulates attack on established ideas and those who represent them because tradition is shaken by *any* change. Thus the age of change makes for the civilization of challenge, until, in the last analysis, those who govern and manage in such a world have to do so through the consent of those they govern *or else dominate them by force*. This is why, in our age, expanding democracy and dominant autocracy are, all the time, so close to one another, and why the one may, at any time, quickly become the other. Fuller democracy is the way forward and autocracy is the regressive alternative.

The struggle for emergence of a new and more democratic

social order, thrusting its way through tradition and habit, inevitably leads to profound changes in education. We can see them around us – changes in all education, of which moral education is one aspect.

The fundamental difference is that we can no longer sell to generation after generation of children and teachers a fixed educational structure and content. Education ceases, on all fronts, to be inculcation, and instead becomes discovery – a personal experience for each child. Hence the revolution now overtaking subject after subject in the curriculum. Education used to be a two-factor process: the teacher who knew and taught, and the child who did not know and learnt. Today it is a dynamic multi-factor process: the information and discipline of subject-matter, the world in which the subject-matter and discipline are seen to be relevant, the teacher as guide and mediator, and the exploring child motivated by his curiosity and his drives for growth and fulfilment.

As with any good system, the new educational system is self-correcting. Subject-matter not relevant to experience and action in the modern world, or irrelevant to the interests of the children, tends to fall out of the curriculum; subject-matter, thought to be essential, but which has lost its appeal, is re-examined to see how its level of motivation can be heightened. The goal of it all is the mature individual capable of dealing with the situations of life: personal, interpersonal, and practical.

Moral education – the education through which essential personal and social values are discovered – has to take all these factors into account. It is, accordingly, due for change as far-reaching as that which is taking place in mathematics, science, languages, and other subjects. The idea that moral education can be assured by parcelling up all desirable values with the surviving tenets of Christian belief is educationally unreliable. Moral education, like any other kind of education, is to be attained by the encouragement of curiosity, questioning, and exploration, not by the imposition of selected ideas. Of course, all schooling involves selection, but good schooling requires the selection of material that will encourage thought, not unquestioning acceptance.

Education, including moral education, may be described as a process of guided personal development. The infant clashing his toy cymbals or tinkling his miniature xylophone on the sitting-room floor will one day, if given the right encouragement, stimulation, and opportunities, attain his full musical stature, whatever that may be – at most a composer; at least someone who knows how to enjoy music. The young child in the infant school playing with materials – sorting, weighing, measuring, matching – is embarking upon the road that, so long as his confidence and interest are sustained, will enable him, in course of time, to partici-pate to the limit of his potentialities in that area of social behaviour we call mathematics. (Adults who wince at the mere sight of a graph or a formula are unlikely to lack endowment for mathem-atics; it is much more likely that their capacity has been blocked and ruined somewhere along the line by authoritarian instruction.)

The relationship between potentiality and exploration in the learning process is particularly well shown in what has happened to school art during the last half-century. Formerly children, if taught art at all, were set to copy models and practise perspective in a way that petrified their potentialities. Over the years, art teaching has been transformed. Instead of having irksome tasks imposed upon him, the child today is encouraged to explore his own powers by using the materials made available to him. By this means he finds out what his powers are, constantly challenges himself to overcome difficulties, and, at the same time, *he discovers the discipline of the medium*. The astounding results of this revolu-tion in art teaching can be seen at any exhibition of children's painting.

Moral education is basically no different from any other form of education. At the start we have the baby – a bundle of energies and potentialities. By the time the child has attained adulthood we hope he will have developed mature moral powers. Whether he does or does not depends on what kind of opportunities and guidance for his moral growth we provide in between. Tradi-tional moral teaching was – and is – authoritarian, imposed, unrelated to personal development. Many of those subjected to such teaching become blocked, resentful, and antagonistic to the whole thing. So we find a good deal of moral illiteracy in society just as we find a good deal of mathematical illiteracy, and for the same reasons – bad education.

To study significant records of struggle and search, as in the Bible, and learn about patterns of belief, like Christianity or Buddhism, are parts of the *content* of moral education; they can no longer be regarded as the *means* to it. Education by inculcation is now a thing of the past on all fronts.

That said, we are still left with a considerable difficulty. Culture *does* depend on sustaining specific knowledge, values and attitudes within society. How, then, are we to assure their continuance in an open, pluralist society if we do not deliberately inculcate them? For a start, we have to accept that an efficient machinery of inculcation is no longer available to us. Inculcation works only if home, school, and society all speak with the same voice. They don't; never again will they echo one another as they did in former times. As recently as the beginning of this century the voices of authority within the community – fathers, schoolmasters, clergymen, doctors – spoke almost in unison on almost any question of behaviour. Today there is a variety that may be experienced as confusion both by the growing child and by his parents. As Dr W. D. Wall says in *The Adolescent Child*: 'The family group may show as many shades of belief and unbelief as there are members; outside, dozens of sects are clamant that theirs is the right and the only way. Politics, ideals, tastes, interests, ambitions, manners, morals – all these and a hundred other most important departments of mental and emotional life offer tangled avenues among which, with more or less conflict, a choice must be made.' Of recent years, the television set, from which almost any idea can come at almost any time, is an additional resident in most homes. At such a time in human history, any attempt to present any set of ideas as totally right, sacrosanct, the source of all virtue, and the answer to all moral problems, cannot be effective. What, then, can?

The task is not as difficult as it may appear, although moral education is by nature complex – a point clearly demonstrated by Wilson, Williams, and Sugarman in their preliminary volume from the Farmington Trust Research Unit, *Introduction to Moral Education*. Once we stop regarding moral education as the passing on of a once-for-all divine revelation about right and wrong, and instead regard it as the transmission of demonstrable principles about living and living together, we need no longer be anxious that essential values will be lost, provided that their preservation is properly attended to by our schools. To embark upon teaching children the principles of swimming, one has only to set about teaching them to swim. The same applies to the principles of life. As soon as we direct education to the aim of teaching children how to live, we shall assure them the opportunity of discovering the right values and attitudes for living. If the values we seek to hand on are valid – as valid, say, as the laws of gravity – then they will be discovered in the real-life experiences to which we introduce the children, and in the discussion of curriculum topics, social problems, and personal problems which should be a part of their exploration of reality. The teacher's task in moral education, as in all education, is to sharpen insight and promote understanding about what, in fact, *is*.

Moral education thus becomes, not a subject, but one facet of the total experience which a good school provides. It may be compared with another educational essential – developing the capacity to think – with which, indeed, it has much in common. A good school seeks to promote clear thinking in every subject and through many activities, such as discussion, taking part in planning school events, and so forth. It may set aside special periods when the development of clear thinking is the specific aim of the allotted time, but it will not depend on these periods to achieve the educational aim; the special periods will serve to supplement and co-ordinate, but will not be expected to do the whole job by themselves. The vital ability to think in an open, changing society is the outcome of total education, not of spasmodic injections of a 'subject'; moral education is much the same.

Moral education, of course, begins at birth, and the role of the home, both in the pre-school period and during the school years, is of immense importance. Here, however, we shall especially

consider moral education in school life, partly because the developmental principles of the early years have already been discussed in
outline, and partly because, in an open, pluralist society, the responsibility for the transmission of the culture and its values largely
devolves upon the schools.

How may the transmission of moral values be facilitated?
For a start, values are caught not taught; although teaching may
assist clarification, values that are received only intellectually and
not reinforced by experience are unlikely to make a lasting
impression. Hence the ethos of the school is of fundamental
importance in moral education. Since teachers will reflect the
pluralism of society, it is imperative that they should together
arrive at common ground about the moral order they wish the
school to promote. Children need the assurance of a consistent
moral climate, which is not the same as a consistent pattern of
belief. They also need the example of their teachers conducting
their affairs and relationships on common, recognizable principles. A common ethos cannot any longer be taken for granted,
but has to be arrived at by staff discussions at which all teachers
can put their own point of view, and the common ground be
gradually discovered.

Second only to the common ethos comes the social structure of
the school. Social isolation inhibits moral growth. A school, then,
should be a warm, friendly community in which every child has
a place, feeling wanted as a person and valued for the contribution
he has to make. The social unit should be a quite small group of
children who work together, help one another, and undertake
simple responsibilities. This kind of social milieu has existed for
a long time in most infant schools, has been spreading rapidly in
junior schools, and is beginning to appear in secondary schools.
It seems likely that all schools before very long will be organized
socially so that they provide for every child a snug base in a small
group, and also experience of other groups, varying in size according to the activity taking place. Such organization makes a big
contribution to moral education because it brings every child into
participation, shared responsibility, and a sense of personal value.
Among the outcomes of such social experience are self-confidence

and self-respect without which personal and moral development are seriously checked. A. H. Maslow, for one, in *Motivation and Personality*, believes that a child's self-respect must be impaired if he has failed to acquire warm and dependable social relationships.

The development of a sense of responsibility, which is one outcome of a good social structure, is obviously an extremely important element in moral education, and one which has been, as yet, inadequately investigated. Responsibility itself has many aspects: responsibility for one's own actions and for one another; responsibility for the well-being of the community of which the individual is a member, and responsibility for relationships between the community and the wider world, including responsibility for a personal contribution beyond one's own community.

Responsibility is learnt through having it, and being clear about what is involved. It is, in fact, the product of the kind of experience that educates this particular relationship. Irresponsibility among teenagers and young adults is not evidence that they are incapable of holding responsibility, but that they have not been given sufficient opportunity to do so. Such insufficiency is double-edged because there is a correlation between the curtailment of responsibility and anti-social aggression: it is deeply frustrating to be denied responsibility – and the dignity that goes with it – after the capacity to handle responsibility has been attained. Experimenting with ways of taking this into account, the headmaster of a London secondary school solved his last-year problem of apathy, aggressiveness, and irresponsibility by giving all his senior pupils the option of becoming 'freemen' of the school, which involved both extra privileges and extra responsibilities.

Study of the capacity for responsibility of adolescents – as, for example, among the rural Xhosa, already described (see page 129) – suggests that we are giving far too little personal responsibility to our young males. Indeed, it seems likely that the restlessness and violence among our young males is, in part, the explosion following excessive tutelage. Student hooliganism – as distinct from legitimate student protest – may spring from this source. Just as some previously over-protected girls go wild in their first year at college as a result of finding themselves free to associate with young men, so may young men, who have been too long denied real responsibility, bubble over into excessive demonstrations against authority once they find a way open to doing so.

It is pertinent that, in an area of Africa where student unrest led to the temporary closure of all teacher training colleges except one, the exception is notable for being carefully designed socially to spread responsibility among all the students. The college is organized in groups of twelve, each one the responsibility of a student 'chief' and his assistant. The students meet in groups and the group leaders hold council meetings to consider complaints and problems as they arise. Each student thus comes to feel responsible for himself and his group and the college community as a whole. At the time of the unrest, this system of intercommunication and shared responsibility enabled the students, with the support of the principal, to make use of the tensions of the time to clarify their own ideas and attitudes without provoking disruption of the community.

The handling of responsibility goes much farther than the sharing of authority. It means that the individual can bring what he is – his ideas, his feelings, his unique self – to the task of considering, planning, and deciding. Young people often feel that their vision of life is scorned and disregarded by those in authority. Responsibility permits them to have their say and make their impact within a socially significant context. They no longer feel gagged and bound by a machinery that seems to have been designed to discount their views. Through participating within a context of responsibility, they develop judgement.

Every school should offer a network of responsibility that draws in every child: systems of helping one another, family groupings, class group organization, tutor groups, house groups, team teaching, discussion, open-plan organization, co-operative projects, student councils, and so forth. A child needs to know what responsibility is in terms of personal experience well before he leaves school. He needs this every bit as much as he needs to know how to read, calculate, be creative, understand his environment, work hard and rewardingly, get along with others, appreciate quality and achievement. To accept responsibility for others as well as for oneself is the prime condition of human fulfilment. Well-planned education for responsibility is already in existence in a number of schools. But whether or not a particular child has the experience at school of responsible involvement of this kind is still a matter of chance. In some areas, his chance will be high; in others, rather poor. An efficient system of moral education requires that such experience shall be as definitely assured for every child, as is, say, physical education at present.

The third strand in a good moral education is the clarification of moral insight to which all subjects can, and should, make a contribution. These informational and emotive aspects of moral education fall under three headings: (a) content that gives an orientation on life and the universe from which the individual can draw a sense of significance and dignity; (b) morally relevant information and ideas derived from the traditional content of the curriculum; and (c) direct consideration of man's religious and moral striving. All three areas should, of course, be approached in an exploratory way, with ample opportunity for questions and discussion.

The importance of orientation for moral education has only recently been grasped. We now realize that to feel lost and unrelated is an alienating, demoralizing, disintegrating experience. Simpler societies had the edge on us here because every individual knew his place within the social order, itself set in a cosmological framework which made sense to people, even if founded on mythology rather than fact. As the original social and ideological framework crumbles, so does it become harder and harder for people to retain a feeling of relatedness and value. But an answer is not to be found in seeking to repair the broken structure; the solution is to reinterpret cosmology and society in terms of expanding knowledge and changed circumstances.

What is the picture we should be offering our children? First the wonder of the infinitely dynamic universe, with its millions of galaxies, and millions of stars within each galaxy, linked to all the exciting explorations of modern astronomy.

Then, the place of our world in this immensity, not as an inconsequential speck in the ocean of space but as of very great significance, because on our earth – no doubt along with other planets attached to other stars – life exists. Then, the story of the evolution of life on this planet, man's recent appearance and struggles, his impressive achievements in learning to control his environment, and now his first tentative adventures beyond the protective sphere of the earth's atmosphere. Finally, man's responsibilities as the custodian of life on this planet, whose future is now in his hands. Children are heartened and enthralled by such a picture. It is contemporary, relevant, indubitable, adventurous, challenging.

Next comes understanding of human life and affairs on this planet with especial reference to the child's own society. This social orientation involves recent history, current struggles, the way society operates, the responsibility of one's own country in world affairs. In its suggestions for courses to help prepare for raising the school-leaving age, the Scottish Department of Education states, in a section on 'Social and Moral Education': 'Before leaving school every pupil should have acquired, within the compass of his ability, a general understanding and appreciation of modern society and should know something of the influences which have created it. He should have some idea of how the state and the local community are organized and run, have a general knowledge of international affairs, and be aware of present-day problems and opportunities.' Social orientation – essential to a sense of belonging and personal involvement and commitment – is an uncertain provision of our schools. Some schools make a first-class job of it, but whether a particular child receives a sound social orientation is, as things are now arranged, a matter of chance. But to give a child a social framework within which to understand his own life is a top educational priority for personal and moral development.

Writing of the educated man in *The Concept of Education*, P. S. Peters states: 'His knowledge and understanding must not be inert either in the sense that they make no difference to his general view of the world, his actions within it and reactions to it *or* in the sense that they involve no concern for the standards immanent in forms of thought and awareness, as well as the ability to attain them.' The context for education is the civilization in which it takes place. The context must be presented as clearly and carefully as are areas of knowledge and skill. We have to till the deserts that lie between, and around, the conventional subjects. Individuals are lost without a valid concept of the whole.

Schools may accept the need to provide orientation on the universe, the world, and society, but complain that they lack the staff to put such orientation across in an informed and interesting way. This may well be so. If it is, then Schools Television should take on the responsibility of supplying co-ordinated orientation courses that *all* secondary schools could use. One way or another it has to be done in order to provide children with a common corpus of information and understanding, clarified by their own questions and discussion. It is vain to hope to build a morally mature nation without providing a factual common ground of understanding that can put individual life in a significant perspective. Moral order is part of a common culture, and a common culture, in a pluralist society, derives from knowledge and experience in which all have shared.

The ordinary school subjects are rich with possibilities for developing and deepening moral insight and feeling. Through English literature children can be given greater understanding of themselves and others, and be confronted, in their imagination, with a variety of moral situations. Literature is about people and their relationships, their feelings, their attitudes, their behaviour, and the consequences of their behaviour – the very stuff of morality. Literature ranges over feeling from love to hate, from lyrical delight to darkest foreboding. In all moods it can stir wonder, excitement, and curiosity about the human condition. It can develop the important qualities of sympathy and compassion.

At the other extreme, mathematics need not be taught only as hard fact and rigid process. It, too, has its moral component, and not only as reverence for a particular kind of truth. The history of mathematics is the story of how man has struggled to find ways of ordering and understanding the universe. The infant can experience this at his level, just as the higher mathematician can experience it at his. The wonder of discovery, the satisfaction of control through discovery, the difficulties of manipulating symbols and processes, and the discipline of precision are equally present for both. In the secondary school, the pupils can be encouraged to study not only mathematical facts, but the social and moral issues arising from statistics, insurance, gambling, and so forth.

History and geography are about the behaviour and habitat of people. Unless reduced to stagnant facts by the academic strait-jacket, they bring children naturally into the arena of human and moral concern: the right use of power, the rule of law, the nature of tyranny, the struggle for freedom, the development of resources, wonder at achievement and courage, compassion for failure and weakness, the dark of despair, the upsurge of hope, and scores of other vital human issues. The arts, in their turn, develop sensitivity, a *sine qua non* of the moral life; any experience which enriches and deepens the inner world of childhood and adolescence enhances personal growth and, therefore, moral growth. All subject areas offer examples of noble lives with which children may identify their aspirations for themselves and nourish their idealism. Children long to be worthy of admiration and need the reassurance that human beings, in spite of frailties and incompleteness, can attain greatness.

The moral aspects of science warrant especial attention because we live in a scientific age. Science offers a continuous story of unremitting courage, effort, and achievement in the struggle against ignorance; it is full of wonder and excitement, whether we look at it in terms of the scientist as a person, the nature of his work, or the social consequences of his discoveries. And with every new discovery comes the moral issue of how it should be used – a question which takes us ever deeper into the qualitative assessment of what matters most.

Furthermore, the world of the scientists – magnificently co-operative, magnificently international in spirit – brings out vividly the values and relationships upon which all human creativity depends: the dedication, the struggle, the humble search for the facts, the leap of inspiration that brings new light and order to where before was darkness and confusion. Between scientist and scientist the only possible relationship is that of mutual integrity and respect. In *Science and Human Values*, Professor J. Bronowski sums it up: 'The society of scientists must be a democracy. . . . Science confronts the work of one man with that of another, and grafts each on each; and it cannot survive without justice and honour and respect between man and man. Only by these means can science pursue its steadfast object, to explore truth. If these values did not exist, then the society of scientists would have to invent them to make the practice of science possible.' The milieu of the scientist is not mechanistic or materialistic; it is personal. The fantastic success of science confirms in a new way the productiveness of human values.

In addition, the curriculum should include time for specific study of man's moral and religious striving. Children, as Piaget has shown, are not sufficiently mature for this before adolescence, but, thereafter, they are themselves deeply concerned about what is right and wrong behaviour in the conduct of their own lives and are capable of discussing situational problems, including their own and one another's, with sensitivity and insight. This provides an opportunity to deal with religious attitudes and beliefs, with the insights of the great moral teachers, with the elementary psychology of human nature – motivation, relationships, behaviour – plus a little sociology and some comparative anthropology. The precise form such specific moral education takes should be sensitive to the particular concerns, interests, and capacities of the young people themselves. No adolescent was ever improved morally by being bored.

Sex education is an important aspect of specific moral education, not because it is to be regarded as something especially charged with the risk of evil-doing, as in the days of prudish morality, but because young people want to know how to deal well with their own sexuality and how best to conduct their relationships with the other sex. Much of sex education can, and should, come in through other subjects: English, history, art, biology, health education, homecraft. But experience has shown that gaps will be left, curiosity remain unsatisfied, and, often, ignorance stay uncorrected if young people are not given definite opportunities to learn and question about sex, in its physical, emotional, and social aspects. Schools that lack the resources to deal effectively with this important aspect of personal and moral development can supplement what they are able to offer internally by drawing in personnel from outside who have been trained to talk to adolescents about sex, and to discuss their doubts and uncertainties with them.

It should be noted that schools that fail to provide adolescents with the information and guidance they need in the conduct of their relationships with the other sex are, in effect, rejecting the adolescents themselves, and that this will be picked up by the adolescents as a rejection, so that their relationships with the school will be impaired in consequence. One cannot undervalue the central reality of the adolescents' lives – the attainment of physical maturity – and expect, at the same time, to retain their trust. Without trust, no efforts at moral education can count for anything.

The attitude to work which arises from experience at school is also of great moral consequence. A person's work is his contribution to the community; he needs to respect his work in order to respect himself, and the quality of his work will reflect how he values his contribution. The task of education is to motivate every child to do his best and to develop a self-critical attitude to personal attainment so that the child strives to improve on his previous performance. Too much failure and too much interpersonal competition quickly undermine a child's morale. Every child needs to feel that what he *can* do will be appreciated and to know that he will be accorded success in proportion to his effort. This keeps him striving courageously. Anything less will undermine his self-confidence and teach him to hate work because it is a source of constantly lost prestige. Children bored or belittled by their school work do not learn what is before them, but they *do* learn habits of indifference and bad application. The habit of slovenly, indifferent work, often charged against some unskilled and semi-skilled adult workers, may well have been picked up at school.

Sometimes a particular school in an area gets such a high reputation for the kind of young workers it produces – although the school is not apparently favoured with especial advantages of intake, staff, or buildings – that all the local employers are eager to get recruits from it. What makes the difference appears to be the self-confidence and personal reliability that the school fosters. The adolescents leaving such schools are not only better workers but happier and more fulfilled young people. The management and methods of such schools justify careful study, since their influence on the personal and moral development of their pupils is exceptional.

Another important moral influence is the internal pastoral care provided by the school. This may be well-meaning but haphazard, or it may take the form of a network of care which ensures that any child in difficulties is quickly noticed and given help, and that a child who is stressed or anxious has someone he trusts to whom he can turn. Such carefully organized pastoral care has a dual role: it quickly rescues children who, if left unhelped too long, may develop obstinate habits that alienate them from the community and pave the way for serious moral breakdown; and it maintains in the school a climate of care which constantly exemplifies the principles of consideration and concern that every good school seeks to engender in its members. Staff conferences to discuss children in difficulties, tutorial and house systems, teacher counsellors, close relations with the school psychological and other services, and with the parents, and the discussion of personal problems in small groups of pupils, with a sympathetic adult in charge, are all part of such a network of care. This will be organized differently in different schools, but needs to be efficiently operating in every school. We have already noted that social isolation, alienation, low attainment, maladjustment and delinquency tend to be found together. We have to treat this syndrome at source – before tendency hardens into habit – in order to raise the standard of moral health in the community as a whole.

At the start of this chapter it was pointed out that the preservation of our culture depends on the effective transfer, from generation to generation, of a basis for common culture. A co-ordinated system of moral education, as outlined above, assures this at the same time as reaching out to every child and assisting him to attain the moral insight he needs in order to deal constructively and sensitively with the decisions of life in an open society. A co-ordinated system assures that each child discovers and learns to apply the personal, interpersonal and social values upon which a democratic society depends; it offers a common background of understanding about society; it provides a common perspective about the place and responsibilities of man in the universe; and it fosters a sense of wonder about the nature of things, of hope for the future, and of admiration and veneration for the noblest and best.

These many aspects need to be drawn to a focus in some way. It is here that the school assembly – or assemblies, if the school is large – can have a powerful consolidating influence. The role of the assembly is to unify in an act of shared social self-consciousness all that the school stands for. Its purpose is to celebrate human aspiration. Its themes are love, compassion, wonder, joy, sorrow, mystery, effort, courage, achievement, hope, responsibility. Its data is human greatness, the commemoration of great lives and great events, including the lives of great religious teachers and great humanitarians; poetry, prose, ideas, and music that speak to the heart of man; inspiring incidents and attainments of the past and present, and news of what the school is achieving and what it seeks to achieve. The assembly should be attractive, positive, and uplifting, with something for every age-group present. Any haranguing that has to be done should be done at some other time. The wealth of material is so vast that it is plainly possible to produce hundreds of different ceremonies without repetition. The assembly should be a daily act of renewal of man's faith in man and the school's conviction of its own purpose.

In this chapter, the ramifications of moral education have only been touched on, and some important aspects – for example, the different approaches appropriate at different ages – have been almost entirely neglected. But perhaps enough has been said to map out the prospect of what has still to be explored and developed. And perhaps enough has also been said to show the great personal and social gain which is attainable by putting into effect what we are beginning to understand are the essentials of personal and moral education in knowledge, skill, understanding, insight, feeling, attitudes, and experience. If our present knowledge about personal and moral development were really acted upon, we might well raise the level of personal life and social responsibility in this country as successfully as we have already raised standards of physical health. Acute physical malnutrition is now rare; it is malnutrition of personality that is still much too common. In the years immediately ahead, education's prime task is to remedy this.

15

SEX TOMORROW

ONE of the problems about writing on moral values in contemporary society is that the past and the future are part of the present. The same ideas can easily be judged by one group to be dangerous innovation and be dismissed by another as old hat. The contrasting viewpoints may both exist within the same street, and often do.

This applies particularly to sex. No ideas within western society have changed with more dramatic speed in the past half-century than those about sex, carrying some people with them and leaving others far behind. To get a perspective on what is happening and so glimpse the prospect of the future we have to search for significant trends that differentiate the present from the past and indicate what the moral order for human sexuality is evolving into. This is important for individual morality on two counts: it sets the pattern for sexual behaviour, and it affects the climate of the home, upon which the moral development of the next generation largely depends.

Let us begin by noting some of the more obvious changes in the attitude to human sexuality that have occurred over the past fifty years or so:

There has been a decline in prudery. Most of us are now pre-
    pared to expose ourselves to sun or sea, when opportunity
    offers, almost naked and quite unashamed.
We now accept our bodies as a fully legitimate source of
    pleasure.
Sexual fulfilment is now regarded, not as a suspect indulgence,
    but as a well-spring of happiness and mental health.
It is now recognized that creative energy is not necessarily the
    product of sublimated sexuality; it is at least as likely to be
    the outcome of a happy sexual relationship.
Woman today has a more important place in society, and is
    more highly valued as a person.
The capacity for sexual passion is now regarded as wholly
    desirable in both sexes.
Birth control is now accepted by all but a minority and is
    discussed without embarrassment.
A cruel, intolerant attitude to divorce has given way to
    compassion. Divorce is a hazard of life; not a sin.
The vindictive attitude to homosexuality and abortion has been
    replaced by humanitarian understanding.

All these changes are clearly gains. Sex in society is in a much
healthier state than when doctors, priests, schoolmasters, and
fathers thought it their duty to terrify adolescents with lies about
the effects of masturbation.

Of course, new attitudes have brought their own problems.
For one thing, the pioneers of emancipation created a new set of
anxieties by presenting sexual fulfilment as easily available through
the mastery of the techniques of love they propounded. This
error has been perpetuated in a number of how-to-make-love
books, which suggest that a highly psychological relationship is
primarily subject to physical skill. To point that out as an over-
simplification is not to minimize the importance of know-how.

These same books also assume that a perpetual high virility is
to be expected in the male and that a woman, unless she is frigid,
will normally experience simultaneous orgasm, provided that
her lover has the necessary acumen. Trying to live up to these

over-stated expectations, men have sometimes come unnecessarily to doubt their manhood and women their capacity for love.

Another disadvantage of emancipation is the commercialization of sex, which the decline in prudery has made possible. This has tended to diminish human love into a kind of press-button sexuality, actuated by the right perfume, soap, and clothes. Again, the transition in attitudes towards sex has itself left many people confused in ideas, or behaviour, or both. None the less, these problems of emancipation, seen against the squalor of traditional sex values, are nothing more than subsidiary growing pains in a movement within society towards healthier sexual attitudes.

The rapid mellowing of attitudes to sex is not due to an expansion of licence, as the old-style moralists seem to suppose, but to the fact that the *situation* has changed. Every human situation gives rise to its own inherent principles of being – the controls and limits that regulate the potential of the situation. When the situation changes, so do the limits. The decline in prudery, the growth in understanding of sex as a desirable and potentially formative influence, the enhancement of women's status, the efficiency and availability of modern contraceptive techniques, and the increased respect for the individual's right to strive for personal fulfilment together create a quite new situation for human sexuality. Limits and controls must inevitably change to meet the logic of the new situation. The task of the present and the future is to redefine principles so that human sexuality will be free not only from outworn inhibitions but also from the chaos that must result if the old rules are dropped and no new principles of control are accepted in their place. An extension of sexual freedom involves an extension of sexual responsibility. The most liberal societies sexually – those of the South Sea islands for example – nevertheless have their underlying order of accepted relationships, values, and good manners. What ought the sexual order of our society to be, now that the taboos have gone? It can be based only on the realities of human sexuality and the values and responsibilities inherent in them.

Sex in a modern democracy, in fact, is to be controlled not by inhibitory edicts from above but by the principles of its own full fruition, discussed, understood, and accepted by each generation in turn. These principles need careful consideration.

As we saw in Chapter Eight, the sexual component of human personality has now to be regarded as an integral part of the whole, needing its own appropriate expression and means of growth at every stage of life, reaching in due course the relationship of mature, passionate love. Such consummation is natural, wholesome, fulfilling. Anthony Storr writes: 'The full development of personality can only take place in a setting of adult loving and being loved.'

We are, each one of us, emerging personalities, in process of growth. We need one another in order to grow, and need a relatedness of depth and significance in order to discover ourselves and actualize ourselves. Some may find the fulfilling relationship in commitment to an ostensibly impersonal aim, but even here there is at least a symbolic union. We talk of a dedicated man as being 'married to his work' and a nun as a 'bride of Christ'. But for the majority of people, including a majority of dedicated people, a deep involvement with others is a condition of fulfilment, and the supreme involvement is the intense relationship of one with one, two people who love one another and bring one another out as they do so.

Of course, individuals vary sexually, as they vary in everything else – which is yet another reason why inflexible rule-of-thumb is an inappropriate way of dealing with something as personal as sex. Some people are more virile than others by nature; some are more passionate than others; some are clearly defined male or female personalities; others hover rather indefinitely around the mid-line of the sex continuum. In human sexuality, as in everything else, nature is prolific with variations. To these inherited differences must be added all the modifications arising primarily from experience: the relaxation or the tension; the freedom or the inhibition; delight in feeling or fear of it; warmth or coldness; and the neurotic distortions of relationship, such as using sex as a thing with which to bolster self-esteem, or as a means of dominating others.

Sex difference must also be taken into account – the built-in elements which have still to be decisively sorted out from cultural influences, but which definitely may be observed from early infancy in monkeys and so, presumably, exist in human children also. Margaret and Harry Harlow reported, thus, on their study of rhesus monkeys:

'The male infant monkeys tend to be rough and aggressive; they threaten other male monkeys and they threaten female monkeys. The female infant monkeys seldom threaten males; they are passive and they retreat from male monkeys – but they never retreat too far. They reserve their threats for female monkeys. Male monkey infants like to play roughly, and female monkeys like to play gently. Older female juveniles are fascinated by baby monkeys long before they can become mothers in their own right. But male juveniles of equivalent age are totally indifferent to baby monkeys.'

Marked differences continue right through primate life as they do also in human life.

Amidst all this variation, there is the unifying factor of the universal search for sexual fulfilment, however it happens to be patterned and experienced in the individual. This exploration is likely to lead, sooner or later, to commitment. As Desmond Morris has pointed out, even the Don Juans who seek to play the love game lightly throughout their lives are liable to find themselves caught up in this enduring unity – the human equivalent of what the ethologists call the pairbond.

Personal sexual fulfilment is attainable only through the implementation of certain principles. One is that it is not possible, in sexual relationships, to be both casual and deep. This is the reason why human sex, if it is to be fully satisfying, has to be something more than the inconsequential enjoyment of individual sexual impulse. Herein lies the frustration of the Cassanovas and the nymphomaniacs. Such people behave as though sexual satisfaction lies in quantity of experience whereas it really lies in quality of experience.

For similar reasons, dishonesty in sex can lead only to incomplete experience. Seduction based on lies and directed to

using the other as an object in the egocentric satisfaction of
physical desire may bring a sense of personal triumph, and the
physical pleasures of the tumescence/detumescence cycle; it
cannot create the reciprocity of person with person which is the
deepest satisfaction of human sexuality and its source of variety
and self-rejuvenation. Personal integrity in human sexuality is
as much a condition of its full flowering as is physical excitement.

The chief interpersonal values governing human sexual fulfilment have already been considered, in Chapter Eight. They are
the same as those governing any other constructive human
relationship – basically, mutual respect, sensitivity and consideration for one another. The escape from egocentricity is as central
to sexual fulfilment as to fulfilment in life as a whole.

Chastity, in its old sense of sexual deprivation, can no longer,
of course, be regarded as an essential value. Whether sexual
development in the adult is experienced over time with one
partner, or more than one, is a matter of circumstances and
individual choice. There is more than one road to sexual fulfilment. Whatever road is followed, there will be pain and suffering
as well as joy and fulfilment. A hopeful love may fade and one
or other partner will be hurt. A one-sided love may be totally
unrequited. But when sex is humanized with human values, all
that happens can be a source of growth, deepening and enriching
the personality, opening the way for greater understanding and
greater fulfilment. Marriage, divorce, and remarriage may be the
road for some. But the future will probably regard the ideal as
to attain an enduring bond before embarking upon marriage – at
least before starting a family – rather than as using marriage to
test whether or not a bond will last.

Some people fear that, once marriage ceases to be regarded as
the precondition to physical love, the result will be a sexual free-
for-all. Such apprehension is groundless because it is based on
assumptions about sex arising from its repression, whereas the
drives at the root of human sexuality are not only physical but
human – so long as they are not reduced to stark physicality by
unnatural denial. The study of sex in simple, uninhibited societies
establishes this very clearly.

The morally formative power of sex arises from the fact that men and women, of their own nature and need, yearn to discover a testing, enduring, comforting, stimulating, companionable, fulfilling, annihilating, and resurrecting bond with a member of the other sex, through which they can find and transform themselves. It is a part of achievement, a part of inspiration, a perennial source of excitement and renewal, a haven, a warmth, a passion, a foundation, a reassurance. The defeated life is, in part, defeated by the death of the hope of finding such a relationship. With men and women everywhere constantly seeking (sometimes unconsciously) for that kind of bond with a member of the other sex – or, if it comes to that, in some cases with a member of the same sex – we do not have to be in doubt about the survival of enduring relationships. Whenever such a relationship develops between a man and a woman, then the partners will usually seek marriage, if only as an announcement to the world, if only as a compliment to one another, if only as a declaration of intent to found a family.

If there were any doubt about this, the attitude of our young adults would set it at rest. At the present time, when personal fulfilment is a frankly overt goal among young people, and when the strictures on premarital relations have been considerably loosened, marriage has never been more popular. But a notable difference about these contemporary young adults is that many of them regard marriage as the extension of personal relations, including sexual relations, into a deeper level of commitment rather than as a concession to Church, State, or Respectability. Having achieved a pairbond, most young people want to confirm it by marriage.

The physical component of a deep pairbond is only now beginning to be valued aright. Desmond Morris believes that the human body's elaborate equipment for love, and the rich potentialities of physical experience thus offered, are attributes selected by human evolution to assure unity between partners and a secure background for the children. This is a further argument for the development of sexual powers prior to marriage, so that the capacity for passionate love may be at its peak, or near its peak, before marriage takes place. Chastity prior to marriage can produce mutual ignorance, clumsiness, inhibition, and lack of warmth, which may postpone for a long period the passionate satisfaction of the partners. This must reduce the strength of the pairbond, if it does not actually inhibit its growth. The resulting mutual exasperation can easily pave the way for a divorce which need not have occurred, or it may produce a home without delight – an unpromising milieu for children.

The need of society, in view of our present knowledge, is to promote quality in marriage. A dead, unstimulating, affectionless home is a dreadful background for a child, impairing all his development: emotional, social, intellectual, and even physical. Harlow and his associates have been studying the affectional network of family life, both in primate and human societies. Five patterns of affectional bonds may be distinguished in the human family: the bond of the child to the mother, the bond of the mother to the child, the bond of the parents together, the bond between father and children, and the bond between the young ones. A further bond, the bond between children in the family and other children – the very important social bond – itself largely arises from the inner security and self-confidence created by the inter-familial bonds. The loving and lively family nest is the basis of future mental and moral health within society.

The force of this has been brought home yet again by the work of Sheldon and Eleanor Glueck in predicting delinquency. The Gluecks have been working for many years at Harvard University (Cambridge, Massachusetts) to discover what factors in the relationships of young children most reliably predict the likelihood of delinquency occurring later on in their lives – a research which opens the way for a sound preventive strategy. The Gluecks have refined their criteria to the point when they have been able to select boys under risk to an accuracy of 85 per cent over a period of ten years, and to predict immunity from risk to an accuracy of over 90 per cent. The work continues, but the most significant factors in prediction, when past and current work is assessed together, seem to be:

1. Freedom of the parents from neurotic traits.
2. The warmth of the relationships between parents and children.
3. The quality of the relationships between the parents.
4. The cohesiveness of the family group as a whole.
5. Understanding and consistency in discipline and supervision.

In this syndrome the relationship between the parents is clearly focal. The central importance of the physical relationship in the whole relationship is plainly implied. A man and woman, happy and fulfilled in their sex life, will find it easier to give their children the generous, undemanding love that children thrive on than will a couple who are shrivelled by physical dissatisfaction and tension, and are tempted to appease their frustration by seeking from their children the warmth they feel to be lacking in their partner. Cohesiveness and discipline also stem back to the warmth and mutuality of the partners: freedom from carping tensions and resentments between the parents is characteristic of the cohesive, robust, adventurous family; discipline is made futile if absence of tenderness and trust between the parents results in the children being used by the parents as the means for trying to score off one another.

All of which reinforces the social value of couples establishing an enduring pairbond – founded as it must be in satisfying physical love – before having children. The new social ideal for human sexuality is not chastity before marriage and fidelity afterwards, but the creation of homes overflowing with love, fun and vitality – the proper background for children. New social attitudes to sex, more attention to education for personal development, and a thorough education for young people in human relationships, including sexual relationships, are all necessary to make possible the creation of such homes.

The sentimentalists may complain that to look at marriage in its developmental aspect is to drive out the romance. This is untrue. There can be nothing more wonderful in human experience than the discovery of two people, one of another, within the encounter of their sincere and loving personalities. This creates in a partnership the excitement and joy of constant discovery and constant renewal. This is the real stuff of life, whereas the sad pattern of fantasy/romance/disillusion often brings a marriage to ashes before the last remnants of the confetti have disappeared from the gutters.

In society today the whole range of matrimonial situations may be observed, from the exultantly happy marriage – founded securely on mutual trust, mutual warmth, mutual affection, mutual tenderness, mutual stimulation, mutual support, and friendship – to the wretchedly miserable marriage kept together by force of circumstances but lacking every quality that makes a partnership satisfying. Between comes a whole spectrum of variations in adequacy and fulfilment, some working quite well, some shaky but still growing, some almost dead but persisting.

Throughout this range of experience, under modern conditions, physical love outside the marriage partnership becomes a possibility. If it occurs, some marriages are strong enough to take it in their stride. Others seem to survive *because of* a supplementary relationship that maintains a balance in the needs of one partner or the other. Other patterns, no doubt, also exist. A degree of risk is unavoidable in the modern situation. Once husbands cease to lock up their wives, and wives cease to hold their husbands on a short lead, the liberating freedom may enrich and strengthen a marriage or expose its frailties. Unhappiness is the germ of infidelity; fulfilment is its antidote. A marriage not strong enough to stand up to a certain amount of testing is not, by modern standards, a marriage at all. The conditions of risk are also the conditions which make marriages of higher quality possible.

It has to be faced, at this point, that there does seem to be a sex difference in sexual need. To quote Anthony Storr again: 'We do know that there seem to be rather basic biological differences between male and female in this respect. The desire for a variety of partners, for instance, though shared by the female to some extent, is much more characteristic of the male. Moreover, males are responsive to a far wider range of sexual stimuli than are females.' These masculine tendencies no doubt vary from individual to individual, and from one time to another in life, but nothing is to be gained by pretending that they do not exist or by condemning them because they do. The frank acceptance of the variation in our sexual natures, between the sexes and within the sexes, still leaves us with full responsibility for our actions but gives them a context of biological reality.

The new approach to divorce takes account of this context in recognizing that absolute fidelity is not the be-all and end-all of marriage. The ideal will continue to be a partnership so rich in potential that exploring the mutual experience of one another is in itself deeply satisfying – strong loves need no paramours. But the ideal will not always be attained, even when good selection of partners becomes more common, and what happens then is the responsibility of the people concerned. The principles governing their actions and decisions should be the human values already mentioned – a much better guide than arbitrary rules that cannot be expected to function properly in an open situation. Because they are impersonal, taboos encourage the cruelty and thought-lessness of despair; instead we need the courage, compassion, and generosity of men and women who accept their responsibility for one another, whatever happens.

The pessimists will say that ordinary people are not reliable enough to be trusted to deal responsibly with their sexual and marital relationships without the sanctions of imposed authority to keep them on the rails, including the authority of the law. If this were true, then ordinary people should not marry at all, since, on that evaluation, they are unfit for the unavoidably high responsibilities of marriage. But it is not true. So much has to be left to personal responsibility today that we must set out to develop responsibility in every individual. Not only marriage but civilization will founder if we fail in this. Ordinary people are quite capable of learning to act responsibly. What kills individual responsibility is the imposition of rules by an external authority. Spoon-feeding of any kind is death to responsibility and maturity. It is only when people know that they have freedom in action that they really begin to think about what their freedom involves. In order to raise the level of responsibility within marriage we have to replace taboos by responsibility throughout the whole area of man–woman relationships.

Up through human history, marriage has not been one thing but many things. Only very slowly, in our tradition, has woman attained equality of status. Polygamy was permitted among the Hebrews until long after the time of Jesus, when a wife's status was so low that she could be divorced by note of hand alone. Even after the establishment of monogamy as the only legal form of marriage, woman was held down as the dependent partner. As late as the seventeenth century, a manual of legal guidance for women warned its readers that their husbands had the legal right to beat them. As a wit put it: 'Husband and wife are one – and the husband is the one.' By the eighteenth century, things had become rather better, but woman was still a cipher, an unresolved compound of witch, angel, and chattel, certainly not a person with any clear status of her own. In Victorian and Edwardian England, marriage, however dusted with the tinsel of romance, was, for women, a stark economic and personal necessity. Without it, her status shrank to that of a social reject. Only in very recent years have women attained legal and economic freedom at all comparable to that of men. It will take some time for this new situation to work itself out – women are a little startled by it and men a little stunned. But, as the new situation is digested, the effect on marriage will be far-reaching.

For the first time in history, the fullness of sexual experience, made possible by the acceptance of woman at her proper personal value, is today made attainable for all people. Man now encounters woman, not as a plaything, or an inferior, but person to person. This equality between the sexes – not yet fully achieved or accepted but on its way – will gradually raise the standard of marriage, because exploitation of one sex by the other will no longer be tolerated, and because the full potentialities of partnership will be sought, not by the occasional couple, but by everyone. Marriages that lack depth of relationship and commitment will just not survive. Marriages in which husband and wife become each other's gaolers will no longer be regarded as virtuous, but as a deplorable waste of human dignity and potentiality.

We are moving into a situation when sex-life and marriage will become increasingly humanized and liberalized, and enriched by the higher demands placed upon them. As this process goes on, a much wider range of possibilities will be accepted in society. Some couples may live together without ever marrying; some may plunge into marriage at first love and risk the consequences; some will marry after a period of maturing personally and physically in the search for the right marriage partner; there will be the occasional woman who wishes to have a child but not a husband; homosexual partnerships will be openly admitted, and there will be some adults of both sexes who prefer to fulfil themselves with a vocation and ordinary friendship rather than through particular, intense relationships. In fact, we shall learn to accept the range of relationships that already exists in society. The mode of sexual life will, within wide limits, be considered a *personal* choice. But trends among young people today suggest that, in the future, society will expect people to run their sexual lives from realistic decisions and responsible attitudes instead of out of muddle and confusion.

The emerging new sex values should not be seen in isolation from the whole contemporary struggle to create a dynamic moral order in society. They are a part of it, and a very important part. The appalling rigidities and pruderies of the past tortured sex, which should be a spring of health and delight, into a major source of neurosis and misery, diminishing moral and creative energy thereby. We can now look forward to a future, already struggling to be born, when uninhibited, but controlled, sexuality within society will enhance the whole quality of life and of marriage. We need this to happen in the interests of humanity, and also because the future will make demands on all the creative vigour that is available in persons and society.

16

CHOICES AND VALUES

LIVING is choosing. Choice is responsibility. The world today is a single vast network of persons, groups, institutions, nations. We live in a *noosphere*, as de Chardin called it, an ambience of thinking and ideas in which everybody is ultimately in communication with everyone else. The world goes on its way by decision and action, and by the ideas and feelings that lie behind the choices or impulses that direct action. Every individual, anywhere in the network, has an effect, however slight, on what happens – we are, today, all far more closely involved in mankind than when John Donne, nearly four hundred years past, reminded his readers that no man is an island, or when St Paul, much longer ago, told the Ephesians: 'We are members one of another.' If we act, we influence; if we don't act, we influence; if we speak, we influence; if we stay silent, we also influence. We influence by the fact of being alive. There is no way of getting out from under this responsibility. We use it creatively when we strive to choose with sincerity, imagination, vision, and compassion.

The moral measure of a modern society is how it chooses and acts in the contemporary choices that face it. The moral measure of a modern man is much the same. We all have to think as hard as we are able, accepting the challenge that any problem we are intelligent enough to envisage as a problem we are capable of thinking about. The hard struggle of life is to get the thinking straight and to act from the straight thinking. That done, there is all the magic of the world to be enjoyed with confidence.

To face the major choices of our age takes us out of range of rules for choice built into the moral codes of our past, because these were composed to suit the set pattern of the times, whereas modern choice must often be concerned with creative innovation in a new situation, for which no precedents exist. This is why professing Christians, who feel they have a special moral guidance to help them, are today often as uncertain and divided about the rights and wrongs of contemporary problems as are those who feel they must depend on their own wits. No controversy is provoked by 'Thou shalt not steal', but what is the actual morality of high profits, vast unearned incomes, planned obsolescence, the wasteful exploitation of resources, or playing the currency market?

There are no established rules to cover atomic war, birth control, the conservation of natural beauty, factory farming, human rights in the modern setting, or a score of other pressing moral issues of our time. In facing these we move into unknown moral territory. These choices of the present force us to search down beneath the moral edicts of the past. We have to strive to get at the dynamics of moral principle. The essential thinking is in its infancy. The fundamental dialogue has only just begun. But we can look at some of the choices before us in order to see if we can, even now, get a little clearer about how it is best to choose.

The first big question must be: 'What kind of future do we want for ourselves, our children, our grandchildren, and the generations after them?' We have looked into this a little already, and some answers to that question come readily enough to mind, although the implementation of each decision will take a great deal of thought, effort, and co-operation. We want to survive, which means the total elimination of war as soon as possible. We want the world to be richly endowed and beautiful, which means quality not quantity as our criterion: population control, conservation not exploitation, people before profits, the preservation and creation of beauty as high priorities. We want all people to have a chance to fulfil themselves: freedom from hunger, disease, impoverishment, indignity, injustice – and a rich, evocative, satisfying, formative education for every child born. These aspirations are no longer dreams, but fully practicable possibilities provided that those who wield power turn their attention to co-operating for the common good. Provided, that is, that the ordinary people of the world get clear enough about the way the world ought to be going and push their leaders hard enough to get it going that way. Hundreds of day-to-day decisions are involved, each for or against a better future.

The biggest responsibility of all is to bother enough to get clear enough to push in the right direction. The force of public opinion can be subtle and powerful, as we have seen in the comparatively peaceful revolutions in Ghana and, originally, in Czechoslovakia. Enough people wanting something with clarity and unity can, in the modern world, achieve almost anything, because people with a purpose make news and the mass media quickly spread their message.

What threatens us, if we do not care enough (and if war is avoided), is not 1984 as Orwell saw it, but the comfortable degradation of the lollipop society. Suppose we abdicate and let the powers that be do it for us in their own way, we shall, almost certainly, get for everyone, in the long run, a world of material plenty. We have only to hand over passively to the élites of power, the technicians, and the computer people, and – provided that the élites achieve a rapprochement (which they are beginning to show signs of doing), and provided that enough scientists play along with the élites – we can have a sugar-coated world of general abundance in a few decades: every family its own electric runabout; milk and bread on the rates (or taxes) in the better-off countries; synthetic protein by the ton to stop any nutritional gaps; full, free medical care; a four-day week; half a dozen television programmes going eighteen hours every day; fun halls to keep fit in; sex or sex-substitutes planned for all; and a range of pharmaceutical aids to convert the sting of painful emotion into a gentle euphoria. Huxley's *Brave New World* – with modifications – no longer fantasy but fact. The necessary technology is already worked out, or well on the way to a solution. It could be a world without want, a world with suffering minimized, a world without burglars, murderers, or obstreperous sexuality – anti-aggression additives to the drinking water, or, for particularly obstinate cases, a tiny electrode embedded in a critical area of the brain, could look after public problems of that kind.

The lollipop society could be a society without vice; anything likely to cause a moralist to frown could be painlessly trimmed away during the formative years. It could also be a benignly contented society. As we learn more and more about the micro-chemistry of the brain, we shall constantly be in a better position to charm away dissatisfactions as the alcoholic does today with his whisky, but then more subtly, ever so subtly, with insignificant side-effects. Later on still – a good deal later, but sometime – we shall be able to do an even better job by modifying the genes that cause the trouble or by intervening in the procreative process in other ways. The right genetic engineering may one day be able to produce populations of personalities with built-in happiness and virtue.

Why not? Old-style morality has nothing to offer, because the lollipop society could meet all its conditions for good behaviour. At this point we are in the substratum beneath the moral codes. We have to reject the lollipop society, not because it lacks virtue but because it lacks the stuff of dynamic life: raw vitality, creativity, adventurousness, discontent, nonconformity, a sense of purpose, the search for more abundant life.

There is no traditional moral reason against the lollipop society; it is the dynamic of human nature that revolts at it – the creative drive in man that cannot be content with any resting-place, but must explore, learn, control, create, move on. Which is why most people will reject for themselves a future of passive ease. They cannot tolerate the thought of living as manipulated automata. They want the adventure, excitement, and risk of life. A world in which everything is tidy, complete, perfectly balanced, impeccably well organized is dull. Given the choice, most people would prefer the uncertainties of 'the beautiful, strange, wide, unpredictable world' to the smoothness of a synthetic paradise in which every need was foreseen and dealt with and every need not foreseen was gently coaxed into oblivion as soon as it emerged.

The moral reason why the lollipop society should be rejected, therefore, is not that it represents a breach of any traditional moral virtues – it could be the most virtuous society ever known – but that it would mean the end of creation on this planet as certainly as if we blew life off its surface and poisoned the sea with an atomic holocaust. Our prime duty is to serve evolution, to keep life varied, exploratory, and open-ended. Science, including eugenic science, is good by this evaluation so long as it increases variety, vitality, potential; it would be evil were it to limit or standardize in terms of *any* conception of what ought to be. The unreleased potentialities in man are totally incalculable. To attempt to freeze them to any pattern would be destructive. This is why Utopias are out, élites untrustworthy, and perfect human types illusions. Utopias are past ideas crystallized into an imagined perfection which always turns out to lack vitality; élites, by their nature, falsely assume the superiority of what they are; perfect types must forever be imperfect because in them is renounced the possibility of positive change.

Supposing we had the power to make men what we wished – and we may have it one day – and therefore had the power to make society what we wished, do any rules exist from which we could plan the blueprints? None do, nor can there ever be such rules. The values beneath the rules are the dynamic values of change and development, and these by their nature cannot be captured by any formulae; sorted out by any computer; analysed in their entirety from the sayings of any moral teacher. The chief virtue is the service of life. The highest act of faith is belief in life. The supreme task is to steer life into new fields of possibility and opportunity.

The urge to reach towards life and bring more to ourselves by bringing out more of ourselves is the primary dynamic in man and the primary source of his moral energy. Old people regret

most not what they have done but what they failed to do –
experiences never known, places never visited, books never read,
tasks never undertaken. This eager appetite for experience, the
discontent of wanting more of life, however much one has, is the
very stuff of being human, a value in its own right because an
aspect of the creative driving-force which is in the universe and
in each one of us. Man is insatiable, because dynamic. Meet all
his needs at one level and that very act will create a new range of
needs; meet those, and others again will come. This is why a
welfare state – wholly desirable at its own level – can never,
simply by taking care of people, assure contentment, because the
measure of its success is that it releases energy to seek *new* goals.
It follows that better education has to go along with better social
care in order to prepare people for fulfilment in terms of the
higher goals.

Everyone wants a world in which human well-being is
maximized. But that is the start; not the finish. The start of what?
No one can say. Our act of faith must be that we believe in what
happens when human vitality and creativity are released.

The young today sense that life could be more satisfying,
want it to be so, but feel themselves caught up in a system that
seems to have nothing to offer but more of the same: ceaseless and
sometimes pointless pressure without enough opportunity for
being. They are looking for some other system that would give
more time for *living*. They do not know whether to play along
with the *status quo* for the prizes or to opt out in search of
something more deeply satisfying.

A big choice for everyone today is how far to accept the
world that 'they' have created, and will continue to create if the
acceptance of the *status quo* is not questioned. So much of it seems
sensible and productive, and yet the feeling cannot be shaken off
that life could, and should, be more rewarding as an experience.
The prizes to be won are wrapped in frustration: 'Getting and
spending we lay waste our powers.' *They* don't seem to care
about that, but *we* do.

Who are *they*? We need to give substance to the symbol. At
first sight it may appear that *they* are all those in power. But it is

not as simple as that because there is power *over* and power *with*. Those who genuinely draw others in to share their authority and decisions are not experienced as *they*. *They* are those who are felt to be using their power arbitrarily. *They* are those in key positions who are too much cut off from contacts and consultation.

The trouble lies in the participation gap. Wisdom and sanity in decision come from people working together co-operatively in autonomous groups to find the answers to problems thrown up by their life situations: at home, at work, out in the world. Ultimately, decisions are likely to fall to the responsibility of an individual, but the decision-maker needs to be in continuous communication with the individuals and groups who are involved in the decisions. And all the evidence shows that, if ideas and aspirations are to be properly communicated and discussed, participation groups should be kept as small as possible.

The participation gap is at present undermining the potential vigour of western democracy. At one end of the scale are the rank-and-file with occasional voting rights; at the other an assortment of leaders, many of them too isolated, many of them struggling and posturing to hold what they have. The social organization between the extremes is, for the most part, either muddled or missing. Which means that far too many people in authority are having to get on – or choose to try to get on – without adequate group involvement and support, and become either arrogant dictators or frightened men, impoverished in their thinking and feeling from lack of communication. These lonely power figures, defending themselves against threat to their status, frightened of innovation or initiative, often huddling together in cliques for mutual support, are, collectively, the 'they' of our society. Meanwhile the ordinary members of the community live unconsulted lives and grow frustrated and resentful.

The *status quo* is no longer good enough. Many systems have to change. The innovation and initiative of more people must be tapped to bring richer resources to thinking and decision, and to make those resources more effective in producing positive results. Dynamically this means that we have to fill in the structure between the bottom and the top of our democracy with participant social organization. Nothing less can release and focus the creative energy we need to solve the problems of our time; nothing less can reduce the present squandering of so much energy in *pointless* conflict.

The world of plenty *and* opportunity *and* potential fulfilment we all want can be brought about only through a rapid expansion of modern participant democracy, active in a regenerated community life – which means, among other things, self-responsible regionalization. *They* can give us only the lollipop society because that is where the impersonal juggernaut of scientific technological society will take us of its own momentum, if left uncorrected. *We* have to humanize the vast machines, mechanical and organizational, that make western society what it is, if we want the machines to enhance the quality of life instead of producing its degradation.

So the biggest choice of all – the controlling choice upon which a good outcome for other choices depends – is the choice of participant, inter-communicating democracy as our style of social life. This structure is gradually forcing its way through. Occasionally its principles are applied by accident and work none the worse for that – as when some forms of system building have improved morale and productivity at the same time by making it necessary to organize labour in small groups of inter-dependent workers. Elsewhere in society – in *some* modern firms, for example, *some* schools, *some* universities – deliberate care is given to promoting effective participant organization. The social truth behind these trends needs to be consciously grasped and applied ever more widely. Shared responsibility and decision-making, and lively inter-communication, are the means to ensure that we end up with a world offering true fulfilment and not the uninspiring pseudo-riches of the lollipop society.

Participant democracy is also the effective means of bridging the gap between the generations. In a world of rapid change, if there is not continuous communication between the older generation and the younger – and the real possibility of influencing one another through this communication – an antagonism develops that drives the generations farther and farther apart.

The young are full of ideas that should be listened to and, where applicable, used. When this does not happen, the apathetic ones contract out of adult society and the energetic embattle themselves against it. Both groups now exist internationally: the hippies and the rebels. That youth should challenge is healthy enough; that youth should be driven to despise the ways of their elders is not. More bridges have to be built and an important decision of the present is how best to build them. The vote at eighteen can be one such bridge.

Women, too, must be brought in more effectively. Men are known to be the more aggressive, more status-conscious sex. Many decisions today can get quickly out of hand if the values of aggression and status – of 'saving face' – are too dominant. The logic of this is to secure a better balance of the sexes in the seats of power. One thing wrong with the world as it is may well be that too many decisions are made purely from the masculine stand-point. Women are the conservers, the civilizers, the protectors. As we move over from the competitive world, with its terrible status battles, to the co-operative world, with its new aspirations and hopes for social and personal fulfilment, we also shift from the extreme masculine end of the spectrum towards the feminine end. The logic of this is to draw more women into decision-making situations at all levels. It is notable that, in the Labour government elected in 1966, some of the wisest measures came from Barbara Castle while at the Ministry of Transport. Accident reduction and noise abatement are both typically feminine, conserving acts. A man would hardly have acted as she did. It is the men who like the 'one last round' and the throaty exhausts.

Let us recapitulate. The future has to be secured by right choices both about what it is to be, and about how to sustain and stimulate the creative potentiality of people. The decisions to secure such a future will often be made ultimately by individuals, or groups in authority, but these individuals, or groups, should be constantly in touch with new thinking through the associations of a vigorous participant democracy, comprised of interacting, interlocking, functional groups that, at the final face-to-face level, must be kept *small*. Such a democracy, to enhance its energy, wisdom, and effectiveness, must give to youth and to women a bigger role than either gets at present. These changes will be brought about partly by more enlightened management at the top and partly by 'us' at the grass-roots insisting on the necessary changes being made to bring us continuously into effective involvement in the decision-making process.

In place of the frenetic, over-competitive, wasteful 'we-and-they' society we can then bring into being a society in which the nation's purposes are felt as community purposes because we have all thought and acted to create them. They will be better, more humane, more imaginative, more interesting purposes because we have. And a primary source of apathy and alienation will have been removed.

The modern moral situation is well exemplified by the new choices that are arising from advances in genetic engineering, and, more urgently, from modern transplant surgery. When is an individual to be considered dead? Under what conditions should organs be available for transplant? Again, if only one kidney of the right kind, or one heart, is available, and two people need it equally badly, by what criteria should the surgeon judge who shall have it? This new kind of choice serves to underline what has already been discussed in this chapter. No traditional moral rules help much. Each case should be judged on its merits, in part on the grounds of surgical prospects, in part on the grounds of personal need, and in part on the grounds of the social value of the individuals concerned. When values clash, which should have precedence? Suppose, for example, the choice were between a young father with two children and a middle-aged physicist with an international reputation? Such a choice could not be settled by rule of thumb; it would have to be discussed by those involved so that every facet of the situation could be considered. Similar controls will be needed to guide, when they come, the possibilities of choosing the sex of babies, of duplicating human beings, of the whole strange world of genetic engineering. Broadcasting on 14 February 1968, Donald Gould, the editor of *New Scientist*, told us that this new world of unexpected choices 'must have a moral philosophy to go along with it'. The principles can only be those of personal and social clarity operating in an alert, integrated, well-informed democracy.

Individual responsibility in association with discussion, communication, and participant decision-making is the key to modern social life, with human and social values used as the criteria of choice. Modern choices are to be made out of the responsibility of being human. A choice becomes a moral choice not by conformity to a rigid standard but through the effort and sincerity involved in accepting the struggle of the choice, in trying to choose wisely, and in action to secure the outcome of wise choice. Around us today there is an international liberation movement of the human spirit concerned to make a new kind of democracy the basis for national and international life. Each of us has to decide where he stands in the struggle.

We can see, gathering now, moves and pressures towards the transformation of society from a *primarily* producer–consumer system to one which *primarily* aims to harness the potential power and wealth of the modern world for the fulfilment of people and societies. The change involves steering society by means of individual responsibility and social control instead of through isolated power figures, cadres, cliques, and bureaucracies. Professor Herbert Marcuse fears that the pluto-democracies will skilfully absorb or repress the forces for change, without changing fundamentally themselves. His warning is justified. On the other hand, the new revolution has allies not only among youth, and the rejected, but among all those at every level of society whose thinking is socially creative, and who feel an acute sense of waste and frustration in the outworn, arbitrary ways of running national and international affairs. We cannot easily predict when and how these forces for change will come to a sufficient focus to transform society. All that we can be sure of is that a major transition is on its way in both capitalist and communist societies. And for each of us is the choice: to participate in the thinking and the struggle to create the future, or to sink into the complacency of accepting the *status quo* without question.

17

YES, TO LIFE

IN Chapter Sixteen we looked at some aspects of the morality of social choice; in this final chapter we shall consider the personal attitude to life appropriate to a contemporary moral order.

Morality, we now see, should be founded on the right use of our powers, not on their denial. This means that a modern moral attitude becomes one of accepting all that adds quality and richness to life: not 'Thou shalt not' but 'Thou shalt wisely, compassionately, creatively'.

The odds against any particular person being born are several millions to one *against*. But we are here. We have it – life. What are we going to do with it?

There is only one possible answer. *Live it* – fully, profoundly, with all our senses aware and awake; as though looking our last 'on all things lovely every hour'. We should take our prize to our hearts and do it justice.

The valid philosophy for living people is life-affirmation. The greatest of all blasphemies is to deny the worth of life. We have to say 'No' often enough to ourselves, other people, and unacceptable actions, but never to life. The right response to life is 'Yes', and we say 'No' only in the service of that bigger 'Yes'.

Yes, to man. If we can't be affirmative about man, we had better live up a mountain, or on a desert island. The communist world, in its rather awkward way – concerned for the people, but not always sufficiently for the person – has a great confidence in man. It's a poor tale if denigrating man, against the evidence – once we look at our species as emerging – turns out to be a characteristic perversion of the western democracies.

Yes, to our bodies and the physical enjoyment of life: our eyes, our ears, the feel of comforting touch, good food and drink, the evocative quality of scents, the movement of our limbs, the touch of wind and rain, the comfort of a hot bath, the snug warmth of bed, the ecstasy of sense in consummation, sleep, the weary muscles of the long climb, the headache of effort pressed beyond energy:

> Body,
> My playmate!
> Neither the master
> Nor the slave,
> A buoyant heart
> Shall bear you along,
> While you cheer my way
> With your lively flame.
>
> But body,
> My playmate,
> You must not flinch
> Nor fail me when
> The moment comes
> To do the impossible.

Thus Dag Hammarskjöld (translated by Auden in *Markings*) in one of the last poems he wrote, before his tragic death.

Yes, to ourselves, the courage to search for ourselves, the confidence to believe in ourselves, self-acceptance without complacency. Yes to spontaneity, *and* to self-control.

The personal quest is also the moral quest. 'Knowing who in fact we are results in Good Being,' writes Aldous Huxley in *Island*, 'and Good Being results in the most appropriate kind of good doing.'

His brother, Julian, in his essay on 'Transhumanism', gives a biologist's measure of what, for all of us, lies beyond our present selves: 'We are beginning to realize that even the most fortunate people are living far below capacity, and that most human beings develop not more than a small fraction of their potential mental and spiritual efficiency. The human race, in fact, is surrounded by a large area of unrealized possibilities, a challenge to the spirit of exploration.'

Claire and William Russell, in *Human Behaviour*, write: 'There is only one real courage, and that is the courage to be oneself, to be happy and to enjoy life.'

Yes, to others, fellow-explorers in the quest for life, source of fun and fellowship, of conflict and kindness, of stimulating challenge and maddening perversity, rich in variety of personality and culture, adorable, detestable, incomprehensible, endearing, clever, dull, pink, black, brown, olive, yellow, two-sexed, and every one, at root, wanting from life the same thing – fulfilment.

Yes, to the past. The long struggle. The search for truth. The striving, the rivalries, the becoming. The blood and pain. The suffering and triumph. The lonely lamp in the quiet room when an idea was born in the sleeping city. The beauty of paint and stone. Exquisite craftsmanship. The passion of great love. The mute inglorious workers who built the future with their labouring care. The folly and the wisdom, the fun and the frowns. Whole libraries of books. A heaven of melody. A multitude of inventions. We are the inheritors. Let us know it in our minds, reverence it in our hearts, and enjoy it with all the power we find in us.

Yes, to our responsibility as persons, as users of the world, as creators of the new, as collaborators with others.

Yes, to work, the dignity of contribution.

Yes, to awareness. Yes, to courage.

Yes, to experience. The time for living is now. Glooming over
past failure, agonizing over future problems, modern man too
often misses the moment as it flies. He hammers at life too much
instead of letting it come to him. Blake wrote:

> He who binds to himself a joy,
> Doth the winged life destroy.

A life too intense, too rushed, too stressed, too much planned and
programmed, so dulls the senses that, in the end, the present is
never lived. In J. B. Priestley's *Out of Town*, Tuby is talking to
Elfreda:

'I'm still a great looker-forward-toer – being idiotic enough to
believe all too often that life's nothing now but will blaze up
again gloriously next Wednesday.'
'Oh – but so am I,' cried Elfreda. 'But is that bad?'
'Certainly it is. You rob yourself of experience. You cheat
yourself out of the present moment. You think life's nothing,
when it's still something, really all you have, because of next
Wednesday. But then next Wednesday's not what you thought
it would be –'
'Because you expect too much. That's what happens to me,
nearly all the time. Then I tell myself what a fool I am. But I
never thought you'd be like that.'
'In theory I'm not. In practice I often am. But it's partly the
fault of our civilization, which encourages us to look back and
look forward at the expense of the present moment. . . .'

We should not take so much thought for the morrow that
it costs us the fullness of the present. 'Here and now!' chanted
the trained mynah birds on Huxley's imagined island, 'Here
and now!' There is magic in every moment when we are totally
there.

Yes, to striving. We are getting a little soft. Because so much
happens at the turn of a switch we expect things to come easily or
we grow impatient. Some things can't be switched on. The most
important things can't. Knowledge can't. Sensitivity can't.
Understanding can't. Wholeness can't. Love can't – the rush of

desire to the loins is not by itself love; nor is the dream stirred in a girl's fancy. Skill can't. Judgement can't. Such qualities of life have to be striven for over time, learnt and refined, and never completely attained. The road forward is always uphill. That is a practical statement of fact, not a puritanical admonishment.

Striving is the engine of personal and social life. We should be awake, critical, constructive, ready to act. So yes, to striving, and the will to strive, and yes, to help for those who have lost the heart to strive, and yes, to hope – always – but especially when the black mood is on.

Yes, to sympathy and compassion and all that is warm and kind.

Yes, to tolerance, including tolerance of our own imperfections. Yes, to the courage to be imperfect.

Yes, to laughter and gaiety and fun.

Yes, to conflict, and the humanity and the will to work things out frankly. Yes, to thinking *and* feeling.

Yes, to dialogue, the fellowship of difference.

Yes, to suffering; to transcend suffering without being over-whelmed with self-pity is to achieve depth and understanding. We cannot come to grips with life at any point if we are not prepared to take the element of suffering that is a part of all significant living. '*Sunt lacrimae rerum*,' wrote Virgil, there are tears in things. Jacquetta Hawkes puts it: 'Our individual lives are of their very nature tragic, yet mind and senses have together grown up out of the darkness to equip us for delight.'

Yes, also, to setbacks, so long as they do not destroy us. The more we survive without getting bitter or being broken, the stronger we become. In the long run what matters is not what happens to us but 'what we do with what happens to us'.

Yes, even, to death. To quote Dag Hammarskjöld again:

> Tomorrow we shall meet,
> Death and I –
> And he shall thrust his sword
> Into one who is wide awake.

And so, indeed, it was.

And this from Robert Browning, whose constructive non-conformity and vigorous life-affirmation startled the prim respectability of Victorian England:

> I was ever a fighter, so – one fight more,
> The best and the last!
> I would hate that death bandaged my eyes, and forbore,
> And bade me creep past.

It is life-affirmation that arms men against death, not life-denial, with all the weakening, cringing guilt that accompanies it.

Yes, to co-operation and seeing mankind as one. The principles of life-affirmation provide for the world moral values with which it can run its affairs in unity and amity. One day, not so far ahead, the world *will* run its affairs this way, for pragmatic wisdom and moral principle are now almost at one and it is only habit or greed or sectional pride that prevents people seeing this. Today, in a fascinating way, morality has become necessity.

Yes, then, to the unity of men. Separations which not so long ago were taken to be natural and inevitable are every day looking more artificial. No longer does the civilization of the East seek to remain in aloof indifference to the world. No longer do Marxists and Catholics regard each other as mutually untouchable. The very sharpness of the colour conflict is provoking thought and concern, as well as hatred and fanaticism, and once the hard men with the old ideas are out of the corridors of power, growth towards world justice seems marginally more likely than its alternative – race war.

As though, in them, the future has already seeded itself, young people around the world, regardless of creed, philosophy, or colour, show they have an idealism in common. The gap between the generations in any nation is often greater than the gap between young people in different nations. The young are getting together in spite of their elders.

The community of mankind is now noticeably nearer than it was thirty years ago. The human race is a quarrelsome family, but it is beginning to look like a family all the same. Any war is everybody's war whoever is doing the fighting. The futility of war, even when it is claimed as right and proper, sickens people. Talk of glory in battle has a hollow ring. The very fact there is fighting at all is felt as a disgrace by all but small boys and those who see their profit or status to be tied up with the outcome. Communist China is not an exception to this. To reject this vast civilization from the United Nations is to reap a fury of resentment. This is picked up by the rest of the world as a terrifying threat. Recognition and reciprocity could alter the situation. The mood of mankind is towards resolving conflict by discussion, whatever bloody battles are now in progress and are still to be.

Each personal 'yes' to life is part of a general affirmation. The forces of life-affirmation in the world are becoming stronger and getting more in focus, even though still weak against old ideas, prejudices, and habits. The principles for the future are, ultimately, everywhere the same, all the way through from the person to mankind: self-fulfilment, *with* others, not at the expense of others; national fulfilment, *with* other nations, not at the expense of other nations; and world fulfilment, but not at the expense of the future.

We in the west have to re-create our philosophy on what is shared of belief and feeling within our own society and within the world – a passionate, life-affirming humanism. We have to explore and map out this area of common ground to give our own society a base, a perspective, a direction, and a unity with the rest of mankind. What, in addition, anyone believes is his personal concern and choice. But we must build our interdependence on values held in common if we are not to be broken and weakened in our purposes.

This is not to ask for a party line – party lines are sectarian stratagems – but for the agreement by all that we can today attain the necessary unity only through what we can all accept: the secular principles of personal, social, national, and world fulfilment.

In spite of all the hazards still around us, we are on the threshold of a new freedom, and a clearer purpose, fashioned to the nature of man. This is a time to take our eyes off our own feet and look forward with mankind, changing the present as we live it. Where there can be action, there can be change, and where there can be change, there is always a way ahead. We have in us creativity enough to solve any problems so long as we latch on to the life-affirming values, and do not strangle our powers through distrust of ourselves and one another.

We who are living now are the hope of all who come after us. By taking hold on life with all that is in us of energy, intelligence, imagination, compassion, and delight, we can find our personal fulfilment and create a better tomorrow. We are the inheritors and the creators. The richness comes from living in that truth. The morality comes from the principles that such living involves.

PRINCIPAL TEXT REFERENCES

CHAPTER ONE

p. 4: – Selby, Charles, *Events To Be Remembered in the History of England*, Lockwood, London, 1875, p. 286. Selby quotes Smollett and adds his own comments. **p. 5:** – The lines are from 'Written in London, 1902', in *The Complete Poetical Works of William Wordsworth*, Macmillan, London, 1924, p. 181. **p. 6:** – Taylor, G. Rattray, *Sex in History*, Ballantine Books, New York, 1954, pp. 206, 207. Pearl, Cyril, *The Girl with the Swansdown Seat* (paperback edition), Signet Books, London, 1958, p. 63. *Criminal Statistics, England and Wales, 1967*, H.M. Stationery Office, London, 1968, Table A. Burke, Thomas, *The Streets of London*, Batsford, London, 1940, pp. 61, 94, 103. **p. 7:** – *Encyclopaedia Britannica*, Vol. 19, 1950, p. 823. I Samuel 15: 3. I Kings 18. **p. 9:** – Barnett, Anthony, *The Human Species*, Penguin Books, Harmondsworth, 1961, p. 209. **p. 14:** – Pearse, I. H., and Crocker, Lucy H., *The Peckham Experiment*, Allen & Unwin, London, 1943, p. 315. Conference Report, *Young Minds at Risk*, National Association for Mental Health, London, 1967, pp. 28, 29.

CHAPTER TWO

p. 17: – Redfield, Robert, *The Primitive World and its Transformations* (paperback edition), Cornell University Press, 1965, p. 16. **p. 18:** – Piddington, Ralph O'Reilly, *Chambers's Encyclopaedia*, Vol. I, 1959, p. 804. Malinowski, B., *Crime and Custom in Savage Society*, Kegan Paul, London, 1947, p. 18. **p. 19:** – ibid., p. 22. **p. 20:** – Church of England Catechism. **p. 21:** – Church of England Communion Service. **p. 23:** – The lines are from 'Hertha', *Oxford Book of English Verse*, Oxford University Press, 1930, p. 977. **p. 24:** – Teilhard de Chardin, Pierre, *The Phenomenon of Man*, Collins, London, 1959. **p. 26:** – Huxley, Sir Julian, *New Bottles for New Wine*, Chatto & Windus, London, 1957. **p. 28:** – Kroeber, A. L., *Anthropology*, Harcourt Brace, New York, 1948, p. 282. Blackham, Harold, *Religion in a Modern Society*, Constable, London, 1966, p. 185. Maslow, A. H., *Towards a Psychology of Being*, D. Van Nostrand, Princeton, N.J., 1962, p. 177.

CHAPTER THREE

p. 31: – The lines are from 'Essay on Man', Epistle II, lines 13–18. **p. 33:** – Greenslade, Rev. Stanley Lawrence, *Chambers's Encyclopaedia*, Vol. I, 1959, p. 774.

p. 35: – Flornoy, Bertrand, *Jivaro*, Elek, London, 1953, p. 77. Redfield, *The Primitive World*, p. 39. Huxley, *New Bottles for New Wine*, p. 23. **p. 37:** – Freud, Sigmund, *An Outline of Psycho-Analysis*, Hogarth Press, London, 1949, p. 72. Storr, Anthony, *Sexual Deviation*, Penguin Books, Harmondsworth, 1964, p. 42. **p. 39:** – Freud, op. cit., p. 7. **p. 44:** – Carstairs, G. M., the quotation is from an address given to the Family Planning Association.

CHAPTER FOUR

p. 47: – Redfield, *The Primitive World*, p. 15. **p. 51:** – Ginsberg, Morris, *On The Diversity of Morals*, Heinemann, London, 1956, p. 110. Redfield, op. cit., pp. 142, 143. **p. 54:** – Toynbee, Arnold J., *A Study of History*, Oxford University Press, 1946, p. 576. **p. 55:** – Trist, Higgin, Murray, and Pollock, *Organizational Choice*, Tavistock Publications, London, 1963, pp. 289–95. **p. 56:** – The Milton quotation is from 'Areopagitica', *Complete Prose Works of John Milton*, Yale University Press, 1959, p. 515. **p. 59:** – MacIntyre, Alasdair, *A Short History of Ethics*, Routledge & Kegan Paul, London, 1967, p. 268. **p. 62:** – Wilson, John, *Reason and Morals*, Cambridge University Press, 1961, p. 152.

CHAPTER FIVE

p. 69: – The lines are from *Macbeth*, Act V, Scene 5, lines 19–28. **p. 71:** – Whitehead, A. N., *Adventures of Ideas*, Penguin Books, Harmondsworth, 1942, p. 86. **p. 73:** – Fromm, Erich, *The Fear of Freedom*, Kegan Paul, London, 1942. The Carlyle quotation is from *Signs of the Times*. Ayer, A. J., in Cranston, Maurice, *Freedom, A New Analysis*, Longmans, Green, London, 1953, p. 88. **p. 76:** – Follett, Mary Parker, in Metcalf, H. C., and Urwick, L., *Dynamic Administration*, Management Publications, Bath, 1941, Chapter 4.

CHAPTER SIX

p. 77: – Riesman, David, *The Lonely Crowd*, Yale University Press, 1950. Fromm, Erich, *The Sane Society*, Routledge & Kegan Paul, London, 1956, p. 120. **p. 80:** – Huxley, *New Wine for New Bottles*, p. 14. **p. 81:** – Storr, Anthony, *The Integrity of the Personality*, Penguin Books, Harmondsworth 1963, p. 166. **p. 82:** – Williams, Leonard, *Samba and the Monkey Mind*, Bodley Head, London, 1965, p. 128.

CHAPTER SEVEN

p. 91: – Carstairs, G. M., *This Island Now*, Penguin Books, Harmondsworth, 1964, pp. 46, 47. **p. 94:** – Piaget, J., *The Moral Judgement of the Child*, Harcourt Brace, New York, 1932. **p. 95:** – Erikson, Erik, *Insight and Responsibility*, Faber & Faber, London, 1966, Chapter 3. **p. 96:** – Adler, Alfred, *What Life Should Mean To You*, Allen & Unwin, London, 1932, Chapter 3. **p. 99:** – Adler, Alfred, *Social Interest, A Challenge to Mankind*, Faber & Faber, London, 1938, Chapter 10. **p. 100:** – Laing, R. D., *The Self and Others*, Tavistock Publications, London, 1961, Chapter 12.

CHAPTER EIGHT

p. 104: – The lines are from 'Rabbi Ben Ezra', Stanza XII. **p. 106:** – St Paul, Epistle to the Romans, 7: 24. St Augustine, *Confessions*, Fontana Books,

London, 1957, p. 40. **p. 107:** – Morgan, Charles, *The Flashing Stream*, Macmillan, London, 1938, p. 17. **p. 108:** – MacMurray, John, *Reason and Emotion*, Faber & Faber, London, 1935, p. 132. Kenyatta, Jomo, *Facing Mount Kenya*, Secker & Warburg, London, 1938, p. 155. **p. 109:** – Bryant, A. T., *The Zulu People*, Shuter & Shooter, Pietermaritzburg, 1949, pp. 568, 569. Mayer, Philip (ed.), *The Social Anthropology of Socialization*, A.S.A. Monograph No. 8, Tavistock Publications, London, in the press. **p. 112:** – Morris, Desmond, *The Naked Ape*, Jonathan Cape, London, 1967. Lilar, Suzanne, *Aspects of Love in Western Society*, Thames & Hudson, London, 1965. **p. 113:** – The lines are from *King Lear*, Act IV, Scene 6, lines 129–30. Suttie, Ian D., *The Origins of Love and Hate*, Kegan Paul, London, 1935, Chapter 6. **p. 116:** – Eppel, E. M. and M., *Adolescents and Morality*, Routledge & Kegan Paul, London, 1966, p. 77. Logan, R. F. L., and Goldberg, E. M., 'Rising Eighteen in a London Suburb', *British Journal of Sociology*, **4**, No. 4, pp. 323–45. **p. 119:** – MacMurray, op. cit., p. 39.

CHAPTER NINE

p. 121: – Allen, Frederick, *Proceedings of the International Congress on Mental Health*, 1948, Vol. 2, H. K. Lewis, London, 1948, pp. 4, 5. **p. 123:** – Fromm, Erich, *Man For Himself*, Routledge & Kegan Paul, London, 1948, p. 216. Storr, Anthony, *Human Aggression*, Allen Lane, The Penguin Press, London, 1968. **p. 124:** – Koestler, Arthur, *The Ghost in the Machine*, Hutchinson, London, 1967, Chapter 25. **p. 125:** – Schaller, George, *The Year of the Gorilla*, Penguin Books, Harmondsworth, 1967. Carpenter, C. R., 'The Howlers of Barro Colorado Island', in *Primate Behaviour*, Holt, Rinehart & Winston, New York, 1965, p. 273. **p. 126:** – ibid, p. 99. **p. 127:** – Lorenz, Konrad, *On Aggression*, Methuen, London, 1966, Chapters 7 and 13, and p. 208. **p. 129:** – Mayer (ed.) *Social Amorphology of Socialization*. **p. 131:** – Musgrove, F., *Youth and the Social Order*, Routledge & Kegan Paul, London, 1964. **p. 132:** – Kortlandt, Adrian, 'Chimpanzees in the Wild', reprinted from *Scientific American* (May 1962).

CHAPTER TEN

p. 137: – The lines are from 'Morality', verse 1. **p. 140:** – The lines are the last lines of the sonnet 'When I have fears that I may cease to be'. **p. 141:** – Maslow, A. H., 'The Good Life of the Self-Actualizing Person', in *Humanist*, **27**, No. 4 (American Humanist Association, Yellow Springs, Ohio). **p. 142:** – The lines are from 'The World'. **p. 143:** – Jung, C. G., *Two Essays on Analytical Psychology*, Ballière, London, 1928, p. 189. **p. 144:** – MacMurray, *Reason and Emotion*, p. 47. **p. 145:** – The first lines are from Oscar Wilde's 'The Ballad of Reading Gaol', in Oscar Wilde, *Plays, Prose Writings and Poems*, Dent, London, 1930, p. 145. The second lines are from 'In Memoriam', Stanza LIII. **p. 147:** – Comfort, Alex, *The Anxiety Makers*, Nelson, London, 1967.

CHAPTER ELEVEN

p. 152: – Asimov, Isaac, *The Universe*, Allen Lane, The Penguin Press, London, 1967, p. 12. **p. 154:** – Morrison, Philip, in *Radio Times* (28 September 1967). **p. 155:** – Harris, W. J., 'The Origin of Life – A Master Molecule?', *The*

Advancement of Science, **24**, No. 121, pp. 326–32. **p. 160:** – Thorpe, W. H., *Science, Man and Morals*, Methuen, London, 1965, p. 151.

CHAPTER TWELVE

p. 164: – Tyndale, William, *The New Testament* (Cambridge University Press, 1938). **p. 166:** – *Doctrine in the Church of England*, S.P.C.K., London, 1938, pp. 82 and 86. Barth, Karl, *The Humanity of God*, Collins, London, 1961. **p. 169:** – Robinson, John, *Honest to God*, S.C.M. Press, London, 1963. Graham, Billy, *Peace With God*, The World's Work, Kingswood, 1954. **p. 170:** – The girls' responses are from an unpublished inquiry. Mitchell, James (ed.), *The God I Want*, Constable, London, 1967. **p. 171:** – Hopkinson, A. Stephan, in ibid., p. 112. **p. 177:** – Huxley, Sir Julian, *Religion Without Revelation*, Watts, London, 1967). **p. 178:** – Isherwood, Margaret, *Faith Without Dogma*, Allen & Unwin, London, 1964.

CHAPTER THIRTEEN

p. 191: – The Wordsworth quotation is from 'Lines on a Yew Tree'.

CHAPTER FOURTEEN

p. 199: – Wall, W. D., *The Adolescent Child*, Methuen, London, 1948, pp. 13, 14. **p. 200:** – Wilson, John, Williams, Norman, and Sugarman, Barry, *Introduction to Moral Education*, Penguin Books, Harmondsworth, 1967. **p. 202:** – Maslow, A. H., *Motivation in Personality*, Harper, New York, 1954. **p. 205:** – Scottish Education Department, *Raising the School Leaving Age*, H.M. Stationery Office, London, 1966, p. 9. Peters, P. S. (ed.), *The Concept of Education*, Routledge & Kegan Paul, London, 1967, p. 9. **p. 208:** – Bronowski, J., *Science and Human Values*, Penguin Books, Harmondsworth, 1964, pp. 69, 70. Flavel, J. H., *The Developmental Psychology of Jean Piaget*, Van Nostrand, Princeton, N.J., 1963.

CHAPTER FIFTEEN

p. 216: – Storr, *The Integrity of the Personality*, p. 177. **p. 217:** – Harlow, Margaret K. and Harry K., 'An Analysis of Love', *Listener* (18 February 1965). **p. 219:** – Morris, *The Naked Ape*, Chapter 2. **p. 220:** – Harlow, H. F., 'Primary Affectional Patterns in Primates', *American Journal of Orthopsychiatry*, **30**, pp. 676–84. Glueck, Sheldon and Eleanor, *Family Environment and Delinquency*, Routledge & Kegan Paul, London, 1962. **p. 222:** – Storr, Anthony, letter in *New Statesman*, (20 September 1963).

CHAPTER SIXTEEN

p. 236: – Marcuse, Herbert, *One-Dimensional Man*, Routledge & Kegan Paul, London, 1964.

CHAPTER SEVENTEEN

p. 238: – Hammarskjöld, Dag, *Markings*, Faber & Faber, London, 1964, p. 171.
p. 239: – Huxley, Aldous, *Island*, Chatto & Windus, London, 1962, p. 39.

Huxley, Sir Julian, 'Transhumanism', in *New Bottles For New Wine*, p. 15.
Russell, Claire and William, *Human Behaviour*, André Deutsch, London, 1961,
p. 369. The lines are from 'Poems from the Note-Book 1793', *The Complete
Writings of William Blake*, Oxford University Press, 1966, p. 179. **p. 240:** –
Priestley, J. B., *Out of Town*, Heinemann, London, 1968, p. 338. **p. 241:** –
Hawkes, Jacquetta, *Man on Earth*, Cresset Press, London, 1954, p. 246.
Hammarskjöld, op. cit., p. 51. **p. 242:** – The lines are from 'Prospice'.

INDEX